The Superfriends Of The Ring

(A Parody Of Tolkien's <u>The Fellowship Of The Ring</u>)

by Paul A. Erickson

CONTENTS

THE PROLOGUE TO THE PROLOGUE

MEMO

RE: Bulbo's Book Was Not Entirely Accurate

From: Galadtameecha, Owner, Elf Resorts International

To: The Allies Of Goodness

The world has changed, and nobody likes change.

I can feel it at the water cooler, I can smell it in the break room. Much that once was is lost, for none now live who remember it. Let me explain.

It seems that in his book *There Goes My Back Again* (published in the Uttermost North as *The Wobbit*), the former contractor/thief Bulbo Bunkins may not have expressed two key concepts in the book with complete accuracy. This has created great confusion and must be addressed.

In case any of us are unclear about these two concepts (I here address myself to the Wizard and Project Manager Pantsoff, in the unlikely event that he is actually reading this memo), let me be specific.

First of all, the ring that Bulbo "won" from the creature Gol-Gol is not a run-of-the-mill Ring Of Invisibility, such as you or I might swap for a Holocaust Cloak or a Wheelbarrow. It is, in fact, the most powerful and evil object in Little Earth.

It seems like it was only yesterday that the Really Great Rings were forged. Three were given to the Elves, of course, because they were the best rings available at the time. Seven were given to the Dwarves, because the great fathers of the dwarves, the creators of the song “Heigh Ho,” also numbered seven. Nine were given to the Kings Of Men, because the Queens Of Women didn't want them; they felt the rings were tacky.

But they were all of them bamboozled, for another ring, a really REALLY great ring was made. In the land of Bordor, in the fires of Mount Dum-da-dum-dum he created it. The Lord and CEO of Bordor Enslavement, Banking And Destruction, Smoron, contracted the forging of a super-ring to control the others. Into it he poured his impatience, his pettiness and his will to grow the corporation through acquisition. He could never have afforded to forge it in Bordor, so instead he hired a skilled craftsman from the Uttermost South who did brilliant work at a very competitive rate. The ring was named after this craftsman: The Juan Ring.

One by one, the freedom-loving lands of Little Earth were either destroyed or bought off through the power of The Ring, but there were some who insisted on collective bargaining. A Nearly Last Alliance of Elves and Men, who were to be allied many more times in the future as The Allies Of Goodness, marched against the Axis Of Evil.

Goblins and trolls and rargs attacked, and they were hideous. The air was filled with arrows and screams and screaming arrows. It was unfortunately cloudy despite a forecast for a mild, sunny morning. The Allies were about to win the day when Smoron made a rare personal appearance. Even though he was an elf, his form was that of a giant warrior wearing uncomfortably spiky armor, which may explain his bad attitude at the time. He was smiting Elves and Men all over the place. He was about to smite Isadora, son of the late King Of Men, Ellen-Doll, but he first stepped on Isadora’s sword, Nasal, and broke it in twain out of sheer spite.

Surprisingly, Isadora took the hilt of Nasal and somehow killed Smoron with it. No one knows how. I didn't see it myself. Enron tells me it was a cheap shot to the groin, but others report that there was a weak spot in Smoron's armor just inside the left breast. In any event, Smoron slowly vanished with a cry of "You cursed brat! Look at what you've done! I'm melting! What a world! Who would have thought a pathetic human like you could destroy my beautiful wickedness? Oh, look out! I'm going! Oh! Oh!"

His size 72 Extra-Tall suit of armor was left behind, useless to Isadora even with significant alterations. But Isadora noticed that The Ring magically re-sized itself. He picked it up but didn't try it on, perhaps because he was wearing gloves. Others say he didn't like it initially because it looked like a wedding band "and I told my wife I would never wear one." But he knew value when he saw it, so he kept it.

On the way home from the battle, Isadora was ambushed by a gang of goblins. They hadn't yet heard that the battle was over and that their *capo di tutti capi* had been vaporized. Isadora had discovered that The Juan Ring would make him invisible, so he dove into a nearby river to escape. What he didn't know was that The Juan Ring would not give him the power to breathe underwater, or hold his breath indefinitely, or swim in full armor. He drowned.

The Ring managed to swim like a scallop, jetting through the water by expanding and contracting, until it came to a new bearer, the most annoying creature imaginable. No one knows for sure, but we can assume he said something like "Well, looky here! I'm gonna call you My Precious, I say, My Precious!"

His name was Gol-Gol, and he was kind of crazy to begin with, but wearing The Juan Ring made him even crazier. Again, we can guess that his internal dialogue, which he always spoke aloud, was something along the lines of "Mine, I say, all mine! With your help, Precious, I'll kill scrawny little goblins and eat them raw, and live in a cave for the next thousand years! Bwa-ha-ha-ha!" That was mostly The Ring talking.

Many years later, The Ring was stolen by the aforementioned thief, Bulbo Bunkins, a Wobbit from Wobbiton. He invoked the ancient rule of Finders Keepers when he removed The Ring from Gol-Gol's dismal home and tucked it into his little waistcoat. Bulbo reports that the last thing he heard Gol-Gol say was "Carn sarn it! Bunkins! We hates, I say, we hates it forever!" He didn't stick around to see what would happen next.

The second concept Bulbo expressed inaccurately in his book was that according to Pantsoff, Smoron had been defeated. While Pantsoff certainly said this, the statement is dangerously false. It is true that The Axis Of Evil was defeated at the Battle Of Six Or Seven Armies, thanks to the last-minute arrivals of The King Of The Eagles and his Squadron Of The Eagles, as well as the skin-changer The Incredible Bjork. But Smoron was not killed by Isadora. He had unmelted and was attempting to rebrand himself as "The Neccomancer," but was thrown out of his corporate headquarters in Murkywood Forest by The White Council. Defeated, he once again began to melt. Pantsoff was supposed to seal his melting remains in an Invincibilium capsule to prevent any future unmeltings, but he was busy posing for a victory portrait at the time.

To sum up, The Juan Ring is far more dangerous than Pantsoff realizes, and Smoron is still at large and dangerous, despite melting twice. If you see Pantsoff, please let him know. Action needs to be taken immediately to avoid market instability that would diminish the fortunes of us all.

Prologue

CONCERNING WOBBITS

This book is largely concerned with wobbits, and from its pages a reader may discover much of their character and a little of their history. Further information will also be found in the The Wobbit A Parody (Of Tolkien's The Hobbit). It is available in both German and the original English from Amazon, as an eBook and as a paperback. Order yours now!

Chapter 1

A LONG EXPECTED BRUNCH

When Mr. Bulbo Bunkins of Bug End announced that he would shortly be celebrating his eleventy-first birthday with a brunch of special magnificence, no one expected that such a wealthy wobbit might only offer a cash bar.

Bulbo was very rich and very peculiar, and regarded by his neighbors as “queer.” Sixty years earlier he had taken a contract job as a consultant which had, against all odds, won him a fortune. Even more peculiar was the fact that he seemed to stop aging. At ninety he was much the same as fifty. At ninety-nine he looked fifty-one. At one-hundred he looked forty-nine. At one-hundred-one he looked fifty again. At one-hundred-ten neighbors began to say "he’s had some work done," but they secretly thought "he has a portrait in his basement that ages instead of him." This was ridiculous, because Bulbo's entire apartment was the basement underneath a beauty salon, and any magic portraits would have to be hidden somewhere else.

“It will have to be paid for,” they said. “He must be using some expensive vitamin therapy for the super-rich, because his diet is horrible and he gets no exercise. Mega-doses aren’t natural, and trouble will come of it!”

But so far, trouble had not come. Although he was cheap by nature, Bulbo had always tipped generously and bribed freely just so his neighbor wobbits would leave him alone. He remained on visiting terms with his relatives (except, of course, the Snackbag-Bunkinses) and was adored by the local riff-raff for his well-publicized but actually rare acts of charity. Like most Dorks (the family on his mother’s side) he had no close friends until his younger cousins were old enough to join him for late nights of role-playing games.

Bulbo's favorite cousin was young Promo Bunkins. Since the mysterious deaths of his parents, Promo had lived with his cousins the Buckiebrands of Buckiebrand Hall in nearby Buckieland. It was easy to remember the mailing address.

At the age of ninety-nine Bulbo adopted Promo and made him his heir. They had the same birthday, September 22, which seemed to Promo to be a suspicious reason to adopt someone. And since Promo was a tweenager at the time, he was not looking forward to having combined birthday parties with Bulbo. A hundred-year-old guy is usually not much fun to party with, even if he looks fifty.

Promo endured twelve years of combined birthday parties, not realizing that Bulbo had something quite exceptional planned for when Promo turned thirty-three, his wobbit "coming of age." Bulbo was going to be eleventy-one, a clearly Dorkish way of saying one hundred eleven. (The Old Dork himself had only reached 130 due to a raw diet and hyperbaric therapy.) 111 is a very respectable age for a wobbit, since they tend to die in middle-age from "death by misadventure" or from illnesses caused by poor personal habits.

In anticipation of the coming event, tongues began to wag in Wobbiton and Buythewater, like the tails of so many animal-shelter dogs. Local wobbit Ham Sammich, known as the Grasper, took this as an opportunity to share his anecdotes about tending the gardens at Bulbo's condo. Bunkins had purchased his apartment below Virginia's Beauty Parlor when he became rich. Trying to live up to his new role of "job creator," he hired Sammich as gardener, primarily because it meant his new servant would never have any duties inside the condo.

Sammich, who Bulbo employed without benefits, was a dreadful old bore. He was old, but actually younger than Bulbo, but because of Bulbo's mysterious eternal middle-age, Sammich acted like his cranky grand-dad. The Grasper attributed his own long life to avoiding work and drinking beer, and did both regularly. He was at an inn called *The Ivy Drip*, where he addressed a small audience. Small even for wobbits.

"Promo's birthday party'll be Wobbiton's biggest event ever! I swear," slurred Ham. "Tha' Misser Bulbo's all right!"

"Sure, Bulbo's all right," said Daddy Shortlegs (a neighbor of the Grasper), "but who's this young Promo Bunkins that lives with him? Bunkins or not, he's really a Buckiebrand from Buckiebrand Hall, where folks are so queer."

"You're right, Dad!" said the Grasper. "And I've never seen tha' young Promo out on a date. Not that there's anything wrong with that. They do have queer ways in Buckieland, across th' Buckiewine River. Still, as long as his 'dad' keeps paying my wages, tha' Promo is all right, too."

"Did I ever tell you the story about the mysterious death of Promo's parents?" the Grasper said. "Promo told me in the strictest confidence, so if you repeat this, tell everyone it's a secret."

"You don't say, Grasper!" said Ted Sandywobbit, the Wobbiton miller, who always liked to butt in.

"Oh, yeah! Prob'ly killed each other! Mr. Drono Bunkins and tha' poor Miss Tremula Buckiebrand. They were paddleboating on a second honeymoon at the Murkywood Wood-Elf Lodge when the paddleboat capsized. Horseplay was suspected, or perhaps even rough-housing. And they were both somehow related to Bulbo. Tha's even more mysterious."

"That doesn't sound mysterious at all," said the miller. He was hard to please. "Not much of a story. More of an anecdote. I hate those paddleboats, all that pedaling. No wonder they fell in."

"Anyway," said Sammich, "Promo went to live with the Buckiebrands until Mr. Bulbo adopted him. What a shock tha' must have been to the Snackbag-Bunkinses. First Bulbo's eternal middle-age, and then a new beneficiary suspiciously being named."

"What about the rootball card collection, and all the silver and gold?" said Daddy. "And the jools?'

"The what?"

"I'm sorry, the 'jewels.' What about them?"

"He never had any jewels," Ham said, "and Mr. Bulbo refused to diversify his portfolio, taking only gold as payment on his contract instead. As for his rootball memorabilia, all of the cards, programs, merchandise, jerseys, and even a rare game ball are all going to Promo."

"But my boy Sham can tell you all about that." Ham's son, Sham Sammich, was following in his father's footsteps, which meant drinking and watching rootball games while on the clock for Mr. Bulbo. There was hardly enough work for one of them. "Sham's a rootball nut! He knows the rules better than a referee. But the game's not the same anymore. Trying to prevent 'concussions.' It's a huge waste of time in my opinion."

"'Horsecollar tackles and false starts!' I says to him. 'Rutabagas and ghost-payrolling are good enough for me and you! Pay attention or you'll get caught goofing off!' I says."

"You can says what you want, but that Bulbo's got strange interests beyond rootball," said Sandywobbit. "Visits from comic book collectors and weird foreign musicians. He's even had dwarves calling after normal business hours, with that old self-employed 'wizard,' Pantsoff. Bug End is a queer place, and its folk queerer. Getting queerer by the moment, in fact."

"Shouldn't you be at your mill, doing your milling, Mr. Sandywobbit?" said Ham. "All I know is my Sham is going to Mr. Bulbo's party. I hope he brings a date."

Days passed and The Day Of Bulbo Bunkins' Party drew near, whether young Promo Bunkins liked it or not. An odd-looking waggon (you or I would call it a "wagon") laden with odd-looking packages and paraphernalia toiled up the hill to Bulbo's condo in the Bug End neighborhood of Wobbiton. It was driven by an odd-looking old man, not a wobbit. He wore immense black wing-tip boots and affected an unnecessary scarf. He had a long, bushy moustache that stuck out beyond the brim of his hat. Many wobbits believed it to be nose hair. The bundles, the cart, and even the horse were each labeled with a large red P.

That was Pantsoff's mark, of course, and it was Pantsoff The Wizard driving the cart. Years as a contractor had made him keenly aware of the business value of Branding, so he put his mark on everything, even things that weren't his. He was famous in Wobbiton for his fireworks, as well as the fires and smokes that often resulted from them. Pantsoff dabbled in project management during the off-season, and in wizardry on a cash-only basis. As the waggon rolled past, some young wobbit toughs shouted after him "What's the 'P' stand for, old man? P as in…" Pantsoff quickly turned and silenced them by flipping a promotional P-rune beverage coaster at their leader's head.

"Run away now, you little punks!" said Pantsoff. "There's more coasters where that came from, and I'm not afraid to use them!"

Outside of Bulbo's condo behind the beauty salon, shortly after dinner, he and Pantsoff sat smoking their pipes. It was a filthy habit Bulbo had picked up on their project with Borin Oakmanfield and the dwarves, and he had trouble quitting it, somehow. He blew an expert smoke ring that rose away over the garden that Ham and his son Sham tended for minimum wage. Pantsoff then blew a series of rings that linked together to spell out *Pantsoff The Wizard, your one-stop project management solution!* As the cloud drifted, it flashed different colors.

"I think I need a holiday," said Bulbo.

"A holiday from what?" said Pantsoff. "You haven't done a day's work since the Oakmanfield Project!"

"A vacation, then. You know, my plan, my secret plan. At the party. My little joke."

"The one about the elf and his proctologist?"

"No," said Bulbo. "The one where I disappear from my own party and leave the bar bill for the Snackbag-Bunkinses."

"Ah," said Pantsoff. "Not much of a joke, really. More of a prank. Who will laugh, I wonder?"

The next day more waggons and even a few carts rolled up to the beauty salon with party-related deliveries. There might have been some grumbling along the lines of "Shop locally!" or "Support small businesses!" but that very week orders started pouring out to community merchants, requiring Bulbo to pay the Wobbiton sales tax. Deliveries were made of bulk-package hors d'oeuvres, boxes of wine, countless rolls of crepe paper decorations and every cheap party commodity you can imagine.

Before long, invitations were mailed in great numbers. The service at the Wobbiton post-office became even slower than ever, and the one in Buythewater township simply closed until vagrants could be rounded up to help. Bulbo blamed these "guest workers" for the low volume of RSVPs. In fact, his pre-stamped response cards reading *Thank you, I shall certainly come, with one guest* were mostly sitting on kitchen counters and dining room tables from Bug End to Bugger Heights. Bulbo was never to get an accurate headcount.

A notice appeared on Bulbo's rickety screen door: 1) MEETINGS BY APPOINTMENT ONLY and below that 2) APPOINTMENTS MUST BE SET AT REGULAR MEETINGS. Bulbo became even more reclusive than normal, plotting and scheming.

One morning, very close to the day of the party, all of Wobbiton was startled awake by a tremendous explosion. It came from a public park near the beauty salon. When wobbits from three neighboring homes went to investigate, they found Pantsoff standing in front of a smoking crater.

"That was some fine wizarding, if I do say so myself" he said to one and all. The blast radius centered in a spot previously occupied by a swing set, a teeter totter and a jungle gym. With the playground equipment blown up, cartloads of tents, tiki-torches and horseshoe pits were brought in directly from the road. Pantsoff paid off the nearby families to cover repairs of shrapnel damage to their homes and to keep them from making any official complaints to the Shirrif's Office. He had plenty of Bulbo's money available for his expenses.

Ham Sammich was soon re-tasked from his fake gardening duties to lead the putting-up of the tents. He introduced himself to everyone by saying "I'm the Tent-Erection Supervisor, you know, who makes sure the laborers are working hard." He called his son Sham the "Erection Foreman" until Sham begged him to stop.

Despite Ham's leadership, the tents were eventually assembled. The finest elf-cooks were brought in from the Murkywood Wood-Elf Lodge, and dwarf engineers were soon digging state-of-the-art latrines. The dwarves suggested that the especially large tree at one end of the park be decorated with festive yet practical strands of toilet paper.

Thursday, September 22 finally dawned. Before the gates were opened, wobbits were already lined up hoping for free breakfast burritos and hazelnut lattes. Bulbo had expected that by having his party at noon on a work-day he would avoid an unmanageably large turnout, but this was not the case. Wobbits far and wide took sick days and arrived, ready to start eating and drinking. Most of them had not returned their RSVPs, and many of them weren't invited at all. Bulbo met his guests and party-crashers in front of the crater Pantsoff had created when he "relocated" the poorly-placed playground equipment. The crater was filled with gifts that Bulbo handed out to all and Sundry. The latter, Mr. Blotto Sundry, was an acquaintance of Bulbo's from *The W Bush*, a small inn on the Buythewater road.

Wobbits give gifts to others on their birthdays. Not very good ones, of course, but it kept the Wobbiton gift-wrap industry booming. And it was a welcome diversion at work to have a birthday gift distribution a couple of times a week. Nobody really liked the gifts: Chia pets, Ginsu knives, blankets with sleeves, but they liked the excitement of getting them. They were usually cheaply made, often with the logos from various dwarf banks or investment companies on them, a sure sign of re-gifting.

Finally the incredible delay caused by the gift-bottleneck at the entrance was over. Everyone had received their gift and found a seat, and the drinking and eating began. There were three official meals: brunch, happy hour, and cocktails. These events were marked chiefly by the fact that there was food available with the drinks that flowed constantly. The rest of the time everyone was drinking as much as possible, since a rumor was circulating that the open bar would become a cash bar once the fireworks started. The drinking went on steadily until sundown.

A skyrocket exploded overhead, the sparks spelling out "Shop in Wobbiton and save! Paid for by the Wobbiton Chamber of Commerce." Two young wobbits watched Pantsoff's fireworks with great interest. One took a quirky little bite out of the fried pickle he was holding as he glanced about furtively. The wobbits ducked into the fireworks tent. The second wobbit, who somehow looked even stupider than the one holding a fried pickle, grabbed a nearby rocket.

"No, no!" said the pickle-wobbit. "Big one! Big one!" The stupid wobbit picked up another rocket so fanciful-looking that it seemed hazardous to launch. "Well? Stick it in the ground!"

"Stick what in the ground?" said the stupid one.

"The skyrocket of course! What did you think I meant?"

"I don't know. Whatever." The stupid wobbit stuck it in the ground. "Got a match?"

"Yeah, your face and my butt!" the first wobbit said, gesturing grandly with his pickle. "Ha! Really though, I don't, do you?"

"Do I what?"

"Do you have a match? Because I don't! Come on, dude!"

"No, I quit smoking. Well, now what do we—Youch!"

Both wobbits suddenly found themselves getting terrifying wedgies. Behind them was a mustachioed old man. He was twice their height, which gave him excellent leverage as he pulled higher and higher on the waistbands of their undies. Soon they were standing uncomfortably on tip-toe, as he addressed them each.

"Mariellen Buckiebrand" he said to the one with the pickle. "And Paraffin Dork. I might have known. Were you really going to set off a skyrocket inside a tent? A tent with clearly posted signs reading 'No Smoking'? A tent filled with fireworks, 190-proof Dwarven Everclear, and Southron-made flammable children's sleepware?"

"We were mostly improvising," said Mariellen. He liked to be called Rock, but everyone called him Mary. "We hadn't thought our plan through this far."

"It was all Mary's idea," said Paraffin. He was often called Puppy, not because of his cute, large eyes, but in recognition of his wisdom, attention-span and self-control.

"Idiots! I should turn you both into Crackerjack. You were about to burn yourselves horribly and ruin my remaining fireworks! But thanks to my intervention there will be plenty of rockets left to chase off any remaining guests at closing time. I just stopped in to get some distilled spirits to liven up Bulbo's punchbowl."

"Here, take a bottle in each hand. My hands are both full," he said as he dragged the wobbits by their underwear out of the tent. "Let's rejoin the party. Bulbo is about to make his speech!"

"Oh no!" cried Mary and Puppy. "Please turn us into Crackerjack, Pantsoff! Candy-coated popcorn, peanuts and a prize! Please!"

Pantsoff and the two young wobbits returned to the party looking for table space that would allow the three of them to sit together. They walked past many Bunkinses and Boffos, and also many Dorks and Buckiebrands. There were various Blobbs (relations of Bulbo's grandmother) and Slobbs (connexions of his Dork grandfather who insisted on spelling "connections" with an "x"). There was a selection of Churroses, Bulgers, Buttcrunchers, Craphouses, Widebodies, Hornhonkers and Smellfoots. The Snackbag-Bunkinses were not forgotten, indeed could not be, since they were famously rude even by wobbit standards. Oboe Snackbag-Bunkins and his wife Earlobia hated Bulbo and liked Promo even less, but they knew if they didn't attend the party they would be openly lampooned by Bulbo in his inevitable after-dinner speech. Pantsoff appeared to be looking forward to it for some reason, but the wobbits he was dragging along would have chewed their own legs off to escape.

Bulbo was about to begin. All his guests were either groggy from too many fried cheese curds, or on a post-sugar-buzz crash from too many deep fried Twinkies, or geezed from too much bulk-purchase beer. They were still eating and drinking, of course, and would continue to do so as long as there were tater tots and box wine within arm's reach.

Bulbo's table was in front of the Party Tree, which was festooned with toilet paper, conveniently close to the Party Latrines. The dwarves that dug them insisted that they be behind the head table to keep the run-off away from the pig-roast area. This had seemed like a smart approach until the wind shifted earlier in the afternoon. Bulbo stood up and cleared his throat.

"Stand up!" shouted a Heckler. The entire Heckler family had come all the way from distant Bugford Falls to eat Bulbo's free food.

"He is standing up!" shouted another. This is how all wobbit speeches begin.

My dear Bunkinses and Boffos, he began again; *and my dear Dorks and Buckiebrands, and Blobbs, and Slobbs, and Churroses, and Hornhonkers, and Bulgers, Buttcrunchers, Widebodies, Craphouses, and Smellfoots.* "SmellFEET!" shouted an elderly wobbit.

"Smell your own feet!" shouted another of the Hecklers.

Smellfoots, insisted Bulbo. *Also my good Snackbag-Bunkinses that I welcome,* Bulbo paused to do air-quotes, *at last, back to my condo behind and below Virginia's Beauty Parlor. Today is my one hundred and eleventh birthday. I am eleventy-one today! One-one-one! Almost one hundred twelve!* He went on like this for some time. It was all so pointless that even the Hecklers were speechless.

Like I said, Eleventy-one years, which is far too short a time to live among such excellent and admirable wobbits! Although when one is with my dear Snackbag-Bunkinses, even eleventy-one days seems like a very long time indeed. Tremendous outburst of approval.

I don't like half of you half as well as you might think, and I know less than half of what you think of me, which is how I like it. There followed a brief silence, broken when one confused wobbit yelled "He's a witch!" Nervously, Bulbo reached into his pocket, as if he was about to draw a gun and shoot his way out. But he had an even better exit planned.

Finally, he said, *I wish to make a couple of announcements. Will the owner of the blue ox-cart next to the latrines please move it immediately, you're double parked. Also, I regret to announce that I am going. I am leaving NOW. GOODBYE!*

Nothing happened. He looked panicky, patted his pockets, took a silver ring off his finger, and reached into his pocket again.

No kidding this time. I am leaving NOW, REALLY. GOODBYE!

He stepped down and vanished. There was a sudden flurry of fresh, hot popcorn falling out of air. The guests all took off their hats and held them up to catch yet more snack food for themselves. Then they noticed that Bulbo was gone.

"Finally!" a Heckler shouted. "I thought he'd never stop talking!"

Every Bunkins, Boffo, Dork, Buckiebrand, Blobb, Slobb, Churros, Bulger, Buttcruncher, Craphouse, Widebody, Hornhonker, and Smellfoot began to talk at once. Mostly they were asking where the dessert carts and Elvish Coffee were. Everyone talked except Promo. He had enjoyed Bulbo's joke, but didn't say so or laugh out loud; he thought it was more of a publicity stunt.

This was too bad, since Bulbo had intended to sneak out of town. To help reduce some of the controversy, Promo ordered that Pantsoff's huge supply of distilled spirits be quietly added to all punch, beer and wine. Given the appetite of the normal wobbit, many of them would forget about Bulbo's joke by morning, if they remembered the evening at all. Before a mickey could be slipped into his beer, though, Promo drained it and left quickly. He didn't want to have to dodge any of Pantsoff's final fireworks.

As for Bulbo Bunkins, you probably realize without being told that he had disappeared using the golden ring you're familiar with; the very magic ring that he had acquired on his journey with the Dwarves of Smithibank as detailed in his book *There Goes My Back Again.* After getting the wrong ring on the first try, he slipped it on his finger, disappeared, and was never seen by any wobbit in Wobbiton again, much like Hootie And The Blowfish.

He walked back to his below-ground condo, listening with a smile to the ka-booms of very low altitude fireworks and the shrieks of slow-moving party guests. Then he stepped down through the screen door into his home, or the "al-u-minium" door as the wobbits liked to say. He took off his tuxedo and put on a worn out dwarven cloak and some tattered corduroy pants so old the corduroy was worn smooth in many spots. He pushed some old Smithibank t-shirts aside in a dresser drawer and found an Elf Army Knife with multiple tools and the traditional red handle. It was only a pocket knife, but for a wobbit it was the size of an average shortsword, or perhaps a very short longsword. Large as it was for him, it fit discreetly into a pocket of the ancient pants.

He reached under his bed, not easy for any wobbit, and pulled out a hole-punched manuscript in a leather three-ring binder, which he put with some spare boxers, a few waistcoats and a swimsuit into a large gladstone bag. Then he swore, dug his tuxedo pants out of the laundry hamper, and took his golden ring out of one of the pockets. It was now attached to a fine chain, an uncanny chain that had been mysteriously absent during his disappearing act at the party. He went to his desk and found a formal looking document and an old bank envelope with a red string and two buttons on the back. He put in the document as well as his ring with its chain, closed the flap and wound the red rope back and forth around and around and around the two buttons. It was a really long string, because the envelope was only for the most important bank business. It said so on the front of the envelope. He wound it some more around and around until he ran out of rope. The envelope was sealed. He swore again, unwound and unwound the string, removed the ring and chain, and found a pen and ink. On the front of the envelope in the "To" column he wrote Promo's name, and in the "From" column he wrote his own. The he put the whole thing back together and put it on the coffee table by his recliner. Then he picked it up and stuck it in his pocket. It was then that Pantsoff walked in.

"You've left the party!" said Bulbo. "The frozen Margaritas must have run out."

"No," said Pantsoff. "There was just no sense in lingering. Too many sloshed wobbits looking for fights as they staggered to their waggons in the parking lot. I'm at a point in my career where I can't be seen duking it out with someone half my height. Did you like my concluding fireworks?"

"I loved watching those rubes run for their lives!" said Bulbo. "But why did you add the popcorn effect to my disappearance? My relatives thought you turned me into Fiddle Faddle!"

"And then they gathered you up and ate you!"

"They like a good snack," said Bulbo. "But it spoils my joke if they suspect you of foul play!"

"Since when is disappearing a joke? I'd call it more of a stage illusion. It's also a great way of drawing attention to the ring you've kept secret since the SmithiBank gig at the Only Mountain. Bulbo, I never know what you're going to do next!"

"I'm going on vacation. I am old, Pantsoff. Not as old as you of course, but old. I don't look it, but I'm beginning to feel it. Come to think of it, I've known you for decades and you've been an old man the whole time. What's with that?"

Pantsoff shrugged.

"Like I was saying, I feel all thin, sort of stretched, if you know what I mean, like when I joined that yoga class by mistake. I need a change! I want to see mountains again, Pantsoff—mountains. I want to see them through a large window in a ski resort, as I sit in a recliner by a roaring fire, sipping mulled wine.

I'll be able to finish the Deluxe Reissue of my book, with a new ending: *and he lived happily ever after to the end of his days.*"

Pantsoff laughed. "That has to be an improvement over all the other endings you tried: *After all, tomorrow is another day* or *Pantsoff, I think this is the beginning of a beautiful friendship,* or *That'll do, pig, that'll do.* But nobody will ever read the book, however it ends. The excerpts you posted at *The W Bush* were horrible!"

"Promo read them, and he thought they were great!"

"He has to," said Pantsoff. "He's your sole heir. He doesn't want you to write him out of your will."

"Good old Promo. You'll keep an eye on him, won't you, Pantsoff?"

"Yes, I will—two eyes, and a foot on his neck, as often as I can spare them. He's a tweenager, after all. If only I weren't so busy with my research on your ring. Say, where is the ring, anyway? We had a deal, you were supposed to give it up."

"Oh, it's here," said Bulbo. "And Promo will get it with everything else: the condo, the rootball cards and collectibles, and of course the silver, gold and all the jools."

"The what?"

"I'm sorry, the 'jewels.' Daddy Shortlegs long suspected I had them, but my stupid gardener has been denying it for years. I'm leaving him and his son to Promo, too. They'll be his problem."

"Yeah, that's great, Bulbo, but where's the ring?

"The what?"

"The ring!" said Pantsoff. "Where is it?"

"It's in an inter-office envelope right there on the mantle, you old idiot! What are you: blind or stupid? I swear, you are the most self-absorbed— oh wait. Here it is in my pocket. No offense, Pantsoff."

"None taken, half-pint. Now reach way up and set it on the mantle."

"Listen, you hulking geezer, where do you get off telling me what to do with my joolery?"

"Easy there, knee-high. Let's not get fussy."

"If I am it is your fault," said Bulbo. "It is mine, I tell you, mine! All mine! Bwa-ha-ha! My precious, I say, precious! Look at me when I talk to you, son! The precious is mine, I say, mine!"

"That voice! Where have I heard that voice?" said Pantsoff. "Now I remember! You sound exactly like the creature you 'won' the ring from, Lady Gol-Gol! And that's not meant as a compliment!"

"Here we go," said Bulbo.

"That's right! Let me tell you for the brazillionth time how potentially dangerous this ring is! Oh, and that 'stretched' feeling you mentioned? Probably caused by the ring! Look at the legal disclaimers for any magic ring, and you'll see things like 'May cause nausea, dry mouth, night hysteria and certain sexual side effects. Not for use by pregnant women, pregnant dwarves, or pregnant elves. Stretched feelings may result.' Give up the ring, Bulbo!"

"Give it up to who? You?"

Pantsoff's eyes flashed above his menacing mustache. The room darkened and he seemed to grow large, which is common when you try to stand up straight in a wobbit's rumpus room. Bulbo gaped at him and scuttled into a corner.

"Eek!" he said.

"Bulbo Bunkins! Do not take me for some conjuror of cheap tricks! I'm a wizard and a project manager, and my mystical Gannt charts all tell me that it is time for you to give up the ring!" Pantsoff appeared to shrink as he re-lit the lamps and sat down. Bulbo peeked out from behind the Lay-Z-Boy.

"Are you d-d-done?" he asked.

"Quite," said Pantsoff. "Now give us a hug!"

"Please, Pantsoff. Not in front of the dwarves." Three dwarves had entered the room with Bulbo's baggage, parcels and paraphernalia. Bulbo quickly recovered from his fright at Pantsoff's cheap trick. "Well, I'm off. I hope there's a market for your research. Give my best to Promo."

"Guys, give us a minute," Pantsoff said to the dwarves, who discreetly took Bulbo's things outside. Pantsoff continued with Bulbo.

"And the ring?"

"The what, now?"

"The ring," said Pantsoff, sighing. "It's still in your pocket."

"Ah, yes," said Bulbo. "So it is." He pulled out the red-rope envelope.

"Great. Is the ring in there, and is it the ring we're talking about? Why don't you open that envelope?"

Bulbo glared at him, and started unwinding the string that kept the envelope's flap closed.

"Take your time," said Pantsoff.

Bulbo finally got the string undone. He opened the envelope, held it out at arm's length, and turned it over. A little while later, the ring dropped out to the floor, now without the enigmatic chain. It landed with a strange "Ka-Boom" sound, and immediately lay flat on the linoleum floor. "There it is. Happy?" He put it back into the envelope.

"Ecstatic," said Pantsoff. "I'm also glad that thing didn't bounce away or roll. I wasn't about to try to get it out from under your chiffarobe."

"It's a home entertainment center."

"Maybe a credenza?"

"Whatever," said Bulbo, as he opened his screen door for the last time and joined the dwarves in the Wobbiton darkness. They walked off, as Bulbo sang quietly to himself a reprise of an old song, not bothering to update the lyrics:

The show must go forever on
So if there's money to be made
I'll once more put my mailshirt on
And kill a dragon again, someday
Or else I'll send a relative
Off to risk his limb and life
To him my magic ring I'll give
And my magic Elf Army Knife

Promo came in soon afterwards. He glanced about the condo and then quietly asked "Is Uncle Bulbo gone yet?"

"Yes, at last," said Pantsoff. "I thought he'd never leave. Oh, he left something for you." He handed Promo the inter-office envelope.

"Don't bother unwinding the string. Inside is his will, and his ring, too. His trust documents and his tax records are in the kitchen."

"Oh, great," said Promo. "How long do I have to keep that stuff? Five years? Seven years? Forever? I hate filing." He stopped complaining for a moment. "You said his magic ring is in there? Cool! I'll never have to pay a cover charge to enter a nightclub again!"

"Promo, you've inherited Bulbo's fortune, so stop thinking small for a change. Actually, don't think about the ring at all. Just put it away. Keep it secret, and keep it safe!"

Later that night the last remaining partygoers were removed, some in wheelbarrows by gardeners looking for new income streams. A final handful of wobbits refused to get into the barrows under any circumstances, wheeled or otherwise, for fear of the dread barrow-wights. Librarians and middle-school teachers were brought in to explain the various definitions of the word "barrow," but when this didn't help, the gardeners left and movers with hand-trucks arrived. Thus accommodated, the final wobbits were carted off, standing upright in their hand-trucks and unworried by the possibilities of barrows or wights.

Night slowly passed, like unconscious wobbits in wheelbarrows. But finally, late the next morning, even the most unconscious of them were up and around again. They eventually gravitated to the Bunkins ancestral condo. When a sizable crowd had gathered, muttering questions about Bulbo and his whereabouts, Promo stepped out of the screen door and read a prepared speech.

"Bulbo Bunkins has left the building. He is leaving Wobbiton to pursue other interests. He's been under a lot of stress lately, and would now like to spend less time with his family. You are trespassing on private property. The Shirriffs will be arriving shortly. Unless your name is on the posted list, get the heck off my lawn." The crowd grumbled and checked the list grudgingly. Promo called their names one by one, and handed out some deeply disappointing gag gifts from Bulbo, reading the labels aloud:

For BORA BUNKINS in memory of a LONG correspondence, with love from Bulbo; on a flaming bag of dog crap. Bora's annual holiday letter was so self-serving that most of the Bunkinses quickly threw it away unopened. Bulbo hoped that the humor (or "humour" as the wobbits would say) of his gift would be appreciated by all. He was insecure as a writer, so he telegraphed his jokes by capitalizing the punchlines.

For LADLELARD DORK for his VERY OWN, from Bulbo; on a flaming bag of dog crap. Ladlelard never picked up after his dog, an immense dachshund. Immense, relative to a wobbit.

For PHYLO CHURROS, hoping it will be useful, from B.B.; on a flaming bag of dog crap. Phylo enjoyed leaving flaming bags of dog crap at his neighbors' front doors on All Hallow's Eve.

For the collection of OUZO BUTTCRUNCHER, from a contributor; on a flaming bag of dog crap. Ouzo collected flaming bags of dog crap, and his collection was admired throughout Wobbiton. At least, by wobbits that liked that sort of thing.

For EARLOBIA SNACKBAG-BUNKINS, as a PRESENT; on a flaming bag of dog crap. Bulbo had taken a lot of crap from her over the years, and now could return the compliment with impunity.

Bulbo had hoped to indulge his love of irony by selecting an individualized and truly insulting gift for each recipient. But as is so often the case, he waited until the last minute and then had to make do with whatever was at hand. He had been busy with the party, after all. At least the notes were personalized.

Despite the hostile nature of the gag gifts, Bulbo also had put aside a great many real gifts that were wanted and welcomed by poor wobbits from the bad side of Wobbiton. These wobbits were so poor they couldn't live in anything as nice as a hole. To many of them he gave bottles of fortified buckie-wine. No wobbits wear shoes, so even the poorest wouldn't want them, but many of them enjoyed the legwarmers Bulbo gave away. To the very poorest, most of whom were in his employ, Bulbo finally made payment for their unused sick days. This was in accordance with a decision made in arbitration years earlier that Bulbo had avoided paying out. When you're the richest wobbit in town, you do what you want.

After everyone else left with their gag gifts, Earlobia Snackbag-Bunkins and her husband Oboe barged into the condo to hassle Promo. Their conversation was rather offensive. Perhaps not as offensive as a flaming bag of dog crap, but still offensive. They offered Promo unsolicited advice on planning a yard sale of Bulbo's belongings, hinting that they would take some of the hard-to-sell items off his hands if he asked them nicely. As they talked, they poked around Bulbo's home office. Earlobia found a pile of musical items left behind by Borin & Company when they surprised Bulbo at brunch sixty years earlier. He had been meaning to return them, but kept forgetting. There were noseflutes, cowbells, some forgotten fiddlesticks, and a pair of spoons that Borin's nephew Bufu had played beautifully.

Realizing they were not suddenly going to be offered some sort of settlement, Oboe tried a new approach. "This whole business stinks. And I'm not just talking about the gag gifts. The will says you're the sole heir, Promo? Sole heir, my Aunt Fanny! I demand to see the will!" Promo went to the mantle, got the red rope envelope and gave it to Oboe, who began unwinding the string.

"I'll be in the kitchen," said Promo. "Let me know when you've got that open." He really wished he could vanish, and then he noticed that Bulbo's ring had mysteriously found its way from the string-tied envelope into his pocket. He fidgeted with it for a moment, and then remembered why he came into the kitchen.

He started making some grilled cheese sandwiches for himself and Mariellen Buckiebrand. Mary was hanging around to avoid returning to Buckiebrand Hall, where it was his day to do the dishes. The two of them had just finished eating when Oboe called to them from the other room that he had the envelope open. It was a very long string, and the Snackbag-Bunkinses were almost as old as Bulbo. They did not benefit from the uncanny side-effects of a magic ring to keep them in perpetual middle-age, so they weren't as vigorous or as insulting as they had been in their prime. But they gave it their best.

"I'll be dipped!" said Oboe. "This will looks legit! Come on, Earlobia, let's get out of here. Curses, foiled again!" As they walked past the pile of dwarven musical accessories, Earlobia picked up a pair of claves and a few fiddlesticks.

"Just let him try to stop us!" she said to her husband. "We're old, and we're entitled, will or no will."

"And after waiting sixty years!" she said. "Fiddlesticks? Spoons! We should take the spoons, too!" Loaded with musical knick-knacks, they stepped out of the condo and slowly stumped off. They would have scuttled, like most wobbits, but for their advanced years. Earlobia stopped for a moment, trying to come up with a more memorable parting line.

Oboe turned to her and said "Forget it, dear. It's Wobbiton."

As they continued to stump back to their own hole, they sneered as they passed Pantsoff, who was heading towards Bulbo's condo. When he arrived there, he banged on the rattly screen door with his staff, which made the door even more rattly.

"Little pigs, little pigs, let me come in!" he shouted as he opened the door.

"Thank goodness it's you, Pantsoff!" said Promo. Never before had anyone ever said that to Pantsoff. "I thought it was Earlobia back again to steal more of Bulbo's old junk. I was ready to use his ring to disappear! Hey, what else does it do, besides providing eternal middle-age and making you disappear? Could I use it to turn the Snackbag-Bunkinses into llamas?

"Easy there, junior," said Pantsoff. "All the facts aren't in on that thing. The last sixty years just haven't been enough time for me to research the ring fully. I keep scheduling time to work on it, and then something else comes up and then the research has to be planned forward a few more years. You know how it is. So, why is it that you had the ring in your pocket at all? Is that secret? Or safe?"

"Well, um, I..."

"Just as I thought. The ring is already calling the shots, just as it was starting to do with Bulbo. Didn't you notice the effect it had on him?"

"Yes," said Promo. "It made him invisible and very rich, and it kept him from ever getting old."

"No, I mean besides that," said Pantsoff. "Any mood swings, irritability, shortness of breath, that sort of thing?"

"Not that I noticed."

"Well, be very careful with it. Try not to wear it, or handle it, or look at it, or think about it too much. But make sure you always know where it is, secret and safe."

"Should Mary be hearing all this?" said Promo. "He's in the kitchen."

"Son of a—" said Pantsoff as Mary walked in. "Mary, from now on you have to keep it secret and safe, too. Understand?"

"Whatever," said Mary as he went to take a nap in the guest room.

"With all these side effects," said Promo, "isn't it kind of dangerous for me to keep it here?"

"Oh my, no!" said Pantsoff. "No need to worry. Just as long as it's secret and safe, and you're not looking at it longingly or thinking about it."

"Great," said Promo. "Are you staying for dinner again?"

"I wish I could, but I can't. There's a guy I've got to talk to about this ring. Gotta run. You'll see me later, unless I see you first. Ha! Good-bye now. Bye!"

Promo saw him to the door. Pantsoff walked off at a surprising pace, but bent, as if carrying a great weight. A great weight, such as a sack of gold coins, one of which Promo discovered to be missing the next day. Promo didn't see him again for a long time.

Chapter 2

A SHADOW ON THE PANTS

The talk did not die down in nine days, but by ninety-nine, Bunkins was more the subject of anecdotes than of actual talk. Despite the many rumors, and despite Bulbo's plan, the bar bill from his party was paid in full by Promo, who settled all claims against Bulbo's estate. Eventually Mad Bunkins, who was said to vanish leaving only an insult and a pile of unwashed dishes, and then reappear with a tinfoil hat and a bag of stray cats, became a favorite character of legend. He would outlive other legends like Robin Took Of Murkywood Forest, or King Argeleb And His Knights Of The Round Table or even Johnny Athelas-Seed.

But prior to the finalization of his status as "legendary," word around Wobbiton was that Bulbo was either crazy, delusional or batty. All agreed that he had run off into the Wild Blue Yonder, searching for new ways of spending his endless fortune and squandering his eternal middle-age.

Promo carried on Bulbo's reputation for goof-balliness. He continued to cash Bulbo's Social Security checks. He threw annual parties in honor of Bulbo's birthday, now insisting on a cash bar and eliminating the sit-down meal, although it snowed appetizers and rained soft drinks, as the disappointed wobbits said later. It was odd that the parties continued, since most of Bulbo's neighbors either believed he was dead or wished he was dead. Odder still was that there was no mention at the parties that it was also Promo's birthday. Oddest of all was the fact that at each party Promo's friends slowly became fatter, grayer, and balder---but Promo did not.

This uncanny but unrecognized youthfulness of Promo's may explain why his friends were mostly younger wobbits, at least, younger at the start. Falcon Boffo and Froderick Blogger were two of these. But his closest friends were the pre-tween vandals that Pantsoff had disciplined at Bulbo's party, Paraffin "Puppy" Dork and Mary Buckiebrand. As self-absorbed as they were, even they noticed that in the seventeen years since Bulbo's party, Promo hadn't aged a bit. He was almost fifty, but he looked younger than the two of them, in their late thirties.

Approaching fifty made Promo uncomfortable, even though wobbits know nothing of our modern colonoscopies or prostate exams. He knew Bulbo was fifty when he was shanghaied by Pantsoff, tricked into becoming a consultant. What if the same thing should happen to him? Could Pantsoff convince him to give up a comfortable, boring life in Wobbiton and instead embrace the constant travel, the uncertain career path, and the lack of health benefits that were the life of a consultant?

There were rumors of strange things happening in the world outside. Wood-Elves, who normally avoided the hustle and bustle of Wobbiton, could now be seen passing through the edges of suburban Bugland Heights in their traditional orange and plaid. Dwarves were on the road in unusual numbers, even though they prefer the subway. Promo got news from them when he could, but it was mostly about a plummeting market and the coming economic meltdown. Even worse, they spoke in whispers about the force behind it all, the dread Competitor.

The wobbits had never heard that name before. They had, however heard of the dread Neccomancer, as legendary as Mad Bunkins himself. He was a figure of darkness, who besmirched the beauty of Little Earth like a shadowy gravy stain on corduroy pants. He had been driven out of his corporate headquarters in Murkywood forest by the White Council, so called because of its disappointing lack of diversity.

The Neccomancer shrewdly relocated to an abandoned corporate campus in the land of Bordor. There he reorganized his operations, rebranding himself as Smoron. He laid off most of his Goblins and replaced them with the slightly larger Porcs, who had been multiplying and dividing in the mountains. Some were able to calculate compound interest. There were trolls, too, no longer stupid but now just a little dim, and able to do collection work. They were armed with dreadful weapons such as really big hammers, and were more than willing to ruin a wobbit's credit rating. There were murmured hints of creatures even more terrible than these, but they had no name, which made them difficult to talk about. Hence the use of murmured hints, rather than scary campfire stories.

Little of this, of course, reached the sometimes pointed ears of ordinary wobbits. Wobbits don't have the attention span required for financial news that doesn't directly and immediately affect them. They prefer scandals and celebrity gossip. Ham Sammich, for example, was working for Promo one afternoon while at the same time drinking at *The Ass-Dragon Inn*. He was discussing the news of the day with Ted Sandywobbit.

"Queer things you do hear these days, Ted."

Ted loved a stimulating discussion. "Ha! Nothing's queerer than you, Ham!"

"Oh yeah?" said Ham. "Well, you're stupid!"

"Queer!"

"Stupid!"

"Queer!"

"Stupid!"

This went on all afternoon. Finally, after a leisurely dinner and more drinks, Ham got up and the two wobbits bid each other goodnight.

"Queer!" said Ted, waving.

"Stupid!" said Ham, as he nodded and stepped out the door.

It was just at this time that Pantsoff reappeared after a long absence. For years after the party he had been away. This was to avoid the legal issues that often followed one his fireworks displays. He'd visit Wobbiton only long enough to do a fireworks show, get paid in cash, empty Promo's larder and then vanish before he could be served any subpoenas. Sham was walking home from *The Ass-Dragon Inn* at the same time that Pantsoff was knocking on Promo's aluminum screen door.

"Open up, Promo!" he said. "I know you're in there. I'm a wizard!"

"I thought you were a Project Manager," said Promo as he opened the door.

"Ha HAA! You are in there, after all," said Pantsoff. "I knew it! Say, you haven't aged a bit since I passed through Wobbiton nine years ago."

"Has it been nine years? Well, you're right, I haven't aged a bit. It's great! But look at you! You've always looked old, Pantsoff, but you look even older than normal. What's the point of living for millennia if you start out looking old and look steadily older the whole time?"

"That's an interesting question coming from you, Promo. Why aren't you curious about your own eternal middle-age?"

"I assumed I inherited it from Uncle Bulbo."

"You inherited it all right. But it's not in your blood, it's in your ring!" said Pantsoff dramatically. "The ring you inherited from Bulbo!"

"Yes, that's what I meant."

"Oh. Well, did you keep it secret? Did you keep it safe? Because it's time I told you how powerful Bulbo's ring really is. You're in great danger!"

"I'm in great danger," said Promo, "and you're just telling me now? You made Bulbo give the ring to me thirteen years ago. You're a little late warning me, aren't you?"

"A Project Manager is never late, my dear wobbit. He provides critical information to his friends exactly when he intends to."

"So you intended to withhold information, putting me in great danger?"

"Um, no, not as such," said Pantsoff. "Actually that whole 'never late' thing sounded much better in my head, before I said it."

"Ah. You were telling me about the ring..."

"Yes! Bulbo's ring! I've learned quite a lot after thirteen years of ring-related due diligence."

"You didn't start researching the ring until after you gave it me? What were you doing during the decades when Bulbo had it?"

"Promo, you must realize there are many other projects in the world besides this one. I am managing several of them."

"Name one."

"I, uh, well, I can't discuss them because, um, it would violate the confidentiality agreement I have with all my clients. It's part of the Wizard's Code that requires my compliance as an accredited member of the White Council."

"Shame on you, Pantsoff, for belonging to a Restricted club."

"Not again, Promo, please. It's not a restricted club, it's a professional association. It's just called the White Council. We're all wizards and sorcerers and so forth."

"Uncle Bulbo always wanted to buy his way in. Couldn't you have just one wobbit in your membership? Perhaps one with a dangerous and powerful magic ring?"

"Speaking of your ring, Promo, I was about to tell you of the danger you're in as its owner. You see, once upon a time, the elves made lots of magic rings that provided a variety of super-powers. Being able to fly, or see through walls, or bend steel in your bare hands, these are just few of the common ones. But your ring, Promo, is one of the Really Great Rings.

"You were going to tell me about how it's dangerous."

"Yes, exactly! Very dangerous indeed. You see, your ring is dangerous to a mortal like yourself. As you know, I'm practically immortal, but even I---"

"You're a terrible braggart, for an immortal. I bet vampires don't blather on about being immortal as much as you do."

"Promo, please. The point is that a mortal that keeps this ring will never die, but never grow, either. He, or she, will only continue, until at last every minute is a weariness."

"Yes, I see, like this conversation."

"And if a mortal uses The Ring's invisibility feature often enough, he *fades*: he becomes, in the end, invisible permanently."

"Don't be ridiculous! Uncle Bulbo used the ring all the time, and he never faded. And Bulbo's descriptions of Gol-Gol never mentioned that he looked faded, either, and he used it since prehistoric wobbit times, for hundreds of years!"

"Yes, well, I have some theories about that, too. Wobbits may be more resistant to The Ring's side effects than mortals of other races. Generally, though, most mortals using The Ring end up taking that long walk in the twilight, under the eye of the dark power that rules the all The Rings!"

"Twilight walks? What the heck are you talking about? And why are you now capitalizing 'The Ring?'"

There was a long, awkward silence. A "snip, snip, snip" sound came from Sham Sammich out in the garden.

Despite the silence, Pantsoff wasn't getting the hint that it was time for him to leave. Promo gave in first, and asked "Is there anything else?"

"Not really, just a few technical matters," said Pantsoff. "The ring can change in size and weight, much like a struggling celebrity. It can slip off your finger if it wants to 'trade up' to a new owner with greater potential."

"Yes, it did that to Bulbo all the time. Go figure. This chain on the ring is pretty weird, too. Sometimes it's there, but sometimes it isn't. What have you learned about that, Pantsoff?"

"Nothing. In all the writings about the ring, even in the appendices, there's not a word about the uncanny chain."

"That's not much of an answer. Is there anyone else I could talk to, perhaps your manager?"

"Oh, you mean Saccharin The White."

"Another racist, Pantsoff?"

"No, of course not. But he doesn't care much for wobbits."

"I see. But not because of racism."

"He has no interest in wobbits because all his market research is on the Really Great Rings. And unlike elves, dwarves and men, no wobbits were included in the focus groups for the Rings, so there was no data available. Not until now. Or rather, not until Bulbo stole the ring from Gol-Gol. But that's a very recent development."

"Bulbo stole the ring almost eighty years ago!"

"Yes. We members of the White Council like to keep our eyes on the Big Picture. I asked Saccharin at one of our regular meetings about the dangers of The Juan Ring, but he told me not to worry about it, that his report would be published very soon. Bulbo seemed fine, so I decided to quietly take the initiative and do some research of my own. And after only seven or eight decades, I can assure you that Bulbo will probably not suffer any permanent side effects from his possession of the ring. Other than his unnaturally long middle age. But most of my time is spent researching wobbits, and my current theory is that you all are virtually immune to most ring-related ailments.

"Wobbits!" said Pantsoff. "You little guys are full of surprises. You can be as soft as expensive toilet paper, or as tough as a two-farthing steak. Nobody in Little Earth knows more about wobbits than me! Not even Smoron himself, until now."

"How did Smoron find out about wobbits?"

"Probably he read the article I published, titled 'Wobbits: Their Immunity To The Juan Ring And Their Value As Slaves.' By the way, could I see that ring of yours for a minute?"

Promo pulled the ring out of the pocket of his little corduroy pants. It was chained to his belt, like a biker's oversized wallet. He unfastened it and handed it to Pantsoff.

"Look at it closely, in the light from the fireplace. Are there any markings on it? Any at all?"

"Um, no?"

"Correct! Remember your answer. Now watch carefully, and don't look away from the ring for even a moment." The wizard threw it suddenly into the fire.

"Hey!" said Promo. "I just had that chimney swept!"

"Wait!" said Pantsoff with a commanding voice, giving a quick look from above his bristling mustache. He held Promo back, and the room became dark and silent, except, of course, for the sound of Sham's snipping in the garden. Pantsoff attempted some misdirecting small talk.

"Have we ever met before? Please tell everyone your name."

"Gimme back my ring, you moron!" said Promo, wriggling.

"Very well. Just keep watching the ring." Pantsoff reached into the fire with some tongs and got the ring. He held it up in front of Promo. "Here, take it. It is quite cool."

"Are you crazy? You're holding it with tongs! You take it!"

"Oh, for Pete's sake! Take the ring, Promo!" He grabbed Promo's hand and dropped the ring into it.

"Hot!" shrieked Promo, followed by "Oh, it is cool. Weird."

"Now, then, were there any marks on it before?"

"No..."

"But how about now? Look closely."

"It looks like there are fiery letters."

"Ta daaa!" said Pantsoff as he flourished broadly, and then bowed. "Thank you! Thank you!"

"Your close-up magic has really improved, Pantsoff. But I can't read the writing. I don't even recognize the language."

"No, because you met your foreign language requirement in high school by taking the Conversational Mermaid class. But I know all the languages of elves, men and porcs, so I will translate it for you." He cleared his throat.

Juan Ring to lay them off, Juan Ring to find them,
Juan Ring to hire them as temps
and with a contract bind them

"It is only two lines of an Olde Elvish verse:"

Three rings for the Elven-kings to make sales calls,
Seven to the Dwarf-lords for performance reviews
Nine for Mortal Men with their brass balls
One for the Dark CEO to use
In the Land Of Bordor where regs don't apply
Juan Ring to lay them off, Juan Ring to find them,
Juan Ring to hire them as temps
and with a contract bind them
In the Land Of Bordor where regs don't apply.

He paused, and then said slowly in a deep voice, "This is the Super-Ring, the Juan Ring."

"'Juan Ring to hire them as temps and with a contract bind them,'" said Promo. "What the heck does that mean?"

"It's Smoron's Mission Statement. No one likes making sales calls or doing performance reviews, and so he tempted the elves and the dwarves with lesser rings that would make these tasks easier. And you know how Mortal Men are. Which means that this is the ring he lost ages ago. He'll do anything to get it back, and it would be really bad if he did."

Fear seemed to stretch out at Promo like an angry middle finger, rising up and flipping him off from the East. "Great! That's the most terrifying set of Core Values I've ever heard," he said. "Now I know why the thing is dangerous. It was conveniently lost for ages until my uncle found it, and then you made him give it to me. Now Smoron, the most mysterious, powerful and hated CEO in Little Earth has returned from the dead and wants it back. And you're telling me I can't give it to him!"

"Exactly! You're even sharper than Bulbo!"

"I wish it need not have happened in my time," said Promo.

"So do I," said Pantsoff. "But what can you do?"

"Why me, Pantsoff?"

"I don't know. Some days you eat the chimera, and some days the chimera eats you. If Smoron gets The Ring, Little Earth will enter a new era of misery. There will be corruption, unfair taxation, gerrymandering, atonal music, unregulated banking, malfeasance, low student test scores, corporate acquisitions, malaise, special interest lobbying, and endless junk mail. Here, let me show you this memo from Galadtameetcha, a member of the White Council. It tells you everything you need to know. You take a look at it, while I listen to Sham snipping in the garden."

Promo read the memo, his lips moving furiously. "Wow! Galadtameetcha really sticks it to you in this thing. And whatever happened to the other rings?"

"Ah!" said Pantsoff. "That is a very long story."

"No surprise there," said Promo.

"Yes, well, the Three Elven Rings the elves hid from Smoron. Of The Seven Dwaven Rings, Smoron made generous mint-condition offers on all of them, but was only able to acquire three. The others had already been dismantled and their various components sold at a huge profit. The Nine Rings Of Men are still held by the original owners, who were long ensnared by them. These great kings of men, great captains of industry, lost their souls. They were once great producers of goods, mighty job creators, but now they are mere shadows. They are yes-men to Smoron's terrible will, making public appearances where he cannot and providing statements for the media.

"Of course, since Smoron put so much of his power and capitol into The Juan Ring, neither he nor his corporate empire can be destroyed while The Ring still exists. To make matters worse, if he recovers it, he will have control over the mysteriously missing Elven Rings, and he will be stronger and wealthier than ever."

"Then why wasn't it destroyed by Isadora?"

"Good question, and one we all asked ourselves. It was Gil-Gameshalad the Elven-King and Ellen-Doll of Westinghouse who overthrew Smoron, though they themselves perished in the deed. Ellen-Doll's son, Isadora is said to have finished him off. He then took the Ring, some say by cutting it off Smoron's hand."

"Gross! That sounds like a cheap shot for a good guy."

"Not as good as we hoped. Men are easily tempted by the Ring, and even though the original plan was that the Ring be immediately destroyed, Isadora gave in to his desire for the ring, the way a dieting wobbit gives in to his desire for a doughnut. He kept it, but it abandoned him, the worst decision the ring ever made. It was on the hand of a king, but then went down a river, and then to the slimy hand of prehistoric wobbit loner: Gol-Gol, of the Moisty Mountains."

"Gol-Gol was a wobbit?"

"Sort of. Long ago there lived by the banks of the Really Great River an underhanded and clay-footed group, the ancestors of the Stool family. They made little boats and bathyspheres out of reeds, and loved the River. The sneakiest of that family was called Beagol. He liked basements and sewers and subways and caves. He had a slightly more normal friend called Treagol. Together, they came up with the whole rhyming name fad that would become so popular with the Dwarves years later.

"The two of them were playing Orco-Polo in the river on day when Treagol found a beautiful golden ring. Beagol snuck up, got one look at it and knew he would stop at nothing to have it."

"'Give us that, Treagol, my love,' he said."

"'Whoa, whoa, whoa!' Treagol said. 'There are a couple of things I object to in that sentence. The easiest one for me to talk about is your demand, without even saying please, for my new ring.'"

"'But it's my birthday, my love, and I wants it.'"

"'Claiming it's your birthday may get you free cake when you're eating at Mithril Tuesdays, but you're not getting anything from me. And this 'my love' stuff has got to stop right now. It's not like we're Elves or something.'"

"'No, my love. Would an elf strangle you, like this?'"

"'Gack!' said Treagol. When Beagol was was done strangling his late best friend, he smiled, took the ring and put it on his finger, and said 'Now you're mine, I say, mine, my precious! Bwa-ha-ha!'"

"Beagol returned home. When his family took even less notice of him than usual, he slowly realized that wearing the ring made him invisible. He found that he couldn't resist using it for pranks and practical jokes. They were mostly of the Fake Haunted House or the I'm Not The One That Farted variety, and neither friends nor family found them to be very funny. They kicked him, and he bit their feet, which is hard to do while you're being kicked. He took to shoplifting and identity theft, and finally his no-nonsense grandmother made him leave town. He stayed in disreputable motels until his money ran out, and then moved into a modest hole in the ground, more of a ditch, actually. He dug an addition which gave him a lot more storage space and a formal dining room. Soon he dug another two rooms, and then more. Eventually he dug his way into the heart of the Moisty Mountains. There he lived off raw fish and careless goblins. The goblins called him Gol-Gol."

"Why?" said Promo. "because of the constant gurgling in his throat?"

"Don't be ridiculous. If that were the case they would have called him Mr. Ahem, or Lord Harumph. No, they called him Gol-Gol because that's what he named himself. He took his pet name for his gramma and used it to reinvent himself. She threw him out, and it was his passive-aggressive attempt at revenge. Some say that his friends call him Lady Gol-Gol because of his big eyes, thin face and long fingers, but this is ridiculous too, because he hasn't had friends for hundreds of years."

"So the ring was trapped with Gol-Gol," said Promo. "Why did it abandon him for Bulbo? It's hardly a promotion, perhaps a lateral move at best."

"The ring was answering the call of Smoron, not daring to ask its master to leave a message instead. It left Gol-Gol for the unlikeliest person imaginable, and by person I mean wobbit. Bulbo was hardly a wise choice for the ring or for Smoron, so we must assume that there was something else at work. Perhaps, and I'm just brainstorming here, Bulbo was *meant* to find the ring, and *not* by its maker. In which case you also were *meant* to have it. And that is an encouraging thought."

"Encouraging for you, perhaps," said Promo. "You're not the one stuck with Little Earth's most dangerous piece of stolen merchandise. So Smoron is looking for it, but maybe he doesn't know I'm the one that has it. And I suppose Gol-Gol is after it, too?"

"Don't worry about that," said Pantsoff. "Gol-Gol's gone to Bordor to rat you out to Smoron."

"Crap!" said Promo. "Now what do I do? Maybe I could find Bulbo and give the ring back to him. Yeah, that's it! It's a pity Bulbo didn't kill Gol-Gol when he had the chance."

"Pity?" said Pantsoff. "It was Pity that stayed his hand. Pity, and Mercy. 'Mercy!' Bulbo said to himself, 'it's a pity I didn't hit Gol-Gol hard enough to kill him. I was sure a shovel-blow to the head would do the trick, but he's just unconscious. No time to finish him off, though, there's goblins ahead. They'll probably kill him and save me the trouble.'" Pantsoff looked down at Promo.

"Uncle Bulbo told you all this?" said Promo. "He actually said all these things?"

"Maybe he did, maybe he didn't. The important thing, Promo, is that you not live in the past."

"Whatever. If Gol-Gol were here right now, I know I could kill him. I could kill Bulbo, too. He's given me this ring that's practically a death sentence. He deserves death."

"Deserves it!" said Pantsoff. "I daresay he does. Many that live deserve death, and many that die deserve life. That's very clever; I'll have to tell that one to Bulbo. He's quite a fan of irony. Seriously, though, you're in real trouble. What do you plan to do?"

"You're the Project Manager! Start managing! You tell me!" said Promo. Then his face suddenly brightened. "Hey, I know! You're on the White Council, you take it!" Promo tossed the ring to a surprised and terrified Pantsoff.

"No!" said Pantsoff. He caught it with the sleeves of his robe and tossed it back to Promo.

"I don't want it," said Promo as he tossed back.

"You keep it," said Pantsoff, batting it back as if it were a live grenade.

"I insist," said Promo, as he returned it with a nice lob.

Pantsoff gathered his wizard robes and jumped onto a wobbit-sized davenport to avoid the ring. It fell to the floor and stopped dead, just like when Bulbo dropped it on the same floor years earlier.

"Cut it out, Promo!" he said. "If I accepted the ring, I could make sales calls without fear, I could deliver performance reviews that would satisfy everyone, and I would of course defeat Smoron. But that would make me the CEO of his parent company, World Domination Solutions. And that's a job I don't want, no matter how good the salary, bonus structure, benefits, 401k and severance package make it appear. It's lonely, the hours are endless, the media hounds you constantly, and everyone's out to get you, both your friends and your enemies. I will not take the ring. You, on the other hand, can keep it with virtually no side effects, like I said. Except for invisibility and a swooning sensation when you use it, and extremely long life with mild ring-related paranoia the rest of the time."

"Until Smoron kills me," said Promo.

"Good point," said Pantsoff. "Maybe you should get out of town for a while. Use a fake name: Guy Incognito, Clark Kent, something like that. How about Mr. Underwear? And take some friends with you. If you're in a group of four wobbits there's a chance that Smoron will kill one of them by mistake, thinking he's killing you. He has spies everywhere, Promo."

Outside, Sham's snipping had somehow grown quiet. Too quiet. With one impossibly quick movement, Pantsoff reached over a table, through a window and then down, pulling in Sham, who was holding a wine glass up to his ear.

"You have your first applicant for the position of Traveling Companion, Promo. Or should I turn him into something unnatural, like a Perpetual Motion Machine, or Blue Food? What do you say, Sham?"

"I'd be happy to travel with Mr. Underpants! Will I have mini-bar privileges?"

Chapter 3

THREE IS A CROWD

"I thought we decided you would leave three weeks ago," said Pantsoff. "You ought to go quietly, but you ought to go. You've been so concerned about keeping your traveling preparations quiet that you haven't made any at all."

"Yeah, I've been really busy," said Promo. "It's been crazy around here. And it would help me to put my itinerary together if you would tell me where I'm going. Is there a plan yet?"

"I've got that all worked out for you. Simply walk southeast until you see a giant volcano. If you need to ask for directions, say that you're looking for the Crotch Of Doom. You can fill in the blanks as you go."

"That's not much of a plan."

"Nonsense!" said Pantsoff. "I once presented a similar plan to your Uncle Bulbo and he did quite well for himself, burgling the treasure from a dragon. He answered his own questions on a just-in-time basis. You'll know you're headed in the right direction because the trip will become more and more dangerous. Of course, you may want to stop off at Enron's Famous Last Waffle House at Riverdale."

"Riverdale!" said Promo. "Little Earth's finest resort! Sham will be delighted! Who will be paying his mini-bar bill, by the way?"

"Oh don't worry about that," said Pantsoff. "I'll have the White Council reimburse all your valid expenses. Be sure to keep your receipts."

One summer's evening, an astonishing piece of news reached *The Ass-Dragon Inn* and *The Ivy Drip*: Mr. Promo had sold his basement condo below Virginia's Beauty Salon. He had sold it to Earlobia Snackbag-Bunkins! It was all part of an improvised attempt at covering his tracks as he left Wobbiton to "downsize his lifestyle" and take advantage of the "booming housing market in the stylish Bug End neighborhood." He told everyone that would listen that he was moving to the more affordable Buckiebrand area.

Most wobbits assumed that Promo had become yet another victim of dwarf banking. The largest dwarf bank, Smithibank ("The Bank For Smithies") was constantly being accused of predatory lending. Promo's neighbors figured that he had mortgaged Mr. Bulbo's prize condo to finance a lavish secret second life, and now was unable to make the inevitable balloon payment. Some of them whispered about foreclosure. It was all a story, of course. The creation and distribution of this story, all to cover his trip to the Crotch Of Doom, was the cleverest thing Promo had ever done. It wasn't elf-clever or dwarf-clever or even wizard-clever, but for a wobbit, it was incredibly brilliant.

Pantsoff hung around Bug End for another two months, all the time nagging Promo about the urgency of the adventure, while at the same time constantly asking Promo to do his laundry, run errands with him, and listen to his anecdotes.

Finally, after Promo refused to lend him a few farthings, Pantsoff decided it was time to leave. "I've got some stuff I've got to do," he said. "I'll be back in a few days, definitely in time for your going-away party. In the meantime, stick to my plan, and be more careful than ever, especially of the Ring. Don't use it. Let me say that again with special emphasis: *don't use it!"* With that, he left.

"Don't use what?" said Promo. "Were you talking to me?"

As one would expect, Pantsoff was nowhere to be found when Promo began packing his things. Box after box of roleplaying game rulebooks, carefully preserved graphic novels, and the last of Bulbo's rootball memorabilia were packed and stacked by the door. Once the packing was mostly done, and the day of the going-away party had arrived, there was still no Pantsoff.

"It's unlike him to pass up a free meal," thought Promo, but he assumed it was due to the wizard's overall unreliability.

On September 20th, two waggons, a wain, and a surrey with a fringe on top all went off to Buckieland, conveying all of Promo's stuff to his new home by way of the Buckiewine bridge.

The "party" took place in the echoey, empty condo. All the wobbits that couldn't avoid Promo's pleas for help with the move were there: Froderick "Blimpy" Blogger, Falcon Boffo, and of course, Mariellen Buckiebrand and Paraffin "Puppy" Dork. They ate traditional moving day fare: pizza delivered from the local Little Steward's franchise and bottles of Ye Olde Style beer.

"Our last meal in the condo," said Promo, when they were done eating. He had been saying things like that all day. He gathered up all the pizza boxes, dirty paper plates, used napkins and empty beer bottles and said "Our last taking out of the garbage" as he carried them towards the back door. The other wobbits rolled their eyes. But Mary grabbed the boxes and bags and dumped them in the empty rumpus room in the middle of the shag carpet, insisting that the trash be left for Earlobia "to help her feel at home." The party was officially over, and Pantsoff had not come. Promo was worried, but also greatly relieved. With no Pantsoff to entertain, there was no need for Promo to go out for more beer.

After kicking around the garbage in the rumpus room, they went through the condo removing all the candles, toilet paper, and anything else that the Earlobia might need as soon as she moved in. Puppy spent forty-five minutes running back and forth making hooting sounds, to enjoy the unusual echo. He eventually tuckered himself out and fell asleep on a built-in sectional with the other wobbits. It was crowded, but better than sleeping on the floor. At some point during the night, Falcon Boffo took a six pack and went home to avoid additional work.

Bright and early at 11:45 the next morning they woke and packed the last boxes of action figures onto a waiting stagecoach. Mary took charge, and drove off with Blimpy to get Promo's studio apartment in Buckieland ready for his arrival. Promo had paid them to do this, but it was worth it. Mary dropped off the key with Earlobia's adult son Loatho. Loatho still lived at home, so he was looking forward to finally having his own room at Bulbo's comparatively spacious condo. As Mary drove away, he and Loatho shook fists at each other in contempt, as was their custom.

Promo and the others brunched on cold pizza and warm beer, then took a nap until dinner, then had more leftovers, and then shouldered their lumpy duffle bags. They were ready to get going when they noticed that Sham had disappeared, causing Promo to search quickly for The Ring until he heard the sound of bottles being opened in the pantry.

"Sham! What the heck are you doing in there?" Promo yelled, but then Sham reappeared, wiping his mouth and offering bottles to all.

"Here you go, gentlemen," Sham knew that Old Mr. Bulbo had become an accomplished home-brewer, and Sham was saying goodbye to the remaining bottles of Bulbo's delicious Earlobia Stout. The handmade label featured a whimsical drawing of a plus-size version of Promo's aunt.

"Good idea," said Puppy. "It wouldn't do to leave any of these about where they might hurt Earlobia's feelings. At least, let's not leave any full ones! Isn't that right? Aye?" They yelled "aye," drank their stouts and soon were walking.

"I'll last for a bit now, Mr. Promo, sir," Sham said. "When are we going to take a bathroom break?"

After the first of many, many bathroom breaks, Sham rejoined Promo and Puppy, and on his head was a stupid little hat which he called a fedora. He said it was stylish, too stylish to wear in Wobbiton. Everyone agreed that, even in the gloom, he looked like an idiot.

In their maroon windbreakers they could hardly be seen in the darkness. Since they were all wobbits, and tired of making small talk about Sham's hat, they made no noise that even a vole or marmoset could hear. Silently, Promo turned and waved goodbye to Wobbiton for the twentieth time.

"I wonder if I shall ever look at that lousy little village again?" he said tragically. Puppy turned to Sham and pantomimed a mocking scene of weeping and vomiting.

They walked on, and the road led through a forest or wood or something. After a half hour or so they took another bathroom break and stopped for the night. They slept in a pile, as wobbits do in the wild. A fox traveling on business stopped and sniffed in case if any of them seemed good to eat.

"Wobbits!" he thought. "Three of them, sleeping out of doors in a heap. There's something mighty queer behind this." He was quite right, but he decided to not get involved, just to be on the safe side.

Morning came as cold and clammy as the hands of a parody writer. The wobbits argued about what to have for breakfast, started a fire, and cooked some bacon, sausage links, sausage patties, three strip steaks, and some eggs. They ate, argued about cleaning up, and while Puppy cleaned the pans, Promo and Sham repacked their lumpy duffle bags. In just a few short hours they were underway.

"This road goes on forever," said Puppy as they stopped for lunch."Where is it we're going? Why? Are we there yet?"

"Do elves live in these woods?" asked Sham.

"Which kind?" asked Promo.

"Why, Wood-Elves, of course."

"I don't know," said Promo. "There might be High Elves, or even Regular Elves."

"What's the difference?" said Sham.

"Well, Wood-Elves live in the woods, and the other kinds, well, they live in the woods, too. But I'm sure there's a difference. I just can't put my finger on it."

"You're both stupid," said Puppy. "There's no such thing as Elves."

"No such thing?" said Sham. "Well, that does it. No one talks like that in front of Sham Sammich. Defend yourself, Mr. Paraffin!" They dueled a bizarre fisticuffs/sissy slap-fight until they noticed Promo, singing softly to himself.

The show must go forever on
So if there's money to be made
I'll once more put my mailshirt on
And kill a dragon again, someday

Or else I'll send a relative
Off to risk his limb and life
To him my magic ring I'll give
And my magic Elf Army Knife

"So Mr. Bulbo's song has come true at last," said Sham. "Here you are, risking limb and life, all for his ring."

"There's been no danger yet that I've noticed," said Promo. "Do you suppose Pantsoff could have been wrong about the whole thing?" He smiled, winked broadly, and they all laughed at Pantsoff. The number and scope of his errors over the years was known to all.

"But you know what Bulbo used to say: 'It's a dangerous business, Promo, going out of your door. You step into the road, and if you don't watch out, you could slip on a banana peel. Or step on a rake and hit yourself in the eye. Or have a piano fall on your head.' He worried about all kinds of crazy stuff. It was pretty difficult to live with him those last years before he left."

Promo stopped talking suddenly. "Did you hear that?" he asked.

"No," said Puppy. "Because you were talking about Bulbo's delusions."

"I wasn't listening to you, sir," said Sham. "I heard a noise, too. A horse." An eerie wind blew some leaves ominously.

"I think we should get off the road," said Promo.

The other two wobbits looked at him.

"What?" said Sham.

"Huh?" said Puppy.

"Get off the road!" shrieked a now panicky Promo. He shoved them into a nearby gully. The sound of a horse drew nearer. Promo didn't want to look, but he couldn't stop himself. He saw a horse and on it was a full-sized man, not a wobbit or dwarf or even an elf. He was thin, in a very dark suit, and had an expensive haircut, but his face was somehow invisible. Promo ducked down again.

The riding executive came very close to the wobbits. Worms and centipedes started wriggling up out of the soil around them. Puppy was mouthing the word "Gross!" to the other two when the rider made a sniffing sound, as if he was about to hold out a milk carton and say "Smell this milk. Does this smell bad to you?"

Promo felt an urge to put on his ring, like when the person next to you at an important event yawns and you want to yawn too, but you know you don't dare. The urge was becoming irresistible, and the rider's fox-like sniffing was now quite annoying. Sham wanted to hand him a tissue.

Sham was at that moment realizing that his fried meat breakfast would soon force him to give away their position to the sniffing rider. He threw a rucksack full of bangers and mash into the woods as a distraction. The uncanny executive was startled. He sniffed again, this time as if he was fighting a kingsfoil allergy. Then he rode off to investigate Sham's decoy.

Once the hoofbeats faded into the distance, Puppy spoke up. "Well, I call that very queer, and I'm a Dork. I know Queer, and that was Queer. It almost seemed like he was looking for us."

"Of course he was looking for us, you moron!" said Promo. "He was looking for me! And the ring! I wish I had known we were being followed."

"Maybe now isn't the time," said Sham, "but I'm reminded that the Grasper had a message for you. Before we left he said 'Hello, Sham.' I said 'Hello, Dad.' He said 'How's the packing coming along?' I said 'Not bad, we just--'"

"Skip to the message, Sham."

"Very good, sir. So Dad says to me *There's been a strange customer here looking for Mr. Promo. I didn't like the sound of him. He seemed nice, but mean at the same time, like he was trying to sell me something I didn't need, perhaps a home equity loan. He sounded right put out when I told him that Mr. Promo had left Wobbiton for good. Hissed at me, he did, even worse than when the dwarves at Smithibank hiss. It gave me a shudder, it did.*

What sort of fellow was he? says I to the Grasper. *Oh, he was a black guy, I'm sure of it. I didn't see his face, because he didn't have one, but he just seemed black. You know what I mean. He spoke funny.*

"I didn't know your dad was a racist," said Promo.

"He's not, Mr. Promo," said Sham. "He's just, um, old."

"That's not an excuse."

"No, sir, it isn't. But there we are."

"Yes. But as I said before, it might have been helpful to know that an evil, uncanny businessman was looking for me before I headed into the wilderness, beyond rescue or aid."

"Indeed, sir."

"Still," said Puppy, "there may be no connection between the Grasper's mysterious stranger and our well-dressed Rider. It may just have been a coincidence that two evil-looking spirits in black both have been looking for you."

"Perhaps it was my imagination, Puppy," said Promo. "But we should get going all the same, in case any more Riders show up. It's miles before we arrive in Buckieland."

As was his habit, Promo started quietly singing a wobbit walking song. Bulbo had written the words and forced them into a public-domain tune. He had planned to sell the song, but no one liked it besides Promo.

Upon the hearth, the fire is red
Beneath the roof a bed
But we're not blue, we like to brag
About our duffle bags
Val-deree, val-derah
Val-deree, val-derah-ha-ha-ha-ha-ha
Val-deree, val-derah
Our lumpy duffle bags

Still round the corner there may wait
New paths and secret gates
Our heads held high, we do not drag
Our lumpy duffle bags
Val-deree, val-derah
Val-deree, val-derah-ha-ha-ha-ha-ha
Val-deree, val-derah
Our lumpy duffle bags

Home is behind, the world ahead
With many paths to tread
But we're not tired and we're not sad
Thanks to our duffle bags
Val-deree, val-derah

Val-deree, val-derah-ha-ha-ha-ha-ha
Val-deree, val-derah
Our lumpy duffle bags

Before the song ended, Puppy spoke up. "I don't know about the two of you, but *my* duffle bag is killing me. Can't we stop for the night?"

"Hush!" said Promo. "I think I heard something!"

Everyone jumped off the road. They soon realized that the noise was not coming from an Executive Rider, but from something altogether different.

"That's singing, Mr. Promo! Elf singing!" said Sham. "Here they come!" At Promo's suggestion the wobbits remained hidden. He remembered that some elves are easily annoyed, like the Wood-Elves Uncle Bulbo ran into on his trip through Murkywood Forest.

"I can hear every word, sir! It's quite amazing, given the acoustical problems common to singing in forests. Too bad I don't know elvish."

But Promo knew elvish, just enough to read the occasional elf billboard, or for ordering in an elf restaurant. This was as much as he could translate:

O Elbopad, Gilettrazor
You never could deny
You are our favorite demi-god
From the days of Elves gone by

O Elbopad, Gilettrazor
We think you are sublime
You kindled all the stars above
In the days of Elves gone by

In days of elves gone by, my dear
In days of elves gone by
We're not dwarves, but you're called Snow White
By the elves of days gone by.

"These are Regular Elves, not those trashy Wood-Elves!" said Promo. "They spoke the name of Elbopad!"

The Regular Elves were all gorgeous. Beautiful and shiny, like disreputable twenty-first century vampires. There were no females among them. They approached and looked directly at the wobbits, who thought themselves cleverly hidden.

"Haloo, Promo!" they said. "What are you doing out so late, and so far from home? Is someone giving away free hot dogs nearby?"

"No," said Promo, "no hot dogs. My friends and I are just out for an evening stroll very far from home. Mind if we tag along? We would welcome your company."

"But we have no need of company," they said. "And wobbits are so dull! What would our friends say if they saw us with you? You're positively shabby!"

Promo felt very out of fashion. And short. He decided to change the subject. "Yes, well, how do you know my name?"

"We've seen you out walking with Bulbo, though you may not have seen us, unfortunately for you."

"And who are you, then, and who is in charge here?"

"We are of the House of Nimrod," said one. "And I am in charge. I am Gildor Inglorion. Perhaps you've heard of me."

"I'm afraid I haven't"

"Yes. I get that a lot. Sometimes I feel like I'm not even here."

"That's tough," said Promo. "Can we join you or not?"

Puppy suddenly stepped forward and interrupted, saying "Oh, pretty elves, tell us of the Black Riders!" as if he was trying to make a good impression. It appeared that he now believed in elves. Passionately.

"Black Riders?" said Gildor. "Were they actually black?"

"Um, no sir," said Sham. "They wore black suits, and they seemed black. You know."

"No we don't know," said Gildor. "But before you say something so offensive that we all get into trouble, you best come with us. You'll be safe for the night. Follow me. And do us a favor, no more talk about the Riding Executives tonight."

The wobbits joined the company of elves, and walked to a beautifully decorated clearing in the woods where a sophisticated dinner party was taking place. The portions were small but the presentation of each plate was magnificent. None of the wobbits knew what they were eating, but they were drinking what must have been Appletinis. Most of the silverware was unfamiliar, and Puppy mistakenly helped himself to a plateful of what turned out to be the centerpiece. He and Sham overindulged until they were quite groggy. As soon as they were snoring some helpful elves changed them into little pyjamas after quick sponge baths. Promo was looking on, feeling strangely uneasy, when Gildor approached him.

"I've been looking all over for you, Promo. Tell me, is Pantsoff mixed up in this adventure of yours?"

"Yes, and he told me nothing about the Executive Riders. So tell me!"

"Pantsoff said nothing? Then I'll say nothing more."

"You haven't said anything!"

"Exactly!" said Gildor, with a portentous look. "If I told you what I know, you would give up your journey in terror."

"Thanks," said Promo. "This little talk has been very reassuring. Maybe you can give me some advice, then. Pantsoff was supposed to leave Wobbiton with us, but he never showed. Since I now know that we're being hunted by demons, do you think it might be a good idea for us to wait with your company until Pantsoff gets here?"

"Promo, let me share an Olde Elf Saying with you: *Do not get mixed up in the affairs of Pantsoff, for his failure could rub off on you.* In other words, you figure it out. This whole project of his is already coming apart, and I don't want to be around when it collapses completely."

"That's interesting," said Promo. "We wobbits have a similar saying. *Here comes Pantsoff. Keep an eye on your wallet.*" They both laughed.

"Then may Elbopad protect you. It appears we understand each other?"

"Probably not, no." Promo was done talking. The exotic liquor was finally catching up with him. He found where Sham and Puppy lay sleeping and threw himself on top of the pile. The next morning, he, too was in pyjamas.

Chapter 4

A SHORT CHAPTER TO TOMATOES

Promo woke to find Sham's knee in his mouth, but he felt refreshed all the same. The elves were gone, much to the disappointment of Sham and Puppy, but they had left a continental breakfast behind for the wobbits.

"Croissants and hot cocoa!" said Sham. "Back home the Grasper and I would have been happy with rubbery bagels and instant coffee!"

Puppy quickly drank three cocoas as soon as he found his pants, and then he burned off the sugar rush by running around and around the grassy clearing as he laughed. Sham kept eating. Promo brooded and spoke quietly to himself.

"It doesn't seem right, bringing Sham and Puppy on this project. Sham just came to see elves and now he's seen them. As for Puppy, who knows why he's here? He certainly doesn't." Puppy was still running in circles.

"I know Pantsoff thought it would be good to have a few extra wobbits along to get between me and any stray arrows, but now that I'm actually being stalked, I almost feel guilty about that. Puppy has no idea of the danger he's in, and Sham has worked for my family for years. Somehow, it seems insensitive to use them as decoys. I'll have to think about this a lot more and maybe send them home later. Perhaps when we arrive at Riverdale." He looked up from his brooding and noticed Sham standing at parade rest, watching him.

"So," said Promo, "let me say again that we're headed into great danger. I was going to keep the terrifying truth from you until it was too late, but since you've been eavesdropping again, I suppose I should tell you the whole story. I'm supposed to carry Bulbo's ring across Little Earth and destroy it, while those Executive Riders are trying to kill me. The ring actually belongs to Smoron, so he'll be trying to kill me, too. I'm unsure now why I agreed to do this, since it appears to lead to my certain death."

"That it does, sir."

"So you'll be going back to Wobbiton?"

"No, sir, I'll be staying with you."

"But why, Sham?"

"Because of the elves, sir. *Don't you leave him* they said to me. *I never intended to,* I said, *and if any more of those Riders come after him, they'll have Sham Sammich to contend with.* Then they laughed, and offered me another pillow."

"Well, it is a pretty funny idea, you fighting those riders."

"Indeed, sir."

"When did the elves talk with you?"

"It was in the middle of the night, sir. I woke up for some reason, and some elves were right there, looking at me very close, and they appeared startled. Then they began talking."

"And what do you think of Elves, now that you've met some?"

"Oh, they're fabulous, sir. Their cooking is excellent, they're very stylish dressers, and they have wonderful singing voices. There's something about them though that I can't quite..."

"...put your finger on?"

"Exactly, sir. They are so old, yet so young. So sad, yet so gay, as it were."

"Not that there's anything wrong with that, though, right Sham?"

"Of course not, sir."

"Are you two still talking?" said Puppy, interrupting. "Let's go! I'm so bored!" He had the duffle bags packed and ready to go, although his packing had made them extra-lumpy.

"Yes, let's go," said Promo. "The elves told me that the ferry across the Buckiewine River is easy to get to if you take their special shortcut. They said we could avoid the traffic and road construction at Woody Forest by taking the bypass through Mudville."

"Mudville? No way! The commute through there is always a mess."

"Puppy, the elves said that was the way to go and I believe them. And they said that a hair stylist they like has his salon there. They recommended I see him for a more contemporary, shorter hairstyle."

"*Short cuts make long delays*," argued Puppy. "But if we must go through Mudville, then we could also stop at a tavern the elves said we should try. It's called *The Canary Perch* and the bartender makes an excellent Mojito."

With this thought, Puppy burst into a one of his favorite songs as they walked:

Ho ho ho to the bottle I go
To heal my heart and drown my woe
Though I can quit any time I pick
Sometimes I drink 'til I get real sick
I like white wine when I'm eating pork
And I like putting whiskey inside this Dork!

He sang verse after verse for hours until Promo interrupted.

"A drinking song while we walk?" Promo was a purist when it came to this sort of thing. "I suppose you sing walking songs while you drink?"

"You're not the boss of me!" Puppy said. "You're the boss of him!" he said, pointing at Sham.

"Mr. Puppy makes a valid point, sir," Sham said.

"Yeah, and another thing--" said Puppy, and then he stopped. "Hey! I know where we are! We're near Buckieland, at Bumfurlong, old Farmer Lamprey's land."

"Oh crap!" said Promo. "Not Farmer Lamprey! The meanest farmer in Little Earth, with those huge, ferocious dogs! He probably still remembers when he caught me stealing a basket of his tomatoes."

"Not to worry, cousin Promo. Me and old Lamprey go way back. You have nothing to worry about."

As they approached the farm with its endless stakes of tomato vines, some towering five feet tall, they heard a tremendous barking and braying, and a loud voice shouting "Killer! McNasty! Blitzen! Come on, lads!"

Three chihuahuas, each large enough to look a wobbit in the eye, surrounded and then began sniffing Promo and his decoys, one dog per wobbit. Pantsoff's "cannon fodder" strategy for Puppy and Sham had paid off: Promo was glad all three dogs weren't all sniffing him at once. It wasn't as bad as when the Rider was sniffing him, but even one huge dog sniffing him was still pretty unnerving. A rugged looking wobbit was with the dogs.

"Hey guys, look," said Puppy. "It's Farmer Lamprey! Farmer Lamprey, it's me, Paraffin Dork! How long has it been? Have you lost some weight? You look great!"

The old tough wobbit slowly smiled. "Well if it isn't Master Paraffin! Good to see you, lad! I was about to set the dogs on you. There's been some queer folk around of late."

"Dorks?" said Promo.

"Elves?" said Sham and Puppy.

"No, a really skinny man on a black horse. The man was black, too."

"Really?" said Promo. "You could see his face?"

"Well, no," said old Lamprey. "He didn't have any face I could see. Just an expensive haircut and a conservatively stylish black suit. But he seemed black, you know?"

"No, I don't know. But go on."

"The fellow says to me 'I come from the home office downtown. Have you seen *Bunkins?'* in a queer voice."

"Go figure," said Puppy.

"'Be off!' I said. 'There's no Bunkins here. He lives in Wobbiton, beneath a beauty salon.'"

"'Bunkins has left' he said in a hiss. 'He is coming. He is not far away. I wish to find him. If he passes this way, will you tell me? I will return with gold."

"'And jools?' I said."

"'What?' he said.'"

"'Jewels!' I said."

"'Sure. Whatever.' he said."

"'I doubt it,' I said. I never trust anyone that won't use contractions when speaking. By then I had stalled him long enough for my dogs to arrive and start their tremendous yipping. He knew

I had the advantage. He gave a sort of hiss. It may have been laughing."

"At least he has a sense of humor," said Puppy.

"He spurred his great horse right at me, but I walked underneath it to get out of the way. He looked around for me, hissed one more time, and rode off. What do you think of that?"

Promo stood silent for a while. Everyone looked at him expectantly. Finally he said "I don't know what to think."

"I'll tell you what to think!" said Lamprey. This was exactly what he had planned to say to Promo anyway. "You'll think about minding your own business and settling down! Your Uncle Bulbo stirred up a lot of trouble with his 'consulting.' I hope you don't have anything like that planned!"

"Why, no, no, not at all! I'm just relocating to Buckieland. That's all. Just relocating."

"Glad to hear it, Master Promo! A very wise choice," said Farmer Lamprey. "I expect you lads are headed to the ferry to cross the Buckiewine River. If you'd like, I could have my wife, Mrs. Lamprey, fix you some supper. Then I could give you a lift to the ferry on my buckieboard waggon."

"The people of Buckieland certainly know how to stick with a theme," said Sham quietly.

"Yes, Farmer Lamprey!" said Promo. "Supper and a ride would be wonderful! Thank you!"

In a short while they all sat down to eat with Mrs. Lamprey and dozens of Lamprey sons and daughters. There was beer in plenty, and buckiewine, and a mighty platter of bacon, lettuce and tomato sandwiches. The BLTs were made with Farmer Lamprey's heirloom tomatoes and Mrs. Lamprey's artisanal pigs. The bread was freshly baked, the lettuce was organic, of course, and the mayonnaise was hand-crafted in small batches. The Lampreys were famous throughout Little Earth for their BLTs, which they sold from buckieboard waggons that travelled far and wide.

While Promo, Sham and Puppy were nibbling at the last crusts, Lamprey got the waggon ready. They heard Mrs. Lamprey saying farewell.

"You be careful of yourself, Lamprey," she said. "No talking to strangers, especially ones in dark, expensive suits. And come straight home after! We have a lot of tomatoes to pick tomorrow!"

"Yes, dear," he said back to her as the guests climbed aboard. They drove out of the gate and soon were at the Buckiewine River Ferry.

"This is just a raft at a little wharf, lit by tiki-lamps," said Sham. "I was expecting an otherworldly being with wings and a wand who would send us across the river magically!"

"You're thinking of the Buckiewine River *Fairy*," said Puppy. "She's twenty miles downriver."

"I understand," said Sham.

"What terrible place to be ambushed by those Riders," said Promo. He looked up as they all heard a galloping in the darkness.

"Quick, onto the ferry!" said Promo. "It's one of the Executive Riders! Come on, Lamprey, while there's still time!"

"Never!" said Lamprey. The Rider came almost into view and stopped. "Don't you come a step closer! What do you want?"

The figure hissed, and the spoke. "I want Bunkins. Have you seen him?" He hissed again, twice, and then cleared his throat. "Pardon me. I've been drinking a lot of milk, and I'm a little phlegmy."

He dismounted, and the wobbits realized the horse was in fact a pony. In the festive light of the tiki-lamps the rider was revealed to be wobbit-sized. "Promo!" he said. "Puppy! Sham! I've been looking all over for you guys! Hello, Farmer Lamprey!"

"Maryellen Buckiebrand, you idiot!" Lamprey said. "I was ready to kill you. What's wrong with you?"

"I got bored waiting for these three, so I crossed the river earlier today and have been looking for them in every tavern I've passed. I also waited for a while with the Buckiewine River Fairy."

"How is she, by the way?" said Puppy.

"She's fine," said Mary. "Business has been a little slow."

"Thanks for almost scaring us to death," said Lamprey. "But since you're all together I best be getting back. Mrs. Lamprey will be worriting with it being so late."

"Did he say 'worriting' just now?" Sham quietly asked Promo.

"He means 'worrying,'" said Promo. "It's a Buckieland thing."

"Very good, sir."

As Promo got back on the ferry boat, Lamprey handed him a basket. "These are for all of you from Mrs. Lamprey," he said. "You can share them with Mr. Mary, if you like, but I wouldn't. It's been a queer day, and he's been the icing on the queer-cake, in a manner of speaking."

"Hey!" said Mary.

They watched as Lamprey and the buckieboard waggon drove back into the night. Suddenly Promo laughed: from the covered basket he held, the scent of BLTs was rising.

Chapter 5

WOBBIT HOT-TUBBING

"Come on, dudes," said Mary. "Let's get across the river. I have a bad feeling about this." Mary led the pony down the ferry path, which was straight, unlike the fairy path downriver. It was decorated with various signs prohibiting boat-rocking, littering, horseplay, roughhousing, smoking, spitting or loud mandolin playing while on the ferry.

Everyone was aboard, and Mary grabbed a nearby pole. He used it to slowly push the raft into the river. Soon they could see the far side, lighted by the windows of Buckiebrand Hall, the ancient home of the Buckiebrands. Mary looked at it sadly.

"I missed Taco Night to meet you, Promo," he said. "You owe me, dude."

"No I don't," said Promo. "I paid you back in Wobbiton."

"You're the boss," said Mary.

The ferry slowly approached the riverbank. Sham was the only member of the party that had never been in Buckieland. He hoped the others wouldn't notice him doing anything "touristy," but he still wanted to take the famous guided tour of Buckiebrand Hall and buy a postcard to send the Grasper. Somehow, ever since they left Bug End, Sham felt like a new wobbit. Travel was broadening him.

He had a strange feeling that he was leaving his old provincial life behind on the opposite bank with Farmer Lamprey and his ferocious chihuahuas. Or perhaps the feeling was from too many BLTs. Either way, it was strange. He looked back one last time, and noticed that Promo was doing the same thing.

"Shall I ever see Farmer Lamprey and his splendid tomatoes again?" Promo asked himself in a dreamy voice. As Sham rolled his eyes, he noticed something in the tiki-light on the bank behind them.

"Excuse me, sir," he said to Promo. "Do you see something moving back there on the bank? It appears to be someone in a dark suit, sniffing the ground."

"Yes," said Promo. "I see him. It looks like he's writing something now, in a notebook."

"Indeed, sir. And now he's putting the notebook into a briefcase. Strange."

"You don't suppose he's one of those Executive Riders, do you Sham?"

"Perhaps, sir. Although he isn't on a horse."

"True," said Promo. "It's a good thing he can't get this boat from the other side of the river."

Promo thought for a moment. "Hey, how would we have gotten across if the boat had been on the wrong side?" Mary just shrugged as they reached the bank.

"That doesn't seem like much of a system," said Promo.

"Yeah," said Mary. "Whatever. Not my problem." Mary began tying up the ferry as the pony and the rest of the party stepped onto the wharf.

It was not far from the Buckiewine River to Promo's new home. They all walked past the raucous music of Buckiebrand Hall just as a chair crashed through a window, landing in front of the wobbits. Mary didn't seem surprised.

"Taco Night can be a little extreme," he said. "I just hope that wasn't my chair. Oh! Here we are!" They had arrived at Promo's new condo. It was a garden apartment, just like back in Wobbiton, with an aluminum screen door. The rest of the building was occupied by a vintage clothing shop.

"Take a look at the place, Promo," said Mary. "I have to return this pony to Buckiebrand Hall, and I'll let Blimpy know you've arrived."

Promo looked around. The apartment was a little tired-looking, somewhere between a "fixer-upper" and a "handyman special." Even though he had no intention of ever living in the place, it was discouraging after the opulence of Bulbo's renovated

Bug End condo. Promo was sitting on the floor, missing everything about Wobbiton, when Mary came in with Froderick "Blimpy" Blogger.

"We're here! Isn't this place great! Look at the epic closet space! And did you see this?" Mary opened a door to a small courtyard, in which there was a large, steaming hot-tub.

"Wahoo!" said Puppy, who left a trail of clothes as he ran to the tub and hopped in.

"Mary," said Promo. "You and Blimpy have outdone yourselves! Come on, Sham! Time to unwind. Mary, Blimpy, are you joining us?"

"You bet!" said Mary. "Where's that basket from Mrs. Lamprey?"

"I'll bring it to the tub for everyone to share," said Promo. "I know you and Blimpy plan to eat all the BLTs."

"We had no such plan!" said Mary. "And Blimpy's on a diet."

"That's right," said Blimpy. He took a sandwich from Promo, removed and ate the bacon, lettuce and tomatoes, and put the soggy pieces of toast back in the basket. "This low-carb program I'm on is great. Yesterday I had a sandwich made of smoked turkey between two slices of roast beef." Blimpy told them about his exciting diet as they undressed and got in the hot-tub. He got a case of beer that Promo had paid for, put it within easy reach, opened one, and got in the tub.

"You displace a lot of water, dude!" said Mary.

"Is that beer low-carb, too?" asked Promo. "Because if it is, I don't want any."

"The beer is fine," said Blimpy. Then he muttered "Everyone picks on the fat guy."

They started in on the sandwiches, and then, while their mouths still full, they all began singing. The only thing wobbits love more than tomatoes is singing. And they all think that they're great singers, just like modern-day Italians. Five wobbits each sang their own song until a clear winner emerged: Puppy. He was singing his drinking/walking song, this time with drinking/bathing-related lyrics:

Sing hey! for a beer at the close of the day

And a hot tub to melt the stress away!
We'll sit and soak 'til we start to wrinkle
O! Promo's Beer is a noble drink!

Well! Beer is fun when it foams on high
In a fountain white beneath the sky.
Old Promo's beer makes a hot-tub fun
When I spray it all over everyone!

There was a terrific shouting from the aforementioned everyone, because Puppy couldn't resist spraying them with beer from a shaken bottle. They were all wet already, but no one liked to see beer being wasted.

Despite Puppy's acting up, there was still plenty of beer to go around, and even some more BLTs, which they enjoyed in hot-tubbing comfort. They continued their soaking, and talked about their upcoming rootball fantasy league draft until Mary changed the subject.

"Promo, what did you mean when you asked Sham about an 'executive rider?' And what was that dark but distinguished looking figure doing, sniffing around on the other side of the river? And what was Farmer Lamprey worriting about when I first rode up?"

"'Worriting,' sir?" said Sham discreetly to Promo.

Promo ignored him. "Yes, well," he said to Mary, "there's a chance we're being followed."

"A 'chance!'" said Puppy. "We're being hunted by terrifying black riders on black horses!"

"They're black?" said Mary. "How can you tell?"

"By the way they're dressed, for one thing."

"Oh stop it, Puppy," said Promo. "You sound like the Grasper."

"I'll thank you, sir, to leave my father--" said Sham.

"The Executive Riders wear black suits, okay?" said Promo. "It seems they may work for Smoron."

"Oh, great!" said Mary.

"Farmer Lamprey said they were black riders," said Puppy.

"No he didn't!" said Promo. "He doesn't know a thing about them."

"I wouldn't be so sure," said Mary. "Old Lamprey is smarter than he looks. He used to take trips into the Scary Olde Forest when he was young, and he has a reputation for knowing a great many strange things. For instance, he once told me there are three kinds of elves!"

"No way!" said Puppy. He and Sham leaned in with interest.

"Well, there's the Wood-Elves, and the Regular Elves, and then there's--"

"Anyway," said Promo, "these Executive Riders are after me. There's a reason why, but I can't tell you. It's too terrifying."

"Does it have something to do with leaving Wobbiton and pretending to move to Buckieland?"

"Pretend to move here!" said Promo, trying to look shocked. "Why, that's ridiculous!"

"Promo," said Mary, "none of us believed you were moving into this condo. Look at it! Other than this hot tub, the place is a dump. But with the tiny amount you gave me to spend, it's the best anyone could do. At the beginning I thought you just wanted to rehab it cheaply and sell it at a huge profit before the first mortgage payment. Then I realized that you weren't broke and certainly didn't need to flip condos to make a living. We knew all along that you had been contracted by Pantsoff to work on this dangerous project."

"If you all know it's dangerous, why are you coming with me?"

"Because we're bored!" said Puppy. "Absolutely nothing happens in Wobbiton!"

"And I'm tired of Buckiebrand Hall," said Mary. "Who wants to live in a dormitory their whole life? I hate sharing the bathroom with a dozen Buckiebrands."

"Sham?" said Promo. "How about you?"

"As you'll recall, sir, I made a promise to Gildor and the Regular Elves that I would stay with you. And, of course, as much as I love and respect my dear father, it's not much fun living with an old guy."

"Tell me about it," said Promo. "When Bulbo left I felt like I had been let out of jail."

"Indeed, sir."

"So we're all going with you," said Mary, "as you carry Bulbo's magic ring to The Crotch Of Doom to be destroyed." Promo glared at Sham.

"You told them?" he said. "Sham, that was a secret! Pantsoff said he would turn you into something unnatural if you told!"

"Actually, sir, you'll remember Mr. Pantsoff said he would turn me into something unnatural if I didn't accompany you. It appeared that bringing Mr. Puppy and Mr. Mary along would be entirely in keeping with his wishes."

"Did you have to tell them about The Ring?"

"I didn't sir. Mr. Mary discovered that on his own."

"Oh really?"

"Come on, Promo!" said Mary. "Every time the Snackbag-Bunkinses were anywhere near Bulbo he'd dig around in his pockets until he found the ring, and then he'd disappear until they were gone. I even tried it out myself."

"You wore the Juan Ring? When? How?"

"Bulbo took it to Bugford Falls to have it cleaned, right before his goodbye party. He said he didn't trust any of the Wobbiton jewelers. I went to the shop, signed Bulbo's name, paid for the cleaning, and took the ring home. After I tried it, I left it inside his screen door with a note saying it had been delivered by the jewelers with their compliments, to encourage Bulbo's future business."

"You signed Bulbo's name? That's identity theft!"

"Whatever. I saved Bulbo a trip to Bugford Falls and the cost of the cleaning."

"But The Ring's dangerous!"

"Not really. I didn't notice any side effects, other than the visions of a huge lidless eye, wreathed in flame."

"So, you know about my plans and the ring. If you really want to come with, that's fine with me."

"Hooray!" said Puppy. "We knew it all along! I wrote a song for the occasion."

"Not that same tune again?"

"No, this one is to the tune of the song the dwarves of SmithiBank sang to Bulbo, before they all left on the dragon project. I heard him singing it, and sampled it without his permission for this song:

> *Now Promo Bunkins bids goodbye to all his kith and kin*
> *And nobody can say for sure if he'll come back again*
> *He'll travel with the three of us from this locality*
> *We'd be delighted to return without fatality*

"That's just the last verse," said Puppy. "I was hoping to have the beginning verses done by now, but the packing took longer than I thought."

"If you had actually helped, it might have gone a little faster," said Promo. "But that's neither here nor there. I'm just glad you're all coming with." Promo kept Pantsoff's idea of bringing along expendable wobbits, the "redshirt" concept, to himself. He also was overcoming his feeling of guilt at putting his friends in harm's way. They all had reasons of their own for joining the project team, and who was Promo Bunkins to stop them? Then another question occurred to Promo, which he asked his team.

"What about the Executive Riders? Would it be safe to wait one day for Pantsoff?"

"That depends on what you think they would do to get at you," said Mary. "To enter Buckieland secretly they'd have to get through The Shrubbery, a wall of bushes that protects us on all sides. It's the mightiest barrier ever created by landscapers. Penetrating it would be impossible for anyone in a nice suit like the Riders. But they could go to the gate and ask to be let in. At night they would probably be turned away, but maybe not. And who knows what would happen if they tried during the day, especially if the gate-guards were at lunch. Overall, I'd say it's pretty dangerous for you here. What exactly was your reason for waiting for Pantsoff?"

"I thought he could lead us, guide us to Riverdale, and help us defend ourselves against the Executive Riders." He looked at the other wobbits, and then everyone burst out laughing.

"Lead us!" chuckled Sham.

"Guide us!" snorted Puppy.

"Help us!" guffawed Mary.

Promo finally stopped laughing, sighed, and said "We leave first thing tomorrow. We'll go through the Scary Olde Forest. That will give us the element of surprise."

"To an extent, yes, sir," said Sham. "Strictly speaking, it will throw the Executive Riders off our trail."

"Yes, Sham, thank you."

"You can count me out," said Blimpy. "There's no way I'm going in the Forest. I'll stay here and pretend to be Promo. I'll go around Buckieland saying things like 'Shall I ever see Aunt Earlobia again,' and I can dress up in your old clothes."

"You couldn't fit into my waistcoat if your life depended on it!" said Promo.

"But you can tell Pantsoff what direction we've gone, if he ever shows up," said Mary. "We'll enter the Forest in daylight, when the trees are sleepy and fairly quiet."

"What's this about sleepy trees, Mr. Mary?" asked Sham. He looked concerned.

"You'll find out soon enough," said Promo. "I'm turning in. See you all in the morning."

Blimpy left, and the others found couches, settees or davenports to sleep on. Even though he was in a comfortable bed, Promo fell into a vague dream, where he heard creatures sniffing and moving in a forest. He dreamed of high towers and salt seas. He dreamed that suddenly a light came in the sky, and there was a noise of thunder.

It may have been all the sandwiches.

Chapter 6

THE SCARY OLDE FOREST

Promo woke suddenly. It was still dark in the room. He never woke this early at home, and had been sleeping poorly for many nights. He hadn't yet adjusted to the difference between the Wobbiton and Buckieland time zones. Promo had no idea that "waggon lag" could be this much trouble.

Mary leaned into the bedroom. "Come on, sleepyhead. Sham's making breakfast in the kitchenette, Puppy just packed the dufflebags, and I've got the ponies parked outside. Let's eat!"

Lounging in the den, the party ate their usual egg-and-salsa burritos and hazelnut lattes. Out front were their ponies, the kind loved by wobbits: dirty little beasts, not very fast, or very bright, but cheap and predictable, much like the wobbits themselves.

They rode for about an hour, with Blimpy walking alongside. Soon The Shrubbery loomed ahead of them.

"Now what do we do?" said Promo. "Bushes are the most impenetrable barrier in Little Earth!"

"Watch this," said Mary. He took hold of one of the lanterns that lined The Shrubbery like streetlights, or lamps down a very long hallway. He turned the lantern slightly, and a section on The Shrubbery swung open as easily as if it had been a stone door. Led by Mary, the party stepped out into the wilderness.

"Goodbye!" called Blimpy. "Have fun destroying The Juan Ring and defeating Smoron! Try not to get spellbound or eaten in The Scary Olde Forest!"

"Thanks for being discreet, Blimpy," said Promo. "If Pantsoff ever shows up, tell him he can catch up with us on the Riverdale Byway."

The section of Shrubbery swung back, leaving Blimpy relatively safe in Buckieland as Mary said "There. We are now on the edge of The Scary Olde Forest."

"Are the stories about it true?" asked Puppy.

"Of course not," said Mary. "At least, not the most famous ones. The one about the wobbit lad who sneezed while in the forest but didn't close his eyes so they shot out of his eye-sockets, that one's false. And the one about the Rat King that lives at the center of the Forest is a myth, too. But The Forest *is* queer, queerer than waking up in strange pyjamas. Things there are very much more alive than things are in Wobbiton."

"Things everywhere are more alive than things are in Wobbiton," said Puppy. "That's why I'm here."

"Agreed," said Mary. "But you know what I mean. The trees don't like strangers. They'll try to trip you with a root, or throw an apple at you. And at night you can hear them whisper to each other, passing news and plots in an unintelligible language."

"How do you know they're plotting if their language is unintelligible?" said Promo. "It sounds like you're assuming the worst."

"The Buckiebrands aren't assuming anything," said Mary. "The trees can move, and sometimes they surround strangers and hem them in. Once a long time ago they even attacked Buckieland itself!"

"Attacked?" said Promo. "How many wobbits were killed?"

"None. We chopped down hundreds of trees and burned them in a huge bonfire. No trees grow in that spot to this day."

"But how did you cut them down? I thought you said they could move."

"They can," said Mary. "But not very quickly. They're trees, for Pete's sake."

"Did they smash any buildings?"

"Oh no. Nothing like that. They just were leaning over The Shrubbery."

"And you killed hundreds of them for that?' said Promo.

"Legend has it they leaned over in a very threatening way."

"They leaned over," said Promo, "so you killed them. That may explain why they dislike strangers."

"Perhaps." said Mary. "Let's get going. We want to be out of The Forest by nightfall."

"Right. The trees may sway at us menacingly."

They entered The Scary Olde Forest, the ponies picking their way among the trees. They tried to avoid the hanging branches and twisted roots, but eventually it seemed that the trees were barring their way. Soon there was too little light to see easily. They all got an uncomfortable feeling that they were being watched with disapproval, as if they were lingering over coffee in a restaurant long after paying the check, or "bill" as the wobbits call it. The feeling steadily grew, until the weakest of the group, Puppy, felt he could stand it no longer. Dorks tend to cry out suddenly when they're afraid, which is often.

"Oi, Oi!" he shouted. "Just let me pass through! Mary's the one you want. His family cut you down, not mine!"

"Oy, Oy?" said Sham. "I didn't know Mr. Dork was Jewish."

"Again with the racism!" said Promo. "And I think he said 'Oi, Oi.'"

"Ah, I see, sir."

Mary was looking from side to side. "This is where the Bonfire Glade is supposed to be."

"So you lost us?" said Promo.

"No, it's not me." said Mary. "It's the trees. They've moved! Oh, the disapproval, the enmity they feel for wobbits!"

"I'd say you trees hate the Buckiebrands, mostly," said Puppy loudly to the trees.

"How they hate us, these queer, ancient trees!" said Mary. "They've been the source of endless sorrow in Buckieland for hundreds of--- Oh, there it is! Bonfire Glade is just over there."

"Over where?"

"Just through those trees."

"Which trees?"

"The ones over there!"

They walked where Mary was pointing, and light improved as they walked forward. Then they were out of the trees in a wide circular space, with the blue morning sky above them. No tree grew there, only an endless variety of weeds, like so many

Wobbiton front yards. It was a dreary place, but it was charming and cheerful compared with The Forest. Or Wobbiton.

On the other side of the clearing there was an opening onto a path. The sunlight encouraged them, and they rode towards the path unafraid. But that encouraged feeling died quickly as the trees crowded back towards them and the air became as warm and stuffy as your grandma's living room. Promo tried to sing an inspiring song, but he couldn't even finish the first verse.

We'll take all the trees, and put them in a tree museum
And we'll charge all the wobbits
a guilder and half just to see 'em
Don't it always seem to go
That you cut down all the trees 'til they're gone...

Gone -- Even as he sang the lyric, his voice faded into silence. The forest, the quiet, the stuffiness all made the song and everything else seem so pointless. The trees seemed to crowd around them, like distant relatives that are insensitive about personal space.

"I don't think they like folk-rock." said Mary. "Do you know any reggae?"

They rode on as the path fell and then rose again. They climbed to the top of a hill that was left bare by the trees without any cutting or burning. It was still morning, but it seemed a lot later by the time they stopped. Mary wanted to share another point of interest.

"See down there? That's the River Willywonka. It's queer. Very queer. The queerest river ever. It's the epicenter of queerness for The Scary Olde Forest, the source of all its ambient queerness."

"You seem really sensitive about queerness," said Promo. "What's up with that?" The others looked where Mary was pointing, but it was misty and they could see nothing. To the west they could not see The Shrubbery nor could they see the Buckiewine Valley at all. To the north they couldn't see the Riverdale Byway. "I want no part of the Willywonka. We should stay well away from it. This forest is bad enough."

"Let's have lunch," said Puppy. It was unseasonably warm, so they ate all the egg salad they brought from Buckieland, which surely wouldn't last in the heat. When the sun finally broke through they could see past The Scary Olde Forest to the Barrow-downs. They were happy to see anything beyond the Forest, although the Barrow-downs was a place with a sinister reputation in wobbit-legend, even more terrifying than the Forest.

"The Barrow-downs," said Promo. "I have no intention of going there, either, though I do intend to take us to Bordor, which is even worse."

"Very good, sir," said Sham. "No sense in looking for trouble, as the Grasper would say."

Puppy was getting impatient, so they repacked all the picnic-ware moved on. They started out on the path that led them to the hill, but it appeared that it would eventually lead them to the River Willywonka.

"Should we stay on the path or not?" said Promo. "How I miss Uncle Bulbo and his constant, unrequested advice. I remember something about 'paths' from his book, something Pantsoff told him when he and the dwarf-bankers entered Murkywood Forest. What was it? Well, we want to avoid the Willywonka, so I guess we should leave the path."

They went north, towards where the Riverdale Byway had to be. At first it seemed like a good choice, but they kept having to veer east. Going north always seemed difficult, because it was slightly uphill or because it forced them to walk against the wind. Puppy often saw interesting shaped leaves to the east, and going east usually allowed the wobbits to stay on their ponies. Mary complained bitterly whenever they had to walk, because he had arranged for the ponies and wanted them to be worth what he paid for them. Even though it was Promo's money.

After only an hour or two they lost all sense of direction, although they knew they had long ceased to go northwards at all. They were being forced eastward and southward, into the heart of the forest and not out of it.

The ground grew soft and boggy, and they discovered springs that fed into a brook. The brook babbled, as you would expect. It went through a weedy bed along banks that were easy to follow. It had become a warm, lazy afternoon. The constant babbling reminded Promo of Bulbo, and made him just as sleepy. The brook became a stream, and as they followed the stream they stepped into a slightly less shady spot.

"I know this clearing!" said Mary. "It's completely clear of trees, except for willows."

The stream became a drowsy river as brown as chocolate, and everywhere there were willows. The clearing was bordered with willows, the river was choked with willow logs, the air was filled with falling willow leaves. If it weren't for the fact that Mary said it was a clearing, the wobbits would have thought the place was a willow forest.

"We're not lost anymore!" said Mary "By the look of the water, I'd say this has to be the River Willywonka."

"Mr. Buckiebrand," said Sham, "you're saying we've arrived at the one place to which Mr. Promo didn't want you to take us, sir?"

"Sure, you can look at it that way if you want," said Mary. "But now I know where we are. Remember, this is the source of The Scary Olde Forest's queerness. I'll go ahead and explore."

To the surprise of all, Mary returned safely. "I've found a path that goes along the Willywonka. If we follow it, and if it continues with the river, we will eventually come out of the Forest. But we'll have to be careful."

"When 'Ifs' and 'Buts' become Candy and Nuts, we'll all have a wonderful Yuletide" said Puppy.

"What in the world are you talking about?" said Mary.

"I'm talking about how much I don't want to follow a sinister river out of a sinister wood. How long will it be before we're out of here? Who made the path, anyway? At this point, why are we even listening to you?"

"The answer to all three questions is 'I don't know.' But if you have any better ideas, I'd like to hear them."

They filed out, following Mary to the path he found. It was paved with willow wood-chips that Puppy enjoyed kicking as they walked. There were willow trunks across the occasional gullies, and every so often there were rest stops with benches and picnic tables made out of willow logs.

The morning warmth gave way to afternoon hot. Sleepy hot. Wobbits are ready for a nap anytime, anywhere, and these wobbits were out on their feet.

"Must nap," said Mary. "Can't keep eyes open. Falling down." He fell over, and then crawled to a gigantic, ancient, gnarled willow. It was definitely the scariest tree in a forest made up of scary trees, but Mary was past caring. He lay down between two great roots, and then rolled over. He pulled the tree root as he rolled, and it wrapped itself around him, like a hideous blanket.

"Must nap," he said. "Too hot."

"No Mary, don't do it," said Promo. He did not like the sound of this at all. "It's not the heat, it's the humidity. We can't nap now. We've got to get out of this forest!" But Mary and the others were too far gone to care. The tree seemed to be humming a show tune. That and the gently falling leaves were enough to put Puppy to sleep. He flopped over into what looked like a pair of willowy jaws, or the bloom of a gigantic venus-flytrap. Puppy and Mary had given themselves up to the spell, and were fast asleep. Sham just stood there, yawning.

It almost sounded to Promo like the tree was singing to him. He thought he could hear the lyrics *Feed me, wobbit / Feed me all night long*. He sat down on the river-bank to bathe his hot, tired feet in the chocolaty brown water. He was soon asleep, too.

Sham was worried. The afternoon was getting late, and he thought this sudden sleepiness uncanny, but not quite queer as Mary had said. "There's more to this than falling leaves and relative humidity. I don't like this big tree. Listen to it, singing about being mean and green now. This won't do at all!"

He staggered off to see what happened to the ponies, and as he recovered them he heard a "Bonk" sound followed by a distinct "Ker-splash." He returned to find Promo in the river with a boot-shaped branch on his chest, holding him in the water. Sham grabbed him by his maroon windbreaker and hauled him out. Promo woke and began spluttering.

"Do you know, Sham" he said at length, "the beastly tree *kicked* me in! I felt it. That boot-shaped branch just kicked me in!"

"If this is what the trees around here are like in the day, sir, I don't want to be here at night. Where are Mr. Dork and Mr. Buckiebrand?"

They discovered that Puppy was trapped behind what appeared to be giant green teeth, and Mary was so completely bound up by roots that only his head and feet could be seen. Promo and Sham struggled frantically to release them. It was quite useless. Promo kicked the tree as hard as he could. Being barefoot, he was lucky he didn't break anything. The tree answered with a loud, deep, raucous laugh.

"What a foul thing to happen," said Promo wildly. "Shall I ever see my friends again?"

"No time for that, sir," said Sham, not even taking a moment to roll his eyes. "May I inquire, sir, as to what weapons we might have packed?"

"Weapons?"

"Yes, sir. Something with which we might compel the tree to release our comrades. A battle-axe, perhaps, or a halberd? A *glaive-guisarme*? Even a sword?"

"No, no, nothing like that."

"Would I be correct, sir, in assuming that Mr. Pantsoff provided you with the packing list for this journey, which you followed faithfully?"

"Yes."

"That would explain the lack of weapons, sir. The same thing happened to your Uncle Bulbo. I recommend we cry for help."

"Really?"

"Indeed, sir."

Promo began running in circles yelling *help, help, help!* He felt desperate, lost and witless, and rightly so.

Suddenly he stopped. He heard singing, not from the tree, but someone else, coming from deep in the forest. It was a fine tenor voice, singing gladly and carelessly.

Just got home from Buckieland
Lock the screen door, oh man!
Got to save the Wobbits, then we'll rest on the porch.
Willywonka sets in, pretty soon I'm singing,
Dude, Dude, Dude, looking out my screen door.

The tree was visibly shaken by the song. It seemed to lean away as a man appeared and came close. He was bearded, with long hair, and was wearing a bathrobe. In one hand he carried a bowling bag, and in the other, a creamy drink in a rocks glass.

"Help!' cried Promo and Sham as they ran towards him.

"Be careful, man!" he said. "There's a beverage here!"

"Our friends are caught in the willow tree!" said Sham. "Their lives are in your hands, sir!"

"Their lives are in my hands." he said. "Yeah, well, that's just, like, your opinion, man. And don't call me sir. My name's Jeff Bombadowski, but you can call me Dude. Or 'His Dudeness' or 'Duder' or 'El Duderino' if you're not into the whole brevity thing."

"The willow's got our friends!"

"That's a bummer," said the Dude. "But this aggression will not stand, man. The Big Willow? I know just the tune for him."

There's a willow doing cartwheels,
A balrog wearing high heels.
Look at all the evil creatures lurking on the lawn.
A watcher in the water wants to grab your daughter
Dude, Dude, Dude, looking out my screen door.

Easterlings and oliphants are playing in the band.
Won't you take a ride to the Crotch Of Doom?
Doo, doo, doo.
Smoron's apparition provided by magician.
Dude, Dude, Dude, looking out my screen door.

The Big Willow shook, and then went as limp as celery left in the back of the fridge. The roots around Mary stood him upright and then pulled quickly off him like string being pulled off a spool, leaving him spinning and then quite dizzy. There was a coughing, retching sound, and then out popped Puppy. He was a little sticky, but happy to be alive.

"Thank you!" said the wobbits.

"Well, um, why don't you come back to my place? There's cream, and coffee liqueur, and vodka. We can relax, man. Maybe do some bowling." He walked off, not waiting as the wobbits gathered their ponies.

They hurried to keep up, but the only thing slower than a wobbit is a wobbit with a wobbit-pony. It was becoming dark, and the path and woods seemed more and more dreamlike. They followed until they saw the Dude again, standing and sipping his beverage. He walked with them a little farther and sang as they approached their destination.

Trolls and creepy barrow-wights are playing in the band.
Won't you take a ride to the Crotch Of Doom?
Doo, doo, doo.
Bother me tomorrow, today I'll buy no sorrows.
Dude, Dude, Dude, looking out my screen door.

And with that the wobbits stood upon the threshold, and the golden light of a bowling alley was all about them.

Chapter 7

IN THE HOUSE OF JEFF BOMBADOWSKI

The four wobbits stepped through a screen door, over a wide stone threshold and stood still, blinking in the dim light. They had been in bowling alleys before, and had even heard of wobbits so wealthy that they had bowling alleys in their homes. But they had never met anyone whose home was in a bowling alley until they met the Dude.

In a chair next to one of the ball return racks sat a woman. Her long yellow hair hung in braids from beneath a helmet with two horns. She wore a belt of gold and a silver breastplate. On her feet were shoes of red and green, with the number "8 1/2" on each heel, so that she seemed ready to bowl.

"Enter, good guests," she said as she stood. The wobbits came a few timid steps into the room, feeling awkward, as if they had come to her door begging for a drink of water and then realized that they weren't wearing any pants.

"No, really, come in," she said, taking Promo by the hand. "Help yourself at the bar. I am Maude, daughter of the Willywonka. Fix yourself a cocktail."

The wobbits looked at her in wonder. Maude was by far the most beautiful female they had ever seen. Not that there's anything wrong with wobbit-lasses, especially to a wobbit-lad, but Maude was, well, different. Their mouths hung open until Puppy shook his head and then broke the silence.

"You're the daughter of a river?" said Puppy. "How does that work?"

"Shut up, stupid!" said Mary in a very loud whisper. Promo knew he had to step in before his cousins got them all kicked out, to be eaten by trees.

"Fuh lubba Muh!" said Promo. He was a little nervous. He tried again.

"Fair lady Maude!" he said. And then, without any thought, he began singing.

Sing Hey! for the beautiful lady Maude
Whose golden hair we will gladly laud
Her striking eyes and her perfect ears
O! Maude looks good as a home-brewed beer

"Hey!" said Puppy, interrupting. "That's my drinking song!" But Promo wasn't listening. He was mentally writing a second verse that would truly express his feeling for their hostess. Before he could embarrass himself further, Maude laughed. She wasn't laughing *at* Promo, which would not have been unusual, but not *with* him, either, since he wasn't laughing. She just laughed.

"That was, um, interesting!" she said kindly. "Cute, in fact! Yes, cute!" Not the impact that Promo had hoped for, but there you are.

"Sit, and let's save the next verse until the Dude joins us. He's tending your tired beasts."

The wobbits sat in chairs that were bolted to the floor at the end of one of the bowling lanes. Promo sat at a sort of desk, the scorekeeper's spot. From outside they could hear singing.

Willywonka's daughter, I love her like I oughter
Dude, Dude, Dude, looking out my screen door.

Maude smiled, and rolled her eyes for the benefit of the wobbits. It was obvious that she heard this song quite often.

"Fair lady," said Promo for a third time. "Who is the Dude?"

"The Dude abides," said Maude.

Promo cocked his head, as if he was a dog being told about escrow accounts. "The Dude abides," said Maude. "He is ever with the wood, and the river, and the bowling alley."

"So he protects everything?"

"Nooo, he doesn't protect anything, not exactly. That might require preparation, and follow-through, and would take time away from his bowling. The Dude abides."

"I see," said Promo, but everyone knew that he didn't. A door opened and in came the Dude. He laughed, and going to Maude, took her hand.

"Here's my lady friend!" he said. "I see yellow cream, and coffee liqueur, and vodka and ice and rocks glasses."

"Yellow cream?" said Promo quietly to Sham. "It's always white at home."

"The Dude is probably using a figure of speech, sir."

"Do we have enough?" said the Dude. "Are we ready to bowl, man?"

"We are," said Maude, "but the guests perhaps are not?"

The Dude smiled, walked past the wobbits and through a doorway. The wobbits followed him into a room warmly lit, with four comfy but casual-looking mattresses on the floor. The windows were hung with heavy curtains. There was a pair of green and red shoes at each mattress. One wall was hung with a rug of eastern design.

"I hope you like the rug," said the Dude. "It ties the whole room together."

Before long, the wobbits were back in the main room. As a rule wobbits don't wear shoes. But since the Dude had produced shoes large enough for wobbit feet, the guests felt it would be impolite to not wear them. He also had bowling balls waiting for them with holes drilled perfectly for wobbit-sized hands. Soon they were all bowling merrily, rolling far better than usual. Even keeping score seemed easy, easier and more natural than asking someone else to do it.

All the cocktails and bowling caught up with the wobbits by the end of the third game, so Maude bid them good night.

"Have peace now," she said, "until the morning! Heed no nightly noises! For nothing passes door and window here, not goblin or troll or zombie or giant leech or umber hulk or marmot." She retired to her bedchamber.

The wobbits sat silently with the Dude, unnerved by the list of things they didn't have to be afraid of. Staying near the Dude seemed like a good idea. They didn't want move or speak, in case that would break the spell that was keeping them safe. But Promo had many questions and he couldn't keep quiet for long.

"So, did you hear us calling for you, Dude? Is that why you came?"

The dude stirred like a man shaken out of a pleasant, cocktail-enhanced dream. "What? Oh, yeah, man. I was just, um, there. I don't really, you know, plan things. But we knew you were coming. We heard that some new shit had come to light. There's a lot of strands to your story, a lot of facets. We had heard about what was happening. Some new shit has come to light."

Tom began singing quietly, as if to himself:

Willywonka river, bowling ball to give her
Willow man was eating wobbits, wanted to eat more.
Forgot about the bowling ball, rescued wobbits so small
Dude, Dude, Dude, coming in his screen door.

The Dude sat quietly. He picked up his rocks glass and took a very small sip of his White Rohirrim. He was completely at peace, but Promo wanted to talk.

"Dude," said Promo, "Maude is really a special lady."

"She's not my special lady, man," he said. "She's just my lady friend."

"Sure, Dude. Have it your way. Tell me about the Big Willow."

"No, not the Big Willow!" said Mary, who was still upset about being eaten and spit out by the Big Willow a few hours earlier.

"Not now, in the dark!" said Puppy, as he held Mary close. "Maybe tomorrow!"

The Dude looked at Promo. "What is with you, man? Your friends are fragile. They're very fragile. Look, we can talk about Big Willow in the morning. Until then, remember that you're completely safe in this bowling alley. No goblin or giant or zombie or shambling mound or tree can harm you. You might want to stay away from the windows. Goodnight!" He smiled and led the wobbits to their room. The wobbits were asleep far more quickly than they imagined possible.

In the dead of night, Promo dreamed he was flying. He was passing over a vast office building. On its top were two men. One was talking and pointing at some charts on easels. The other was flipping idly through a handout, pretending to listen. He seemed more and more irritated until finally he leaped up, ran to the edge of the roof and jumped off. Suddenly a shadow passed across the moon. It swept down on the falling figure and bore him away. It was a great eagle. Promo heard the cry "Noooo!' from the rooftop, and then he heard galloping, terrifying galloping. "Galloping that terrifying could only mean one thing: Executive Riders!" thought Promo. He wakened, got a glass of water and went back to bed. He soon was dreaming about flying through the night sky again, but this time with Maude.

Puppy lay at his side dreaming pleasantly, but then he began dreaming of noises coming through the windows. There was a shuffling, and a tapping and scratching at the windows, and a groaning sound, and the moaned word "Brains!" over and over. He wakened, and was about to make sure the windows were closed, but some half-remembered words from the Dude stopped him. He couldn't recall any details, and while he was trying to remember he fell back asleep.

It was the sound of water that Mary heard falling into his quiet sleep. He dreamed he had borrowed Pantsoff's hat, and had cast a spell upon a broom to make it carry water for him. The broom filled a cistern but wouldn't stop, even when Mary hacked it to bits with an axe. The cistern was overflowing and Mary thought "I shall be drowned!" Then he woke up, and was relieved to find his sheets were dry. Soon he was asleep again.

As far as he could remember, Sham slept through the night in deep content. He normally drank beer, and the mixed drinks had hit him hard.

They woke up, all four at once, in the morning light. There was no sign of the Dude or Maude, and the wobbits were very hungry. As far as they could remember there was no actual food consumed during the previous night's bowling. Other than the cream in the White Rohirrims, which did look quite yellow in the golden light of the bowling alley.

While searching for breakfast they found the Dude in a deep sleep. Promo touched his shoulder gently.

"Dude? Good morning, Dude," he said.

The Dude's eyes opened. "Hey, man! This is, like, a private residence, man!" he said. "Oh, it's you. What do you want?" He didn't sound angry, but it seemed like he was used to sleeping in.

"Have you had breakfast yet?" said Mary.

"No," said the Dude.

"Do you mind if we have some?" said Puppy.

"Go ahead," said the Dude.

"We'll gladly help ourselves," said Promo. "Tell us, Dude, where is your kitchen?"

"There's no food there," he said. "But there's some out front by the shoe rack."

The wobbits were soon helping themselves to the finest bowling alley snack food they had ever eaten. Golden pretzels, fresh peanuts, even potato chips, or "crisps" as the wobbits called them, all in little single serving bags hanging in a display. To their surprise they found some tonic water in the bar to wash it all down. They weren't quite ready to start in on the hard stuff just yet. Especially not Sham, who looked a bit dehydrated.

While they were eating, neither the Dude nor Maude appeared. Promo went over to the screen door to look for them outside and saw that it was pouring rain. Then he saw the Dude, walking towards the door through the rain, completely undisturbed by it. He was soaked, but undisturbed. He came in the door and said to the wobbits "It looks like it's raining, man. Time for a hot bath."

He returned to his chambers as the wobbits finished their snacks. After about an hour, they went to see if he was all right. The four wobbits found him in his bathtub, surrounded by candles, sipping a White Rohirrim with his eyes closed.

"Ahem," said Promo.

The Dude didn't respond.

"Dude?' said Promo.

"Yes?" said the Dude, his eyes still closed.

"What do we do now?"

"Nothing, man. It's raining. This is Maude's errand day. We can all bowl when she gets back. I suppose you want to talk until then."

Almost at random, the Dude started to talk. He told them many remarkable stories, of seven-ten splits, twelfth frames, and beverages. Moving constantly in and out of his talk was the Big Willow. The Dude's words laid bare the dark and strange thoughts of trees, and their hatred for the Buckiebrands that burned them, the woodsmen that cut them down, the birds that steal their twigs, the squirrels that tickle them, and the dogs that pee on them. Big Willow was in charge of all the trees in the Willywonka Valley, and the day was soon coming when---

Suddenly the Dude's talk left the woods and went leaping up the young Willywonka, over waterfalls and pebbles, past flowers and bunny rabbits until it came to the Downer Downs. The babbling brook was quickly forgotten as the Dude spoke of the dread Real Barrows and their ancient burial mounds and the wights within. He spoke of fortresses and warring kings. He spoke of abductions, ransoms, dismemberments, poisonings, rug thefts, and desperate battles of sword against bowling ball. Fortresses were burned, and dead kings had gold poured upon their biers, and beers poured upon their gold. And they were buried in real barrows, and green grass grew over all, and no one would mow it, fearing the wights that would come forth with their gaudy jewelry.

The wobbits shuddered. Tales of the wights were common at slumber parties and summer camp weenie-roasts, just as common as tales of the chupacabra and the mothman. But as the wobbits stopped shuddering and glancing knowingly at each other, they found that the Dude's lengthy ramble had drifted from campfire ghost-stories back to charming anecdotes about butterflies and pizza.

Promo hadn't interrupted with a question for hours, and he could resist no longer. "Who are you, Dude?"

"I'm unemployed," he said. "I'm the Dude. The Dude abides. I've been abiding since before the kings and the wights, since before Big Willow and the Willywonka, since before The Man showed up and twisted everything with his voodoo economics."

"Smoron!" cried the wobbits as one. They heard something shuffling and groaning at the door. Something moaning for brains? No, that wasn't it at all. It was Maude, back from running some errands. She was carrying a couple of bags, and Promo quickly helped her.

"Hi, Dude," she said. "I see your friends are still here. Will they be joining us for bowling?"

It was now evening. The wobbits had spent all the day listening to the Dude. He finally got out of the tub, and as the wobbits put on their bowling shoes, and he put on a loose, colorful shirt with an open collar and a single pocket. Above the pocket was stitched his name: "Dude," and on the back was the name of an old team sponsor: "Lamprey Farms."

"You know Farmer Lamprey?" asked Puppy.

"Oh, yeah," said the Dude. "He and I go way back. We've bowled in a lot of leagues together. He even sponsored us a couple of times. Paid the entrance fee and bought the shirts. He knows things." As the Dude talked, it became clear that he knew a few things, too, that he must have been told by Farmer Lamprey, and by Gildor Inglorion.

"You talk to the elves?" said Promo. "Did they tell you about The Ring?"

"Promo!" yelled the other wobbits.

"What ring?' said the Dude. "Oh! The Juan Ring! Let's see it."

To his own astonishment, Promo handed him the ring. None of the other wobbits were astonished.

The Dude looked at it and laughed. Then he put it on his finger. A moment later the wobbits gasped. There was no sign of him disappearing! As if to prove his point he tried it on as an earring, a nose ring, and a lip ring. Still, he did not disappear. Then he flipped it up in the air --- and it vanished with a flash! Promo gave a cry, but then the Dude pulled it out of Sham's ear. Everyone applauded politely as he handed it back to Promo.

This all seemed suspicious to Promo. He waited until the Dude was in the middle of a story of bowlers and their queer ways of ball polishing. Then he put on the ring and walked quietly towards the door.

"Hey, man!" cried the Dude. He was looking right at the invisible Promo. "Where are you going? The Dude abides! We've got to talk. A lot of new shit has come to light. Your case has a lot of ins and outs, a lot of interested parties. Take off the Ring, man!"

They began bowling, and talking. The Dude gave them directions over the Downer Downs, and past the Real Barrows, which he told them to avoid. They didn't need to be afraid --- but they should mind their own business. He advised them to pass the barrows on the west-side if they should chance to stray near one. Then he taught them a rhyme to sing, if they should fall into danger the next day:

Hippogryphs and psychophants are playing in the band
If they catch us we will not be seen again!
Dude, Dude, Dude!
Won't you come and meet us, before these monsters eat us
Dude, Dude, Dude, come on out your back door!

The wobbits sang this ridiculous song until they were sick of it, which was twice. Then they bowled and drank and laughed with the Dude and his lady friend Maude.

Chapter 8

FOG ON THE DOWNER DOWNS

That night they heard no noises. Promo dreamed again. In his dream he saw Pantsoff talking with a panicky-looking Puppy Dork on the battlements of a besieged city. He spoke of their deaths, and after. He said they would be reunited in a land of pale light behind a grey rain curtain, the light growing stronger to turn the veil all to glass and silver, until at last the curtain was rolled back, and a far green country opened before them under a swift sunrise. The whole thing sounded a little far-fetched to Promo, but it seemed to be comforting to Puppy.

The vision melted into waking. The sun was shining again. After a breakfast of bowling alley snacks, the wobbits packed and readied their ponies. They were about to leave when the Dude looked out the screen door and waved goodbye to them in a sincere but slightly absent fashion. It didn't seem like they would get much more out of the Dude, so they got on their ponies and rode a path that soon went alongside a ridge.

"Nuts!" cried Promo. "I knew I forgot something. We didn't say goodbye to Maude!" But there at the top of the ridge was Maude, the sun glinting off her silver breastplate. She waited patiently as they rode their overworked ponies up to her. Eventually they were close enough to speak together.

"Speed now, fair wobbits! Go with a blessing on your footsteps. Make haste while the sun shines!"

"I thought the expression was 'Make *hay* while the sun shines,'" said Puppy quietly to Mary.

"Shut up, you guys!" said Promo in a fierce whisper. He turned to Maude and took a deep breath. Before he could begin to sing, Maude gently touched a finger to his lips.

"No more words, wobbit-friend." she said. "Farewell. Shh!"

As they rode back down, Puppy muttered, "For that we rode up a ridge?"

They wound their way along the floor of the hollow, where it was warm and hazy. There was no tree nor any visible water; it was a country of grass and short springy turf, silent except for the whispers of the air over the edges of the land, like a vast, untamed golf course.

"A hundred wobbit-landscapers could work day and night and never keep it all mown," said Sham with wonder. They had reached the top of a hill and to the north could faintly glimpse a long, dark line.

"That is a line of trees that grow along the Byway," said Mary. "Some say they were planted in the old days."

"If they were planted and not wild, does that mean they won't lean over us threateningly?" said Promo.

Mary looked hurt. "I can't believe you'd say that after a tree ate me and Puppy!"

"That was one tree," said Promo. "A troublemaker. Most trees, even the wild ones, are quiet and law-abiding, don't you think, Sham?"

"I'm afraid I'm not at liberty to say, sir."

"So we're all agreed to ride without delay towards the road," Promo said. He saw to the east that the green hills were covered with mounds, and that some of the mounds were dotted with standing stones, like jagged teeth sticking out of green gums.

"Reminds me of the Grasper," said Promo. "Now what was it that the Dude said about those stones? I'm sure it'll come to me. Maybe if we break for lunch, I'll remember." They found a tall, standing stone to eat near, and unpacked their snack lunches just to the east of it. The stone remained strangely cool despite the hot sun. Their ponies wandered about, looking for carrots.

The next thing they knew, they were all waking up from another inadvertent nap. It was now cold and foggy, and the sun was well on its way to setting. "I can't believe we keep falling asleep!" said Mary.

"What's done is done," said Promo. "But going forward we've got to stop taking naps in uncanny, dangerous places." They all agreed, and quickly packed their picnic baskets, pillows and quilts back onto the ponies. They couldn't see the road anymore because of the fog, but they had a pretty good idea where it was. They led the ponies into a deep fog bank, knowing that if they could march in a straight line long enough, they would get to the Byway.

Their going was very slow, until Promo saw a hopeful sign: a darkness looming in the mist on either side. In between must surely be the north-gate of the Downer Downs.

"Come on!" he called back over his shoulder. "Once we pass through, we'll practically be at the Byway. Our troubles are over!" He hurried closer, but the dark shapes shrunk down to more standing stones, two of them this time. They seemed almost ominous, but that may have been because of the growing darkness and the cold mist. What was it the Dude said about the standing stones? As he walked between them, the darkness level went from "late cocktails on the patio" dark to "cloudy night in the country" dark. Promo was on the verge of remembering the Dude's advice when he noticed that the others had not followed him.

"Sham!" he called. "Mary! Puppy! Stop kidding around, you guys!" He eventually realized that this wasn't a prank, and panic set in quickly. He began running about and yelling "Guys!" His pony sensed that things were not going well, so he bolted. It seemed to Promo that he was running up a hill, or perhaps a mound of some sort. When he reached the top he noticed that it was now completely dark.

"Where have you gone, you morons?" he cried miserably.

There was no reply. He heard the wind hiss over the grass like a gigantic snake, which was of no comfort. Then he heard a desperate, pleading cry for help. He headed toward it. Soon there was a shape to his right: a real barrow! Things were worse than he thought.

"You idiots! Where are you?" he called.

"We're all here," said a strangely deep voice. "All three of us, including the one in the stupid little hat."

"Puppy?" said Promo. "How are you making your voice sound so deep? I thought you were a tenor."

"Come here, little wobbit," said the voice that didn't quite sound like Puppy. "Let's get together. I am waiting!"

Promo knew at that point that he was not talking to Puppy, because Puppy had never kept a conversation going for that long. Since it wasn't Puppy, who was it?

"No way!" said Promo. He did not run, but was becoming weak in the knees. If this was a barrow, then the voice must belong to---

He passed out.

When he came to himself, he knew by the slightly different character to the darkness that he was imprisoned in a real barrow. Suddenly, a song began: a cold murmur, rising and falling like a low moan from the ground. Out of the formless stream of sad but terrible sounds, strings of lyrics would now and again shape themselves. Grim, hard, cold lyrics, heartless and miserable.

My wobbits, I can't get,
can't get enough of your life, babe
Boys, I don't know, I don't know why
Can't get enough of your life, babe
Being dead I can't get used to
No matter how I try
The more life you give, the more I want
And baby, that's no lie

Promo had been taken by the most dread kind of wight imaginable: a Barry Wight. Promo felt he was probably already under the crooned, basso-profundo spell of the Barry Wight, terrified and unable to move from the cold stone on which he lay.

That notwithstanding, there is a seed of courage that lays hidden in the heart of the fattest and most timid wobbit. Promo was friends with the fattest and most timid wobbit of all, Froderick "Blimpy" Blogger, so he knew this to be true. It took every bit of that courage for Promo to even look around. But he found his courage and did look around. It was becoming less dark.

In a cold, green glow he saw Sham, Mary and Puppy lying on stones like his. They were deathly pale and clad in tattered white robes. "That's a really unflattering color on Sham," he thought. About them lay many treasures, but they were cheap and gaudy, just what you'd expect from a wight. On their heads were gold circlets, and there were gold chains about their waists, and on their chests were huge gold medallions with jeweled letters that spelled "Wight." Across their three necks lay one long, naked sword: they were lying very close together.

Behind his head Promo heard a creaking and scraping sound. Finding even more courage, he turned and looked, and saw a long arm groping, walking on its fingers towards Sham, its index and middle fingers taking little, horrifying steps. It was headed towards the hilt of the sword that lay across the three wobbit-necks, and it was only a few tiny finger-steps from its destination!

For a moment, Promo wondered if he could escape using The Ring. Pantsoff, if he ever showed up, certainly wouldn't care if Promo abandoned his friends. They were expendable, after all. But using the ring to escape alone seemed like the sort of thing Bulbo would do in one of his less admirable moments, of which there were many during his adventure decades ago. Promo forced himself to "be the bigger wobbit," stop wondering, and spring into action. The wight's hand was getting closer.

As Sham had pointed out earlier, the wobbits had gone on their dangerous adventure totally unarmed. But there were plenty of old-school swords lying about the real barrow, ancient swords, from when the Barry Wight was just a lad. Some of oldest ones were from a time before sword design had become fairly standard: there were swords with two or three points instead of one, there were swords that were wider than they were long, there were two-handed swords with two hilts side-by-side like a hedge-clipper, and there was one with no hilt at all, just a pointed blade at either end. Promo looked around and quickly found a regular short-sword. Summoning the last of his remaining hidden courage, he hacked and hewed at the crawling hand. It tried to side-step Promo with its tiny finger-steps, but Promo was too fast, and the hand was cut away from the uncanny arm. The sword shattered, so it was good that Promo didn't have a sword of his own to use. It would have been ruined. In the dark, Promo heard a deep, pained voice say "Oh, man!"

All at once, back into Promo's mind came the memory of the Dude's song. He had only to sing it, and the Dude would come. Better late than never, Promo started singing:

Hippogryphs and psychophants are playing in the band
If they catch us we will not be seen again!
Dude, Dude, Dude!
Won't you come and meet us, before these monsters eat us
Dude, Dude, Dude, come on out your back door!

There was a brief silence, and then Promo heard an answering voice singing:

Just left the bowling alley
Goodbye Maude, by golly
Got to save the Wobbits, like I did two days before.
Came quickly, we can all see, I didn't think you'd call me
Dude, Dude, Dude, running out my screen door.

Then he heard stones rumbling and falling, and saw light streaming in, and there was the Dude stepping into the real barrow. He was in his bathrobe and flip-flops. Though it looked like he had just gotten out of bed, it's also true that the Dude looked like that most of the time. He glanced around, thought for a minute and then sang:

Barry wights and killer trees are both pains in the neck.
In the parlance of our times: Please go to heck!
Doo, doo, doo.
Tired of all these monsters, I'll need a twelve-step sponsor
Dude, Dude, Dude, really miss my screen door.

At these words there was a bellow, and then a long trailing howl into an unguessable distance, and then silence, which was soon broken by Promo.

"Dude! Are we ever glad to see you!"

"Help me get your sleeping friends out of here," said the Dude. "You know, into the fresh air, man. Here, you take this one's feet."

"We're wobbits," said Promo. "You should be able to drag two of us out by yourself."

"True, man. And you should be able to keep your friends from taking naps with monsters."

"Have it your way, Dude. I've got his feet." They carried the others one by one into the sunlight. As Promo left the real barrow for the last time he thought he saw the wight's severed hand limping about on its index finger. The Dude went in, saw it, and there was a cry of "Bummer, man!" followed by a stabbing sound. After few more minutes he walked out, carrying the gaudy wight-treasure: gold medallions, platinum teeth grills, silver spoons, and bronzed baby shoes. He laid these in the sun.

"Quickly, um, Promo," said the Dude. "Let's get them out of this, like, wight-wear." He took the robes off Sham and Puppy, while Promo disrobed Mary. He had given up arguing with the Dude.

There the Dude stood, and he looked down upon the three motionless wobbits. He cleared his throat and began another reprise:

Wake up now my wobbit lads, it's time for you to go!
I got the wight, that's all you need to know.
Doo, Doo, Doo
Wake up and get going, I should be home bowling,
Dude, Dude, Dude, closed behind my screen door.

The wobbits stirred, stretched their arms, rubbed their eyes and then suddenly sprang up.

"What the---" began Mary. He stopped and a faraway look came into his eyes. "Of course. I remember. The men of Carn Poan came upon us in the night, and we were worsted. No, we wore worsted wool! No!" Then it seemed like his head cleared. "Where the heck are my pants?" He looked around and realized he was naked, as were Sham and Puppy.

"Maude might have some clothes for you guys," said the Dude. "Just be free and run around naked in the sunlight for a while, okay?" and the next thing anyone knew, he was gone. He didn't disappear, he didn't run off, he was just not there anymore.

They ran around naked as the Dude said, especially Puppy. It warmed them up and brought their color back. By the time they had completed a few laps around the burial mound, the Dude was walking into their midst. He had pants, bowling shirts and bowling shoes for all the wobbits, including Promo.

"So you won't feel left out, man." said the Dude to Promo. "Maude says 'Hello.'"

Knowing that the clothes came from Maude, Promo tore off his own clothes as if they had insulted him, and soon he was wearing a bowling shirt with *The Ivy Drip Tavern* emblazoned on the back. He felt splendid.

"Here," said the Dude as he handed out long daggers from the wight's treasure. "Since you can't keep out of trouble, you should at least be armed, man. Like, what happened to your swords, anyway?"

"Pantsoff didn't think we needed any," said Promo.

"He must not be party to the new shit that's come to light."

"Indeed not, sir," said Sham.

"Oh yeah, I found your ponies, too," the Dude said as six ponies walked up: the four ponies the wobbits rode, their spare, and one other, who was larger and fatter than the others.

"This guy is Fatso Pumpkin," said the Dude, patting Fatso. "He's kept an eye on your ponies for a while. He and I go way back."

"Don't you think your pony minds being given such an offensive name?" said Promo.

"Offensive?" said the Dude. "Like Blimpy Blogger?"

"How do you know Blimpy?" said Promo.

"The Dude abides, man," said the Dude.

"I need a beverage," said the Dude. "You guys could probably use one, too." Before Promo could complain that it was still mid-morning, everyone had a White Rohirrim in their hand. The cream had a strengthening effect and soon they all felt a little better.

As they drank, the Dude dug through the treasure pile. He had found an aluminum briefcase, and began putting the smallest and most valuable-looking items into it.

"It's important I maintain my liquidity," he said. "My accountant tells me my financial situation is very, like, complex. You can take whatever treasure you want, man, and leave the rest for anyone that needs it. I'm cool with that."

At last they set off, and the Dude rode with them. Perhaps he had decided that the next rescue would be easier if he was with the wobbits in the first place, instead of having to find them and then rescue them. As they rode, the Dude sang in a strange language that was unknown to the wobbits, an ancient language whose words seemed mainly to be those of bowling and cocktails.

When they reached the Byway it was early evening. "Well! Here we are at last!" said Promo.

"Thanks to your short cut we only lost two days," said Mary.

"True," said Promo, "but it may also have thrown the Executive Riders off our trail. I'm sure it must have." What with the Killer Willow and the Barry Wight, they had forgotten about the other monsters that were after them. Promo decided to change the subject. "So, Dude, now what do we do?"

"I don't know, man! Get on with your mission, quest, thing, man. If I was you, I'd take this road about four miles to the next village, Whee under Whee-hill, where you'll find an inn called *The Dancing Doughnut*. I know the owner, his name is Barleycorn Butterface. He makes a pretty good White Rohirrim. You can stay there for the night and start the next day refreshed."

The wobbits tempted him with cocktails if he would stay with them until *The Dancing Doughnut,* but the Dude was already riding Fatso Pumpkin back to his bowling alley. They heard him singing:

Happy as a baboon, gonna be with Maude soon
Dude, Dude, Dude, walking though my screen door

He turned and waved, and wished the wobbits well, and then he and the pony were gone.

"I am sorry to take leave of The Dude," said Sham. "He is, as the Grasper would say, a 'caution' and no mistake. It will be some time before we see anyone better, or queerer. Not that there's anything wrong with that. And I must admit I'm looking forward to visiting *The Dancing Doughnut* he spoke of. One hopes it's like *The Ass-Dragon Inn* back home. What sort of people live in Whee?"

"There's huge ugly folks," said Mary, "and there's regular wobbits like us. And *The Dancing Doughnut* is supposed to be epic. Some of my buddies from Buckiebrand Hall used to go there for Farthing Beer Night."

"Great," said Promo. "All the same, let's not make ourselves too much at home. Please remember --- especially you, Puppy --- that the name Bunkins must not be given. Refer to me as Mr. Underwear. That way, no one will be suspicious."

They rode off into the evening. Puppy was trying to memorize Promo's alias. Promo was thinking about Maude. Sham and Mary were wondering if tonight was Farthing Beer Night.

Chapter 9

AT THE SIGN OF *THE DANCING DOUGHNUT*

Farthing Beer Night was a popular night indeed in the village of Whee. Whee was the principle village of Whee-land, a small inhabited region surrounded by the suburbs of Straddle, Crumbe and Piechart on the edge of the Chartwood Forest.

The Men of Whee were cheerful and short. The Women of Whee were cheerful and somewhat shorter. They weren't wobbit short, or even dwarf short, but just shorter than you are, unless you're really short or a very young child. They liked nothing more than eating carrots and belching as they stood in the rain, or drinking beer in pubs with their pet ferrets. They were friendly and familiar with Wobbits, Dwarves and Elves, but didn't much care for Wights or Killer Trees.

In the wild lands beyond Whee there were mysterious wanderers that the Whee-Men didn't much care for either, called Rangers. They were taller, darker and handsomer than the Men Of Whee, which explains a great deal of their dislike. They were said to have strange powers of sight and hearing perhaps due to their healthy outdoor lifestyle, offset only by beer-drinking and pipe-smoking in moderation. Their appearances in Whee were rare, but they always brought news and incredible stories. The Whee-landers enjoyed the infotainment, but never befriended the Rangers that brought it, despite the famous Whee cheerfulness. Cheerfulness, tempered by standoffishness.

There were also many families of wobbits in Whee-land. The Big Folk and the Little Folk (as they called each other in mixed company) were on friendly terms, each minding their own business and keeping to their own kind. They all claimed their schools were separate but equal, but each secretly believed that their own schools were better. Nowhere else in the world was this peculiar (and pointless) arrangement tolerated.

The village of Whee was protected on all sides by an impenetrable Little Earth shrubbery. Where the Byway pierced the mighty bushes there was a gate, guarded by a retired shirriff, a gatekeeper who kept comfy and warm in a small lodge just inside. There was another gate on the opposite side of Whee to take the Byway out of town. Travelers often rode straight through town without enjoying any of the quaint shoppes or the cheerfulness of the locals. The Whee Chamber Of Commerce planned to someday put twists and turns in the Byway. They hoped this would compel visitors to get a more complete look at all the restaurants and espresso bars that Whee had to offer.

Down on the road there was an inn. It had been built ages ago, when traffic on the roads had been far greater, before the current recession had caused a dropoff in both business and vacation travel. *Strange as news from Whee* was still a saying in Wobbiton, descending from those days when news, sports and weather from all over Little Earth could be heard at the inn.

The innkeeper was an important person. First and foremost, he controlled the sale of beer, wine and hard liquor in Whee-land. Second, *The Dancing Doughnut* made the best doughnuts in the Northwest, giving the inn important revenue during the hours before liquor was legally available. Finally, anyone that wanted to be the center of attention, or spread a rumor, or pry into the affairs of others went to the inn to hear from Rangers or speak with dwarves, traveling on business from their retail banks, mortgage lending houses, and investment firms in the mountains.

It was dark, and white stars were shining when Promo and his companions came at last to the West-gate of Whee. Since normal business hours were long over, the gate was shut. There was a hole through which visiting wobbits could call for the gatekeeper. There was slightly higher hole for dwarves, one above that for Whee-landers, a higher one for rangers and elves, and a still higher one for seldom-seen Giraffe-Men of the East. Promo called to the gatekeeper. He called back.

"Do you have any idea what time it is?" he asked. "Who do you think you are, creating a disturbance at this hour?"

"We don't know what time it is, although it must be late," said Promo. "And we are four wobbits. We are journeying east and seek shelter for the night."

"Four wobbits! From Wobbiton, based on your out-of-town accent."

"Whatever!" said Promo. "Are you going to let us in or not?"

"What business takes you east of Whee, and what are your names?"

"Our business and our names are out own!"

"That may be," said the gatekeeper, "but it's my job to ask questions after nightfall. If you choose not to answer, I'll have to ask you to empty your pockets into some dog food dishes, remove your belts, and put all your toiletries in 3.5 ounce bottles."

Puppy stepped forward. "We are wobbits from Buckieland, and we have a fancy to stay at the inn here and enjoy Farthing Beer Night. This is Mr. Underwear. My name is Seymour Bottoms. This gentleman is Hugh Jazz, and with him is our servant, Holden McGroin."

"Very well, sirs, come in, come in." The gate opened, and the wobbits entered. Promo wondered why the gatekeeper was so suspicious, and if anyone had been asking about a party of wobbits. Could it have been Pantsoff? He might have finally caught up with them while they were delayed in the Old Scary Forest and the Downer Downs. Something about the gatekeeper made Promo uneasy, something other than his bad complexion, stringy hair, and missing teeth.

The wobbits rode up a gentle slope, passed shops and soon were in front of an inn. The main building was two stories tall, with two smaller wings and an arch that lead into a courtyard, where there was a pool and patio bar area. Both were closed. Over the door was painted in white letters: *The Dancing Doughnut by Barleycorn Butterface. A Best Uttermost-Western Hotel.*

"I wonder if it's a franchise," said Sham, "or if these hotels are company-owned?" No one could answer him.

Promo went to the front desk to check in while the others waited for their ponies to be valet-parked. He stood there for a moment until a harried, overweight and sweaty man with a tray full of mai tais and daiquiris came to help him.

"Good evening, little master," he said, bending down. "What may you be wanting?"

"Um, what?" said Promo.

"How can I help you? Pardon me, but tonight is Pirate Night in the bar."

"Is that the same as Farthing Beer Night?"

"I'm afraid not, that was last night. Tonight all rum drinks are half price if you talk like a pirate. Or, 'All the rum drinks you may be wanting arrrr half price if you be talking like a pirate.'" And then he added "'Matey. Begging your pardon.'"

"No eye-patch?" asked Promo.

"No. I can't pour drinks accurately without my depth perception. Like I said, 'What may you be wanting?' Checking in, sir?"

"Yes, there are four of us, and we're waiting for someone to take our ponies. Are you Mr. Butterface?"

"That's right, Barleycorn Butterface at your service. And you're from Wobbiton, by the sound of your outrageous accent."

"Well, we're not pirates, that's for sure." They both laughed.

"Say, that reminds me," said Barleycorn. "Something about Wobbiton. Oh, well, it'll come. Your names, sir?"

"Yes, Messrs. Jazz, Bottoms and McGroin are with the ponies. My name is Mr. Underwear."

"Underwear?" said Mr. Butterface. "I almost remembered that time. It's always crazy here on Pirate Night."

"Knob!" he shouted. "Move those hairy feet to the front desk now, Knob!" He looked for Knob behind him. "Guests with ponies! Knob!" He stopped yelling when he realized he was looking over and past Knob, who was a wobbit.

"Don't you want me at the bar, Mr. Butterface?" said Knob.

"Have Rob tend bar."

"Rob's doing the valet parking tonight."

"I forgot about that," said Barleycorn. "Man, it's busy tonight. Help these gentlemen to their rooms with their bags, parcels and paraphernalia. And have Rob take care of their ponies. Enjoy your stay, Mr.---"

"Mr. Underwear," said Promo.

"Say, that reminds me," said Barleycorn, who was then called to lounge to deliver his tray of drinks. "We'll talk later!" he said over his shoulder.

Rob came for the ponies, and Knob led the wobbits to a suite of rooms designed to accommodate wobbits. All hotels in Little Earth had a few such rooms as a matter of regulatory compliance. Knob brought in the luggage.

"I recommend you order room service for dinner,' he said. "There are drawbacks to being 36 inches tall with large, bare feet when you're in an tavern filled with tall drunks wearing boots. But maybe after the dinner rush is over it might be quiet enough for you to visit the lounge."

Promo placed his order, and soon Knob was back with nachos, club sandwiches and Ye Olde Style beer, as well as coffee and Barleycorn's famous Dancing Doughnuts, which didn't actually dance but were pretty tasty. It was all homelike enough but amazingly overpriced. Knob's gratuity had already been added to the bill, as well as a charge for room-service.

"This is criminal!" said Mary, looking at the bill.

"Yeah!" said Puppy as he chewed. "Where's our shrimp cocktail?"

Later, the company visited the inn's lounge. Warm, dim lighting gave it an intimate ambiance, and also made careful cleaning unnecessary. Barleycorn was at the bar, talking to several dwarves and a few strange-looking men. Sitting in booths and at tables were some men of Whee, a collection of local wobbits (telling Big Folk Jokes amongst themselves), a few more dwarves and a sasquatch. In the corner, a blue-green creature with antennas, big bug eyes and sucker-tipped fingers argued with a man wearing a vest and boots, which he had on the table.

"Seems like a nice enough place," said Mary.

"Remember to keep your receipts, everyone," said Promo as they walked in.

They were invited by the Whee-wobbits to join their group, while behind them there was some commotion at the corner table, and the man in the boots walked out. The Whee-wobbits were cheerful, like the Whee-men, but very inquisitive. Promo tried to explain their journey in the vague terms Pantsoff often used: "We're going on a trip, to see a guy about a thing." This didn't satisfy the locals, so Promo explained that it was for a book he was writing. This led to even more questions. He then said that the book would be self-published. With that, all interest in Promo vanished, and his companions began talking.

There was talk from the men and dwarves about trouble brewing away south. Refugees were starting to arrive in Whee, and while the Whee-folk are cheerful, they can only put up with so many jobless out-of-towners. One strange-looking man, a squint-eyed, ill-favored fellow, started talking politics.

"We need someone running Little Earth who can cut government spending and encourage economic growth with tax relief," he said. "Then the wealth will trickle down from the One Per Cent to us little people. And to the even littler wobbits! Arrr!" Then he ordered a half-priced pina colada.

Puppy, after a few mai tais, was now feeling quite at home and began chatting gaily about events in Wobbiton. Not that there's anything wrong with that, but it was making Promo uneasy. One of the Whee-landers who had been to Wobbiton was asking questions about who the Underwears were related to, and where they lived.

Promo suddenly noticed a strange-looking but handsome man in the shadows. He was listening intently to the wobbit-talk.

"There's a great many strange-looking men here tonight," said Promo to Sham.

"Indeed, sir," said Sham. "It's as if we were at a collectable card game tournament."

The man wore a travel-stained long coat wrapped about him, and a fedora. It was technically the same sort of hat that Sham wore, but this hat was neither little nor stupid. It was mysterious, and though it overshadowed his face, it did not hide the gleam of his eyes as he watched the wobbits. He was smoking a pipe. There was a beer and a plate of little hamburgers in front of him.

"Who is that?" said Promo to Butterface as he took another drink order.

"The handsome, mysterious one?" said Butterface. "I don't rightly know. He's one of the wandering folk, Rangers we call them. That one there we call Slider, because of all those greasy little burgers he eats. I mostly make them for wobbits, but he always orders them, usually with fries. Funny you should ask about him, because---"

"You mean chips, sir?" said Sham.

"You wobbits and your strange expressions! Fries are served hot with burgers. Chips are flat and round, and you buy them in a little bag."

"No, those are crisps," said Promo. "Chips are the ones that are served hot, usually with fried fish."

"You never know what you're going to hear next in Whee! Wobbits from Wobbiton!" said Butterface. "Say, that reminds me, what was it now? It's on the tip of my tongue."

Promo noticed that Slider was now looking at him. He was flattered, but unnerved. When Slider beckoned him to come over, Promo couldn't refuse. As Promo sat down, Slider removed his fedora, revealing a shaggy head of dark hair flecked with grey, the tough but sensitive good looks of a warrior-poet, and dreamy grey eyes. No one this handsome had ever been in Wobbiton,

"I am called Slider," he said in quiet, confident voice. "I am very pleased to meet you, Master --- Underwear, if that is indeed your real name."

"Yes, Underwear, that's right," said Promo stiffly. He felt flustered under the gaze of those incredible eyes. He realized he had his hand in his pants pocket, nervously fidgeting with his ring. For some reason, he wanted to put it on.

"Well, Master Underwear, your young friends should stick to beer. The rum seems to be loosening their tongues, and there are queer folk about, if you know what I mean."

Promo was alarmed to see that Puppy was standing on a table, and soon began singing.

I have a friend from who's from Wobbiton
He's on a quest and he likes good rum
He still has many miles to go
He's in this pub and his name's Promo!

"Just as I thought," said Slider. "Who knows what secrets he'll give away by the time he gets to the refrain? You'd better do something quick, Promo!" Puppy started the second verse.

I have a friend who's a real great guy,
He has big feet and he's three feet high.
His uncle found a ring, spelunkin'
He's in this pub and name is...

"Hey everybody, look at me!" said Promo, as he jumped on a table, too. His hand went back into his trouser pocket, clutching at the ring.

"You just can't stand it when I'm the center of attention, can you, Promo?" said Puppy, as he jumped down, discouraged.

"That's right," said Promo to the crowd. "The name's Promo Underwear, and I'm writing a book about about my travels through---" and then the table, off-balance without Puppy, tipped over. Promo fell, and the ring flew out of his pocket and up into the air. It was mysteriously without any chain. Promo reached for it, but it fell onto his finger like a game of ring toss.

Promo looked around to discover that the tavern had become a dreamworld. Everyone was moving in photo-negative slo-mo. There was a whooshing sound, like the flushing of a huge, hideous toilet, and then, a vision of an eye. Promo heard deafening, ghastly whispering.

"Join the firm, Promo! We get paid in stock options, and you'll get a company waggon! Join us! Don't be a loser!" The speaker sounded a little hoarse.

Terrified by the talk of compensation, Promo rolled under a table and managed to pull the ring off his finger.

"Uncle Bulbo wore this ring hundreds of times around the condo, but he never mentioned any hallucinations!" Promo found himself back in the real world.

A muscular hand grabbed him, and dragged him into a dark booth, while the rest of the lounge ran about in confusion over Promo's unexplained disappearance. The strange-looking ill-favored fellow nodded and winked to a strange-looking Bree-lander who had a single conjoined eyebrow, and they discreetly walked out. Promo noticed that the hand grasping his bowling shirt belonged to Slider, who started haranguing him.

"You draw far too much attention to yourself... Mr. Underwear."

"That's my name, don't wear it out," said Promo weakly. "What do you want?"

"A little more caution from you. That is no trinket you carry."

"Trinket? What? Me? I don't know what you're talking about!"

"Let's go to your room. I'll *wring* the truth out of you yet."

When they arrived at Promo's room, Slider bumped his head a few times, and then sat, taking up most of a wobbit-sized love-seat.

"I hate these wobbit-rooms," he said. "Anyway, are you frightened?"

"I wouldn't say I'm 'frightened,' as such," said Promo. "Startled, yes, and concerned, but---" He jumped suddenly at a noise in the hallway. Slider drew his sword, which was only half a sword. The way he held it, however, it looked quite dangerous, even in the close confines of a wobbit-room. The door flew open, and the other three wobbits burst in.

"That's quite enough of that, my good man!" said Sham. He was standing in a Marquis-Of-Queensbury, put-up-your-dukes pose. "We'll thank you to unhand Mr. Promo and sheath your half-weapon."

"Well said, Sham," said Slider. "You have a stout heart."

"He has a stout everything. Look at him!"

"Shut up, Puppy!" said Mary.

"Why don't we continue this back in the lounge," said Slider. "I have a bad feeling about this room. And maybe one of you could buy me a beer."

Chapter 10

SLIDER, AND A LETTER FROM PANTSOFF

"So who are you, exactly?" said Mary, as Butterface went to get a round of drinks for the table.

"I am called Slider," he answered. "Your friend Promo promised he'd talk with me. Now here we all are, at a table for five. Do we need separate checks?"

"No," said Promo. "This will be my treat. What did you need to tell me?"

"Many dark things," said Slider. "I cannot disappear, unlike you, Promo, but I can keep my yap shut and listen, unlike you, Puppy. For instance, I recently was in the Downer Downs crouching in the bushes when I overheard four wobbits talking. One of them said *Please remember --- especially you, Puppy --- that the name Bunkins must not be given. Refer to me as Mr. Underwear. That way, no one will be suspicious.* Mr. Underwear? That's the worst alias I've ever heard!"

"Begging your pardon, sir," said Sham, "but I believe 'Holden McGroin,' the alias I was given, is far worse."

"Fair enough," said Slider. "But really! 'Mr. Underwear?' How did you come up with that?"

"It was Pantsoff's idea," said Promo.

"Yeah, that sounds like one of his," said Slider. "Do you usually take his advice?"

"Do you usually hide in the bushes, eavesdropping?" asked Promo.

"That doesn't make him a bad person, sir," said Sham.

"Even so," said Promo. "I'd like an answer, Slider."

"I was trying to quickly and discreetly find a wobbit named Promo Bunkins. I had learned that he was carrying out of Wobbiton a 'secret' that concerned me and my friends."

"He must be party to the new shit that's come to light!" said Mary.

"I am indeed. And I also know that there are Executive Riders in Whee!"

"No way!" said Puppy.

"Yes, way," said Slider. "Of course, the Shrubbery around Whee is completely impenetrable, but they're in all the same. One knocked down the gate and squished the gatekeeper. Another one snuck in while the squished gatekeeper's replacement was on break. The rest bribed their way in."

"Bribed!" said Mary. "How?"

"Here in Whee, not everyone is honest or cheerful, despite what you've heard from the Chamber Of Commerce. Bill Furface, for example. He's the guy with the one massive eyebrow."

"The unibrow?" said Mary.

"Yes," said Slider. "He's always up to no good. He left the tavern with the squinty southerner right after your nightclub act. If I were a betting man, I'd bet they're having a meeting with the Executive Riders right now."

The wobbits sat silent and terrified.

"What happened to our drink order?" said Slider. "Barleycorn is a great guy and all, but how long does it take to pour five beers? Anyway, based on what I've seen, you desperately need a guide for your trip to Riverdale and the Last Waffle House Of The West. That would be me. I know all the lands between Wobbiton and the Moisty Mountains. I've wandered over them for many years, selflessly guarding innocents like you from evildoers, with never a thought about vacation time or health insurance or retirement. And I'm older than I look. How old do you think I am? Go ahead, guess."

"I don't know," said Promo. "Thirty-five, thirty-nine, maybe?"

"Not even close. But thanks. It must be all the fresh air and exercise I get hunting trolls."

At that moment Barleycorn arrived with the drinks, sweaty and puffing. "Sorry about the delay, guys. I have some guests that are still upset about your magic show, Mr. Underwear. They thought they were going to have to pay a cover charge or something. Now then, what was I going to ask you?"

"Is that a letter in your pocket, addressed to Promo Bunkins?" said Slider.

"Now I remember! I have a letter for you," he said to Promo.

"Well, um, what does that letter have to do with me? My name's Underwear! Mr. Underwear."

"True," said Barleycorn. "But I was told that a Mr. Bunkins would be checking in under the assumed name of Underwear. I was given a description, as well: *A wobbit, short, slightly overweight, about three feet tall, curly brown hair, short, furry size 14 bare feet, possibly pointed ears.* Come to think of it, that could be any of you. Which one of you is Bunkins? He said it was important."

"Who's this 'he' you refer to?" said Promo.

"Pantsoff the Wizard!" said Barleycorn. "He was in the middle of a big project management contract. Nice enough old guy, does a lot of entertaining, not a great tipper, though."

"So what about the letter?" said Promo.

"What letter? Oh this one! Yes, well, about three months ago he walks into my office, right through the door that says 'Authorized Personnel Only,' and says *Barley, my man!* and I says *What are you doing in my office?* And he says *I'm here on important business.* Then I says *Nevertheless, rules are rules, so if you'll step outside---"*

"The point, Barleycorn?" said Promo.

"Please, sir," said Sham. "I like it. Let's allow the story to evolve."

"Go ahead," said Slider.

"Be sure to get this letter to Rohan Express in time for their next-day delivery. I'll pay you back, of course, says he. *You can count on me,* I says. And here it is, as promised." Then he read proudly aloud: "'MR. PROMO BUNKINS, BUG END, WOBBITON.'"

"Give me that!" said Promo as he snatched the letter. "Why didn't you send it? It sat here in Whee for three months!"

"Yes, well, about that," said Barleycorn. "It's actually a kind of funny story. You see, it was Farthing Beer Night, and I says to Knob, I says---"

"Whatever," said Mary. "So now what?"

"You need to be careful," said Barleycorn. "Those thin black men have been here, asking for you!"

"Not again!" said Promo. "Barley, what makes you say the Executive Riders were black?"

"Well, their suits were black, and it was the way they spoke. I'm pretty sure they said that they wanted to 'axe' you some questions."

"I'm disappointed to hear this kind of nonsense in a community as diverse as Whee," said Promo. "Really, Barleycorn! Can't we all just get along?"

"Let's not start throwing stones, Mr. Bunkins," said Barleycorn. "At least I'm not taking up with some homeless man."

"Homeless!" said Slider. "And who should he take up with? A fat innkeeper who only remembers his own name because people shout it at him all day?"

"I'm not that fat!" said Barleycorn.

"Hey!" said Promo. He was shocked that Slider had taken such a cheap shot at a man with a weight problem. He knew he needed to change the subject. "Is anyone curious about what's in the letter? Why don't I read it aloud? I hope it doesn't disclose any shocking secrets!"

"Go ahead," said Barleycorn, visibly hurt. "I have to do some sweeping up in the back, or something." He hurried away.

"And we need a 5:30 wake up call," said Mary. "With four room-service continental breakfasts, too." Barleycorn didn't answer.

"Well?" said Slider. "Read the letter!"

"Yeah!" said Mary and Puppy. "Read it! Read it!"

Promo opened the letter. It was written on Barleycorn's Dancing Doughnut official letterhead. Promo recognized Pantsoff's handwriting from the many IOUs Pantsoff had written over the years. It read as follows:

THE DANCING DOUGHNUT, WHEE, Midyear's Day, 1418.

Dear Promo,

Things couldn't be better! My plan is going off without a hitch, and is exceeding my expectations. The only bad news is that I will not be able to attend your farewell party. You can buy me a beer some other time. By the way, I suggest you leave Wobbiton at once. Nothing bad, mind you, just don't delay at all. Leave a message for me in Whee at The Dancing Doughnut if I haven't caught up with you by then. You can trust the manager (Butterface). You may meet an old co-worker of mine on The Road: a Man, tall, dark, very handsome, and extremely handy in a tight spot. His name is Slider. He has been briefed on our project and will help you. Make for Riverdale. If, for any reason, I am not there, Enron will advise you. He is the Riverdale General Manager.

Very truly yours,

PANTSOFF.

PS. Do not use the you-know-what again, wink-wink. And don't travel by night. But there's nothing to worry about!

PPS. Just to be on the safe side, make sure that the tall, dark stranger is actually Slider before you invite him along. The Executive Riders are also tall and dark, not that there's any chance you'll meet one of them! Anyway, there are many strange men at The Dancing Doughnut, especially on Pirate Night (arrr, matey!). Slider's non-alias is Orogarn.

All that is gold does not glitter
Not all those who wander are lost
You can't tell a book by its cover
A rolling stone gathers no moss
Renewed shall be blade that was broken
The crownless again shall be king
Overnight his best dress shirt is soakin'
'Round the collar shall be no more ring

I hope Butterface sends this promptly. If not, we may all be doomed. No worries! If he forgets, I shall turn him into popcorn.

Farewell! -P

"Barleycorn was recommended to us by both Pantsoff and the Dude," said Promo. "Forgetting an important letter is what I'd expect from a friend of Pantsoff's. But I thought the Dude had better judgement."

"Sir, perhaps the Dude sees qualities in Barleycorn that he judges more important than memory," said Sham. "Such as the mixing of cocktails."

"Good point, Sham," said Promo. "So here we are, with Pantsoff's endorsement of Slider. Which is unfortunate."

"Yeah, Slider," said Mary. "We were starting to like you. But any friend of Pantsoff's---"

"I get that a lot," said Slider. "But I am who I say I am, and you'll need my help getting to Riverdale. I had hoped you'd accept me based on my good looks." He spoke like he was kidding, but the wobbits could see that he wasn't.

"Come on, guys!" said Puppy. "Handsome is as handsome does, as the Dork family has said for generations. Although I never understood what that meant, until now."

"I don't know," said Mary. "This guy comes out of nowhere, says he's our friend, claiming to be this fellow Slider---"

"I *am* Slider, so let's stop horsing around!" he said as he suddenly stood up, looking tall and menacing (compared to the wobbits). Sham, Mary and Puppy were terrified, but not Promo.

"Yes," Promo said. "You're very tall and menacing, just like Pantsoff when he does that same trick. He did it all the time back at Bulbo's condo at Bug End."

"I am Orogarn, son of Orogarni," Slider continued, ignoring the interruption, "and if by life or death I can save you, Promo, I will. The others will have to look after themselves."

"I intended to ask you to join us as soon as I saw you," said Promo. "I figured an employee of the Enemy would feel fair, but be found foul. Pantsoff's poem is your perfect portrait, and I would feel the fool if you were not found fine. If you understand."

"I'm not sure I do," said Slider, "but I think you're saying I'm to be your guide, which is a relief. And yes, the poem is about me. You've already seen my sword, or what's left of it."

"How did you break it?" asked Puppy.

"It was like that when I got it." Slider said this with such finality that even Puppy was discouraged from further questioning.

"Anyway, I'm going to have it fixed when we get to Riverdale. There's a shop there called the Swordatorium, where Enron will have it completely rebuilt. But as for tomorrow, we leave early for Carrottop, an old lookout post. Pantsoff said he would try to meet us there unless something comes up."

"You spoke with Pantsoff?" said Promo. "We need to talk with him! I don't know what I'm supposed to do with all these receipts."

"Yes, well, he's been missing. The Executive Riders are being blamed."

"Oh no!"

"Pantsoff may have fallen victim to one of their weapons, like the Black Breath," said Slider. "It causes sleep disorders, feelings of depression, night terrors, and loss of appetite."

Suddenly Butterface burst into the room. "Those Riders! They're back, looking for you!"

"Promo," said Slider, "you and the others stay here with me. It's too dangerous for you to return to your rooms, so Butterface will go get your luggage."

"Right away!" said Barleycorn. "Knob!" he yelled. "Go get the luggage for Mr. Underwear and his group and bring it here!"

While waiting for Knob, they had coffee and some dancing doughnuts. Soon Knob appeared with their lumpy duffle-bags slung about him and a cart he was pushing.

"I used some rolled up blankets and pillows to make a decoy wobbit in each bed," he said. "The dummy of Mr. Underwear is especially lifelike."

"Fine work, Knob," said Slider. "Goodnight, gentlemen." Butterface and Knob returned to the lobby and front desk of the inn. Once they left, Slider barricaded the door and shuttered the windows.

"You four get some sleep," he said to the wobbits. "We've got a big day tomorrow and I don't want anyone getting cranky."

The wobbits bedded down on the floor, and after some giggling and toenail painting, fell asleep. Slider sat in a chair facing the door, put his half-a-sword on his knees, and poured himself another cup of coffee.

Chapter 11

A KNIFE, RIGHT IN THE PILLOWS

As the wobbits prepared for sleep in Whee, Promo's fake home in Buckieland stood quiet. Blimpy Blogger peered out the door in his nightshirt, nightcap and socks. He had felt sensations of fear all afternoon, but this is not unusual for any wobbit. By bedtime, though, he wondered if perhaps there was something actually wrong in Buckieland. Sure enough, he saw a thin, creeping figure in a black suit entering the back yard from the alley.

Three shadows wearing black, or perhaps dark charcoal, took up positions outside the house. One at the front door, one at the back, and one at the door by the hot tub in the courtyard. The Executive Riders used the Multiple Simultaneous Entry doctrine whenever possible, to disorient their victims and eliminate any possibility of escape. They waited motionless for hours to gain the element of surprise, and then the figure in front drew a blade that gleamed in its own light. There was a soft and heavy blow upon the door, as soft and heavy as the Dude's velvet bowling bag.

"Is Mr. Bunkins available? I must speak with him about an incredible opportunity," said a professional yet menacing voice.

There was another blow upon the door, and the cheap lock popped open. At that moment the same thing happened to the back door. The courtyard door crashed in. Three conservatively dressed figures entered.

From the trees nearby came the honking of a mighty horn.

AWAKE! FOES! FIE! FOUL! AWAKE!

Blimpy Blogger had not been idle. He had been running, which is a brave choice for an overweight wobbit. As soon as he saw the three shadowy figures, he knew he didn't want to find out why they would visit in the middle of the night. He ran as far as he could, to the end of the block, where he collapsed on a doorstep. "Rick! Rick, help me!" he cried in his terror and confusion. "Rick, hide me! Do something! You must help me! Rick! Rick!" Despite the babbled nonsense, Blimpy's neighbor Rick got the idea there were enemies in Buckieland, perhaps searching for letters of transit, or leaning over their Shrubbery in a threatening fashion. And then other neighbors started honking horns and yelling.

AWAKE! FEE! FI! FO! FUM! AWAKE!

The Buckiebrands were honking the Horn Of Buckieland, which hadn't been honked since New Year's Eve. Other than every New Years Eve, it hadn't been honked for a hundred years. Back then, during the famous Fell Winter when the Buckiebrand River froze over, the Horn was honked to warn of invading yeti and snow snakes.

The dark, slender figures knew they would never be able to withstand dozens of wobbits, all honking horns and yelling. They crept quickly back to their horses and galloped down the street. The Ring and Bunkins were gone, and without a forwarding address the Riders were helpless. Galloping through the gate they had smashed on their way in, and over the guards they squished earlier, they vanished from Buckieland.

Promo's dreams were troubled with the noise of galloping hooves and gasping wobbits, and a far off honking and yelling. He opened his eyes and heard Knob outside the door with the wakeup call Mary ordered. Slider had opened the drapes and light poured in after what seemed like an extremely short night.

Once Slider had un-barricaded the door, they all went back to check their wobbit-room. Sure enough, the blankets had been slashed, the pillows had all suffered multiple stab wounds, and the coconut that Knob had used to simulate Promo's head showed signs of blunt instrument trauma.

Barleycorn was devastated. "Mayhem in my rooms, attempted murder of my guests, brand new pillows and blankets ruined. And why is there coconut strewn about? Things aren't like they used to be. This recession is going to ruin us all."

"Yeah, that's tough," said Mary. "You better tell Room Service to make that five continental breakfasts, and we need them right away. Oh, and have the valet bring our ponies around to the front, too. Chop-chop."

"Yes, little master," said Butterface. "Watch how I hurry."

He was back in no time at all. "I regret to inform you," he said without a trace of sarcasm, "that your ponies are missing. So is every other pony, horse, unicorn and hippogryph in the place. And there was something else, what was it--- Now I remember! Your breakfasts should be here momentarily." Barleycorn went back to the front desk with an improved opinion of himself.

"Sir, perhaps they haven't searched everywhere," said Sham. "Our ponies could be in the Exercise Room, or at the Pool, or in the Business Center, perhaps?"

"No, Sham," said Slider, "I'm sure they're gone. But I've seen those ponies, and I'm pretty sure that they were just slowing you down. Of course, this means you'll have to carry your own dufflebags. The ponies would have been useful for carrying food, though. There's absolutely no place to eat between here and Riverdale except for the occasional Pizza Hovel or maybe a Knave In The Box."

Knob arrived with breakfast. "Where should I put this?" he said.

"Oh, by the desk is fine," said Promo. As he was signing for the gratuity, he said, "Knob, isn't there an Avis Rent-A-Horse around here? Or we could buy a used horse if you could direct us to a HorseMax. Could you check around? I'll make it worth your while."

In the end there was more than three hours delay, but Promo was used to this. It had been practically impossible to get Puppy out of bed since their journey began. Knob came back from his pony search with the news that there was only one pony available in all of Whee: a worn-out, high-mileage beater owned by Bill Furface.

"Bill Furface?" said Promo. "That figures. It's probably a trick. The pony will probably explode as soon as he starts trotting, or gallop uncontrollably off the nearest cliff."

"No," said Slider. "If I know Bill Furface, his main interest is making money. He probably raised his unibrow in delight when you approached him, Knob. What's his price? Three times the Blue Book value?"

Butterface ended up paying for the pony, after having Mary sign a document: it stated that Mary held Butterface blameless for the loss of his five ponies, and it exonerated both *The Dancing Doughnut* and Best Uttermost-Western Hotels And Resorts. Later they learned that Mary's ponies were not stolen but driven off, and they eventually found their way back to the Dude's bowling alley where they rejoined their friend Fatty Pumpkin. After some time to unwind, the ponies were traded by the Dude back to Butterface in exchange for a few cases each of coffee liqueur and vodka. Knob treated them well at *The Dancing Doughnut*, and they avoided the trip to Bordor and the Crotch Of Doom. But they missed a very nice time at Enron's Last Waffle House Resort in Riverdale.

In the meanwhile, there were a lot of angry guests from the south whose horses had also vanished. Barleycorn chose to avoid any paperwork by putting the blame on someone else.

"Where's your friend, the squinty-eyed one?" he said. "He's run off, and so have your horses. You travel with a horse thief, and then your horses disappear. Do the math! How is this my fault? I should be suing you!" The southerners then began bickering about who was actually friends with Mr. Squinty-Eyes.

The wobbits repacked for a trip with one pony, heaping as much stuff as possible into a set of enormous saddlebags. As they packed, all of Whee came to gawk at them in front of the inn, what with Promo's vanishing trick, the gatekeeper squished by Executive Riders, the horse theft, and now the famous vagrant Slider joining the adventurers. Butterface put up a grandstand and had Knob selling tickets, making out well from the excitement. Busybodies came from as far as Straddle, Crumbe and Piechart to see the wobbits depart.

"Mr. Butterface," said Promo in front of the inn, in a loud voice to benefit the paying customers in the grandstand, "I hope, in a future time of peace and prosperity, to visit your inn once again." He reached up and shook Barleycorn's hand as the crowd cheered.

"Thank you, Mr. Underwear," said Barleycorn in a fine stage voice, "The replacement cost of the damaged furnishings has been added to your bill under Incidentals, along with this morning's room service. I hope you enjoyed your stay." He grandly presented the bill, accepted Promo's payment, and waved to the crowd.

"Be sure to keep that receipt, sir," said Sham. "There's still a chance that we might find Mr. Pantsoff and be reimbursed."

They tramped off. The pony was the most cheerful of the lot, despite his burdens, because anything was better than being owned by Bill Furface. Bill refused to care for the pony, so that he would always be the better-looking of the two. Sham led the pony, and they both were calmly munching apples. Knob had given him a pocketful. The apples were very small and his pants had huge pockets.

The last house they passed on the edge of town was ill-kept and had an enormous, impenetrable hedge. It belonged Bill Furface. At one of the windows Promo saw a familiar, squinty-eyed face.

"So that's where the squinty southerner ended up! He looks more than a little goblinish, don't you think, Sham?'

"I wouldn't know, sir. I try to avoid making racist observations."

"*Touche*, Sham," said Promo.

Over the hedge peered a massive eyebrow with an ugly face below it. "Hello, loser!" Furface said to Slider. "Found some rubes from out of town to buy you a hot meal, I see." He turned to the wobbits. "Enjoy your travels with Slider, and keep an eye on your valuables. Shammie, don't abuse my poor pony!"

"Indeed, sir," said Sham as he hurled an apple at Furface. It hit him square in the nose. "What a waste. I should have used a road-apple."

At last they left the village behind. By the time they were taking their first coffee break they could see the cottages and condos of Straddle. To the north of the road was Crumbe, and hidden in the Chartwood Forest was Piechart.

"Time for some off-roading" said Slider. "This shortcut will make it harder for the Executive Riders to find us."

"We've heard that one before, right, Promo?" said Mary. "Winter's only a few months away. Do we have time for another shortcut?"

"Laugh it up, fuzz-foot," said Slider. "This isn't my first journey. I've been traveling this wilderness for decades. Trust me."

For the next couple of days the walking was pleasant enough, other than the constant threat of Executive Riders, Barry Wights and Carnivorous Willows. The wobbits discovered that Slider didn't like a lot of chit-chat. This was very hard on Puppy, who liked playing noisy travel games like I Spy and Slug Bug. Adolescent wobbits love playing Slug Bug: you punch the shoulder of your companion whenever you see a bug of any sort, including spiders and millipedes.

The Bilgewater Bog would have been a great venue for Slug Bug. Insects of all sizes and species attacked the wobbits relentlessly.

"What do you suppose they live on when they can't get wobbit?" said Sham.

"Mostly shoggoths and nightgaunts," said Slider.

"Why aren't you getting bitten?" said Mary as he slapped his neck, killing four mosquitos, two horseflies and a cicada.

"You have to let them know who's boss," said Slider. "Stop walking for a moment and I'll show you." He stood quietly, and after an unusually long time a midge zeroed in on him, leading an entire midge squadron. In one movement Slider drew his half-a-sword and cut the lead midge in half. He stood waiting for the next bug as the two pieces of dead midge struck the ground, but the rest of the midges aborted their mission and flew past Slider on either side, never to return. Slider cleaned the tiny bit of midge-blood off his sword and sheathed it.

"You see what I mean?"

The wobbits spent the night being tormented by gnats while listening to giant crickets crashing about in the darkness. The crickets sang a deep-voiced *neek-breek* song that Promo found unnerving as he mentally calculated the size of the insect based on their tone.

It took another day of walking to get out of the bog and marsh, only to end up in a swamp and bayou. That night Promo was kept awake by the constant *neek-breek* sound of the distant neekerbreekers. He saw flashing lights in the eastern sky and noticed a faint smell of popcorn. He saw that Slider was also awake.

"What's that? Lightning?" he said.

"No," said Slider. "It seems to be flashing up into the sky from the hills."

"So it's probably nothing," said Promo. "Right?"

On the fifth day they saw a line of hills, with a taller one standing alone. "That is Carrottop," said Slider. "I suppose we should head that way."

"What do you mean?" said Promo. "Didn't Pantsoff tell you to meet him there?"

"He did, but it's unlikely that we'll arrive there at the same time he does. The guy is never on time for anything. We're far more likely to run into Executive Riders. They'll be there to look for us. The place an incredible view. If we wait there, any beasts or birds for miles around will be able to see us, and not all the birds can be trusted. Yesterday I saw a hummingbird giving me a dirty look."

"Walking for a week to get to this place where we don't want to be wasn't a very good idea, then?" said Promo.

"No, it wasn't," said Slider. "It was part of Pantsoff's plan."

"I understand," said Promo. "Now what?"

They snuck up as best they could and camped out of sight nearby. The next morning was cold, with a sky as clear and blue as Slider's eyes. They had their usual light breakfast of granola bars. Thanks to their low-fat diet and constant walking, the wobbits were starting to get into shape. They had all lost many unwanted pounds and inches.

"If we lose any more weight," said Mary, "we'll look like that wight back in the Downer Downs!"

"Yeah!" said Puppy. "Or put me in a black suit, and I'll look like one of those Executive Riders!" He and Mary laughed raucously.

"Shut up, you idiots!" said Slider, with surprising earnestness.

The hills drew nearer, or at least appeared to, because actually it was Slider and the wobbits that were drawing nearer to the hills. After yet another day of walking they were at the feet of the hills. They camped, and in the morning they began their climb to the ankles of the hills, hoping to be at the knees by lunchtime. It was the fifth of October.

Mary looked up uneasily. "Slider?" he said. "Can I ask you a wight-related question without you yelling at me, like yesterday?"

"Sure, kid, go ahead. It's all the loose talk about the Executive Riders that was bothering me."

"Great. So, Carrottop has sort of a real barrow look to it. There aren't any wights around here, are there? I mean, you seem like a pretty tough guy and all, but you're not the Dude, no offense."

"I get it, Mary," said Slider. "None taken. And no, there aren't any real barrows on Carrottop. It used to be a watchtower. It is said that Ellen-Doll stood up there watching for the arrival of Gil-Gameshalad out of the West, in the days of the Next To The Last Alliance."

"Boring!" cried Puppy, who began randomly throwing rocks.

"Who was Gil-Gameshalad?" asked Promo.

"Here we go" muttered Mary to Puppy, as they both rolled their eyes.

Gil-gameshalad was an elven king
He was in charge of everything
He gave out ice-cold beer for free
To little folks like you and me.

His sword was bright, his lance was keen
The sharpest dresser you've ever seen
One day he marched, this well-dressed guy
To Bordor, where regs don't apply

Everyone turned towards Slider, but he wasn't the one singing. It was Sham, who had a surprisingly deep baritone voice.

"Hey!" said Puppy. "That's the tune to my drinking song!"

"Puppy, give it up!" said Mary. "It's not your tune. It's a public domain folk song. You can't collect royalties on it"

"Humph," said Puppy. "Those are stupid lyrics. The whole thing sounds pretty unbelievable to me. Only a moron would march to Bordor!"

"Do not speak that name so loudly!" said Slider.

"Can't we talk about anything?" said Puppy.

By midday they were at Carrottop, and there was nothing else to do but investigate it, despite the chance of being seen. There were no empty liquor bottles, crumpled memos, or any other sign of Pantsoff.

"We've approached Carrottop stealthily," said Slider, "and there don't appear to be any Executive Riders up there. Time to go take a look."

They climbed to the top, where they found scorch marks and bits of popcorn. "No sign of Pantsoff," said Puppy. "Let's head back to Buckiebrand Hall."

"Not so fast," said Slider. "Look here." He pointed to a piece of Pantsoff's merchandising. It was a promotional calendar, turned to October, where his P-rune was plainly visible. The inspirational message for the month was "TEAMWORK - What other people do to make you look good." October the third had been circled hurriedly in charcoal.

"On the one hand, this may mean nothing. Pantsoff gives these calendars to everyone, and I often find them littering the wilderness. It must cost him a fortune. On the other hand, this is a pretty out-of-the-way spot. Not even other Rangers stop here very often."

"There are other Rangers?" said Promo. But Slider didn't say much in reply. It was like when James Bond mentions the other double-O agents.

"Do you have to be good-looking to be a Ranger?" said Mary.

"Not any more," said Slider. The wobbits looked at him expectantly, as if he was about to ask for their resumes, but he was paying little attention to them. "Let me get back to my point. If Pantsoff did leave this calendar as a message to us, it appears that he only had enough time to indicate that he was here on the third and was in a hurry. He may have been in hurry because he was fighting Executive Riders, or because he was late for a meeting where he was going to close the deal of a lifetime. Or, perhaps he just couldn't be bothered with leaving us a real message that would actually tell us something. In any case, we should probably make our way to Riverdale. That's where he was headed next."

"More walking?" said Puppy. "Aren't we there yet? When are we gonna get there?"

"Alone, I can walk there in six days," said Slider. "With you four, it will take a probably take a fortnight."

"A fortnight!" said Puppy.

"Yes, that means two weeks, sir," said Sham.

Promo was trying to ignore Puppy by staring back down at the Byway towards home. He was alarmed to see two specks heading their way. The two specks were riding two speck-like horses.

"Hey, Slider," he said. "I hate to interrupt your important talk with Puppy, but you should take a look at this." He pointed at the specks. Slider immediately flung himself on the ground, and dragged Promo with him.

"Hit the deck!" said Slider. Sham and Mary dropped to the ground.

"What?" said Puppy. "What's going on?" Sham and Mary pulled him down, and Mary covered his mouth.

"Are either of those specks Executive Rider shaped?" said Promo.

"Perhaps, Mr. Slider, we should be moving along," said Sham.

"Those are indeed Riders," said Slider, "but there is nowhere we could go before nightfall. We should make our stand here. I think I'd prefer a straight fight to all this sneaking around."

"Do you think they've seen us? Back at the Lamprey farm they seemed to be smelling us," said Promo.

"Yes, they smell us," said Slider. "And they smell money, the money we represent. They don't see wobbits or people like we do. All they see are the potential earnings they would generate from hiring us to work part-time without benefits, or the potential savings they could accrue from firing us and outsourcing our jobs to someone even cheaper."

"The Riders just see us as dollar signs?"

"That's right. Although their horses can see us, and so can their contractors like Bill Furface and that treacherous hummingbird. But for now, we should prepare. I noticed some firewood that Pantsoff left behind. We can use that to defend ourselves. The Executive Riders do not love fire, and fear those who wield it."

"Because fire serves all of Little Earth for free?" said Mary.

"No, because the Riders are flammable," said Slider. "They hate the idea that anything might damage their expensive suits. Let's dig in while we have a chance."

The wobbits filled sandbags while Slider quickly hunted, skinned and cooked a deer. After a huge meal of venison, Slider lit a pipe and took the first watch. Sham was washing up the dinner things while Mary and Puppy were playing the hand-slap game. Ignoring their cries of "You flinched!" and "No I didn't," Promo sat next to Slider.

"What do you know about Gil-Gameshalad?" said Promo.

"You're boring me!" cried Puppy, interrupting his game of Slapsies just to complain.

"Sham was saying that Gil-Gameshalad went to Bordor," Promo said.

"We must not speak of this with the employees of the Enemy at hand," said Slider.

"Again?" said Puppy. "The only thing worse than these stories is when you're afraid to tell them."

"Okay, tough guy," said Slider. "I will tell you another tale, that of Tinroofiel, but briefly, for it is a long tale of which the end is not known."

"No surprise there," said Puppy. "I'm all ears." He then had a pantomime heart attack and flopped down as if dead. Slider ignored him, and began:

The grass was long, the leaves were green
Tomato vines grew tall and fair

And in the shed a kerosene
Lamp all the night was glimmering.
Tinroofiel was cooking there
Upon a small hot plate unseen
She wore a hat to keep her hair
Out of the soup pot simmering.

"Hey!" said Puppy. "That's my song again! Everyone keeps stealing it!"

"No, Puppy," said Slider. "The Lay Of Tinroofiel is completely different. While my song and yours both use iambic tetrameter, listen to the rhyme scheme. Your song uses a predictable AABBCC while mine uses a fun ABACBABC. And of course, in mine the tune of the first four lines repeats in the last four, while in yours the tune of the third and fourth lines is repeated in the fifth and sixth. Here, listen." Slider sang Puppy's drinking song:

Ho ho ho to the bottle I go
To heal my heart and drown my woe
Though I can quit any time I pick
Sometimes I drink 'til I get real sick
I like white wine when I'm eating pork
And I like putting whiskey inside this Dork!

"He's got you, Puppy," said Mary. "You have no copyright case here. They're two completely different songs."

"Dang!" said Puppy. "How's a singer-songwriter supposed to ever get a breakout hit?"

"You just need to discover your own sound, kid," said Slider. "Now where was I? Tinroofiel was making tomato soup for Darin, I believe?" He cleared his throat.

"Slider, look!" said Puppy. "Executive Riders!"

"Puppy, come on!" said Promo. "Let him sing the rest of his song."

"Sorry guys," said Slider. "I see them too. Some familiar-looking black shapes. Suffice it to say, the song goes on like that for about a dozen verses. She makes tomato basil soup, he enjoys it, then things begin to go downhill. Now, stay close to the fire, facing out. Keep a burning stick handy."

"Should we draw our swords?" said Promo.

"Sure, go for it," said Slider.

Shadowy figures began to approach on foot from the distance. There appeared to be five of them, but Promo was so terrified that there seemed to be a dozen. Worse than his terror was the overwhelming desire he felt to put on the Ring. It wasn't part of a plan to escape or fight, it was an absolute desire, like the desire to do long-ignored tidying when you should be working on your taxes. It was all he could think of. Then he thought "Resistance is futile" and drew out the Ring on its uncanny chain. He slipped the Ring on the forefinger of his left hand: if he should somehow run into the Dude's special lady, Maude, he didn't want her to think that he was now wearing a wedding ring.

With the Ring on, the dark shapes became terribly clear to Promo. Instead of seeing tailored black suits, stylish haircuts and expensive briefcases, he saw beneath their dark disguises. There were five tall yet portly figures dressed in the universal and eternal garb of the capitalist: top hats, mustaches, striped pants and cutaway coats. Behind their monocles burned keen and merciless eyes. In their soft, manicured hands were walking sticks of steel. Forgetting Slider's advice, Promo ignored his long, flaming stick and raised his barrow sword instead, and it seemed to flicker red. The lead capitalist, who looked like a hideous combination of Mr. Monopoly and the Planter's Peanut Man, bore down upon Promo. In one hand he held his walking stick and in the other a knife: both glowed with a pale light. He sprang forward with walking stick raised, to give Promo an otherworldly thrashing.

At that moment Promo threw himself at the ground and then heard himself crying aloud *O Elbowpad! Gilletrazor!* Then he struck with all his might, as Isadora did at Smoron: a cheap shot at his enemy's ghastly crotch. He heard an understandably shrill cry, and then felt something painful in his left shoulder. *That's probably going to leave a mark* he thought, and then he started to swoon. He thought *I really wish I wasn't swooning in front of Slider. That guy is so awesome.* Then he saw Slider leaping out of the darkness with a long, flaming stick in each hand. He fought the swoon off long enough to think *Awesome!* and then he slipped the

Ring from his finger. Finally he thought *I wonder what happened to the Ring's chain?*

Chapter 12

CANTER TO THE CROSSING

When Promo woke he was still clutching the Ring, and lying near a heap of long, flaming sticks arranged into a campfire.

"These long, flaming sticks would be handy for battling Executive Riders," he said. "Where am I? Where is the Pale Capitalist? Where is the chain for my Ring?"

The others were delighted Promo was still alive, but could only tell him that they had seen five dark specks that turned out to be the men in dark suits. Sham explained that Promo disappeared when things looked especially desperate, as Uncle Bulbo had often done. He heard Promo's voice speaking a foreign language, investigated, and found him visible again but wounded. Slider returned to the campsite and told Puppy to put Promo near the fire. Then he extinguished Promo's sleeve and told Puppy to move him not quite so near to the fire. This was when Promo woke up.

Slider spoke quietly with him. Then he said to the others "I have good news and bad news."

"Let's have the good news first," said Mary.

"The Executive Riders have gone."

"That's it?" said Mary.

"Also, Promo isn't dead yet."

"We knew that," said Mary. "How about the bad news?"

"The bad news is that the Executive Riders will be back. We can't be caught here again, but there's nowhere the four of you could possibly go that's any safer. But that doesn't matter because of Promo's poisoned, mortal wound."

"I'm dying?" said Promo.

"Yeah, kid, although I had hoped to break this to you a little more gently. Also, we've got to eat the rest of that venison soon before it goes bad. That's it though. No more bad news at the moment. And now if you'll excuse me, I'm going to run off again. I'll be back soon. Get some rest."

"No problem," said Promo. "I'll try to stay alive until you return."

Shortly after a disappointing sunrise, Slider returned. He woke the wobbits to show them a pair of black suit pants, with pleats and cuffs. There was a jagged tear right beneath the fly.

"It is the mark of Promo's cheap shot," he said. "But a ruined business suit is the only hurt his sword did this Executive Rider. More deadly was the name of Elbowpad. This, on the other hand, was quite deadly to Promo," he said, holding up a very pointy looking dagger. It was jagged along the edge, and the tip was broken off.

"The tip of this dagger broke off in Promo's shoulder. The weapons-smiths at Bordor Cutlery are compelled to do hurried, shoddy work."

"That would explain the incredible pain," said Promo. "I thought maybe I had dislocated it when I stabbed that guy in the groin."

"Now watch this," said Slider. He held up the dagger in direct sunlight, and the blade vanished like smoke in the air. "That's cheap work! As deadly as this weapon is, they can only be used at night. There's a companion model that can only be used during the day. If you unsheathe it at night it turns into beef jerky."

He removed some leaves from a pouch at his belt. "These may help you, Promo. They are the leaves of the doublemint plant."

"How did you find them in the dark, Mr. Slider?" said Sham.

"In Ranger School they teach you how to find them blindfolded, by their scent."

He paused long enough for the wobbits to be impressed. "They can heal wounds and chewing them freshens your breath."

"So what do I do with them?" said Promo. "Smoke them?"

"No, don't be ridiculous," said Slider. "That's if you're using them to cure a cough or sore throat due to a summer cold. Sham, boil some water."

"You're going to make them into a tea?"

"Yes, doublemint tea is pretty good with a light breakfast. I'm famished! Bring out the leftover doughnuts, too, Sham! But in your case, Promo, I'm going to simply chew up the leaves and them poke them into your mortal wound."

"Isn't that likely to cause an infection?" said Promo. "When was the last time you washed your hands? Or brushed your teeth?"

"Infection!" said Slider. "You've got a shard of Vorpal Blade in you. By this time tomorrow you'll be begging for an infection." Then, after chewing some of the doublemint leaves, he jammed a few little wads of leaves into the wound.

"Ouch!" said Promo. "Look, if this is a mortal wound couldn't you just let me die in peace?"

"Did I say the wound was mortal? I meant to say 'mostly mortal,' which is entirely different. I suppose you were looking forward to a land of pale light behind a grey rain curtain and then a far green country opened before you under a swift sunrise? Not just yet, Promo Bunkins."

The next morning they headed south. They walked, or in Puppy's case wandered, for eleven tedious days. The entire time Promo's arm was killing him, quite literally. The landscape became even more bleak. There were very large footprints everywhere, and many skeletons to be stepped over.

"We're now in troll country," said Slider. "We'll take a break, but be on your guard, boys. Promo, I can give you your next dose of doublemint in about forty-five minutes. Sham, stay here with him. Puppy, you find a campsite and Mary, you keep an eye on Puppy. I'm going to hunt for lunch."

Puppy headed straight for a dangerous-looking cave. "Look you guys! Cool! A cave! Let's picnic here!" Before Mary could intervene, Puppy was carelessly pulling duffle-bags off their pony and flinging them on the ground at the entrance to the cave. He was about to spread out blankets for them all to sit on when he saw three trolls.

"Trolls!" he screamed, as he ran back and forth. "Very large ones! Help me! Help!"

"Here we come, Puppy," said Slider calmly. He slowly walked over with Mary.

"Yes! I see what you mean," said Mary. "Not to worry, I'll take care of them." Mary stepped in front of the nearest troll and mooned him. Slider smiled patiently.

"Here Mr. Troll, bite my ass! What's that? You can't, because you turned to stone decades ago? How about you others? No?" He pulled up his pants.

"They're all stone," said Puppy.

"Duh!" said Mary. "It's broad daylight, you moron."

"Good one, Mary," said Slider as they high-fived each other. "And these aren't just any trolls. Don't you remember Bulbo's story? These are the same very large trolls that were going to eat Borin Oakmanfield and his dwarves. Pantsoff tricked them into arguing until sunrise, which of course turned them to stone. You might also notice that there's a message carved into the one on the right. It says 'For Project Management, Hire Pantsoff!' That guy never quits!"

"He can't get a lot of foot traffic around here,' said Mary. "Who would see this sort of advertising?"

"It must be niche marketing," said Slider. "And over here's the hole where Pantsoff dug up the treasure. He and Bulbo embezzled it from the dwarves on the trip home."

"It's not like the dwarves needed it," said Puppy.

"Where are the trolls' very large clothes?" said Mary.

"All traces of their clothes have been worn away by decades of wind and rain," said Slider. "Please don't let Promo see them. In his weakened condition, I'm afraid the sight of their very large whoosies and whatsies might be too much for him to bear." Mary and Puppy carefully draped the trolls' private parts with some spare tablecloths while Slider trapped, dressed and stewed some rabbits. Then they explained the situation to Sham, and had him bring Promo over for a light lunch of hasenpfeffer and lager.

"Look, Mr. Promo!" Sham said. "Mr. Bulbo's Trolls!"

"Yes," said Promo. He ate his stew with great enthusiasm for someone who was dying. "What a hideous place for a picnic. And why are they wearing red and white checked loincloths?"

"Best not to ask, sir," said Sham. "Say, this reminds me of a song:"

Troll sat on an old stone
Munching on an old bone
Many years he gnawed it near
'Cause he was very poor
Meat was hard to come by
Done by and a-gum by
Dude Dude Dude coming out his back door

The Dude had bowling shoes on
Said "Like, who is that yon
Looks like it's a shin bone
From my dear, late Uncle Tim
You're munching on a hunk a
My favorite dear old Uncle
Troll, Troll, Troll, please stop chewing on him

"Sam!" said Puppy. "You're singing a song about the Dude! Are you saying that you knew about the Dude before he rescued us from the Killer Willow? Why didn't you speak up?"

"I didn't feel it was my place, sir."

"Wait a minute!" said Mary. "The Dude has a deceased uncle? He doesn't seem like the type of guy to have a family."

"Except for Maude," said Promo. "Shall I ever see her horned helmet again?"

"Here we go," said Mary, as Puppy pantomimed tears flying out of his eyes.

"Enough singing!" said Promo. "If I must die, shut up and let me die. Or, if you really want to get me some medical care at Riverdale, perhaps we should do a little more walking before dark."

They tidied and repacked, and then marched for a while longer. As it started to get dark, they heard the *clip-clop-clippity-clop* of ominous hooves. Puppy and Mary started to burrow for safety when they heard the rider greet them with the words *May Goclubbing!* The voice was so articulate and well-modulated that they knew the rider must be of the Elven-folk. He was blonde, of course, and very stylishly dressed with a perfect complexion. To Promo he looked fabulous. He also appeared to have light streaming from his incredibly clear skin, like a very tasteful novelty lamp. The wobbits had hoped to talk with the strikingly attractive elf as he dismounted, but he went straight to Slider and the two began talking quietly and urgently.

"Garfunkel!" said Slider. "What are you doing here? I was expecting my girlfriend!"

"She's working," said Garfunkel. "It's been crazy at Riverdale. We're hosting two conventions at the same time. She couldn't get away, and sends her regrets."

"It's just that she keeps telling me that we need to spend more time together if we really want to build our relationship. Quality time, she said."

"I understand, Orogarn. Relationships are tough. But perhaps we should focus on Promo and his wound. I'm here to help him get to Riverdale."

"Of course," said Slider. He turned to the wobbits. "Guys, this is Garfunkel, one of Riverdale's finest. That's Mary, and the one over there that's staring at you is Puppy, and that's Sham carrying Promo, the one with the bad shoulder."

"You're from Riverdale?" said Promo. "So Pantsoff must have arrived there by now?"

"Pantsoff? No, not yet. We have his reservation and Enron, our manager, has insisted we keep it open. We could have rented that suite twice by now. But I've been on the road for a while, so perhaps he's arrived. I'm sure he's fine. You know Pantsoff. I'm just glad you're in one piece, Promo. The roads are choked with Executive Riders. I've been chasing them all over the place."

"You chase Executive Riders?" said Mary. "You must be a total badass!" He looked at Slider critically.

"Hold on there, tough guy," said Garfunkel. "There's only a half-dozen elves in all Little Earth that can stand up to the Executive Riders. Orogarn here scared off five of them with a broken sword and two long, flaming sticks. I'm not sure I could take on even one Rider if I had to protect four wobbits while I was doing it. And Orgarn isn't an elf, so he's got that working against him."

"Tell me about it," said Slider.

"Pardon me, gentlemen," said Sham, "but shouldn't we be looking after Mr. Promo?"

"Good point, Sham," said Slider. "Here, Garfunkel, look at this." He showed the hilt of the Rider's knife.

"Ah! The Nightime-Only Vorpal Blade," said Garfunkel. "Part of Bordor Cutlery's newest strategy to gain shelf space. A retailer that sells Vorpal Blades has to sell both the night model and the day model, allowing less shelf space for any competitor's soul-stealing dagger. And even if it never is exposed to daylight it might only be usable once, because of a blade-breakage problem they refuse to correct. Hold onto that, Orogarn. Enron would love to see it."

"And the wound, sir?" said Sham.

"Let me take a look," said Garfunkel. "Promo, you're going to feel some pressure. Then there will be a slight stinging sensation. Your eyes may water a little." He removed Promo's bandage and probed the wound.

"Yeow!" said Promo.

"Sorry about that. Orogarn, this is a great field dressing. You Rangers still are excellent at First Aid. What did you use on this, doublemint? And it didn't get infected? Nice work."

"You can heal the wound, sir?" said Sham.

"Goodness no!" said Garfunkel. "But let me try one thing." He breathed heavily on his hands, and then clapped them once and held them together for a moment. Then he laid them on Promo's wound. The icy pain lessened, and Promo looked at him with amazement. "It's an Elf thing. I can give you one of those every four hours for up to two days. After that, you'll probably be dead."

"Then we'd better get going," said Slider.

"Yes," said Garfunkel. "Promo, you'll ride my horse."

"No I won't," said Promo. "Look how tall that thing is! I'll fall off and break my neck!"

"You won't fall off. This is an elf-horse."

"You have special horses?" said Mary.

"Of course we do! And no one, not even a wobbit, ever falls off. This horse's gallop is so smooth, light and breezy that it feels like his hooves barely touch the ground."

"Go figure," said Mary as he nudged Puppy.

"They have special everything," said Puppy.

They resumed their march and Garfunkel led them. They walked almost all night, despite Puppy's non-stop complaining and fake stumbling. Not until the gray of dawn did Garfunkel allow them to stop. The wobbits slept in their traditional heap for just five hours, and it was long after coffee-break time before they were on the road again.

As they walked, Puppy was so relentless in his fussing that Garfunkel finally said "Here," and handed him a very elegant hip flask. "Just take a sip, and pass it around." The liquor within was clear, had no taste, and left no sensation in the mouth. Puppy wasn't sure that he actually drank anything at all. A moment later, though, he felt like he had just knocked back a pot of espresso with lots of sugar. He started walking very quickly.

"Give me some of that!" said Mary. He took the flask, drank, and passed it along before catching up with Puppy. In this way, they covered nearly twenty miles by nightfall.

They started early again the next morning. The wobbits were very disappointed that Garfunkel did not offer his flask. By afternoon they entered a pine forest and just past it they could see the Brewing River and the Ford Of Riverdale.

"This is exactly where I would set up an ambush," said Slider.

"Fly, you fools!" said Garfunkel moments later. "Executive Riders!"

He was right, of course, but it was a few moments before the others knew what was happening. Then the Riders came through the wood and headed straight for Promo.

Promo hesitated. He could see the Riders in their Olde-Time Capitalist aspect, with glittering white spats and bow ties, and their dread walking sticks raised on high. He hesitated, as if they had sent him a terrible email commanding him to wait.

"Ride on!" cried Garfunkel. Then he called to the horse in elf-tongue: *Nolo Contendere, Assfelloff!*

Assfelloff sprang away, and Promo did not fall. In an attempt to confuse the Riders, Promo's horse galloped back and forth dramatically among the pine trees. At one point it ran in circles around one tree several times. Slider and the others were soon far behind. They were terrified, because Promo appeared to them as lifeless as a discolored rubber mannequin, motionless on the horse. Assfelloff finally was able to dodge past the Riders and cross the river at the ford. There were nine of them, some in the river and some remaining on the far bank. This was their chance. The Riders could easily cross the river, capture Promo while he was defenseless and alone, and take The Ring. But they chose, as villains always do, to instead taunt him at their moment of triumph.

"Come back!" said the Boss Capitalist. "Come back! You have a big meeting in Bordor! If we start the paperwork now you could be on our payroll this time next week!"

"By Elbowpad, you shall not have The Ring," said Promo. "And I'm independently wealthy, so I don't need a job!"

"Of course you need a job! You need the medical coverage! And no one is ever wealthy enough! Am I right?" The Boss's horse stepped into the river.

At that moment there came a roaring and a rushing, a noise of loud waters. Promo saw the river rise, and in the white water there seemed to be the images of white, frothy kayakers furiously paddling their boats, bearing down on the Executive Riders. They swept the Riders under and away. Behind the Riders on shore, Promo saw the dazzling figure of a charging Garfunkel. With him was a non-dazzling and slightly disappointed figure waving a half-a-sword. In the rear were three very short figures, hanging back. But the force of Garfunkel, and possibly that of Slider, panicked the Rider rear-guard, who ran into the waves and were swept away with their colleagues.

Then Promo felt himself falling, despite Assfelloff's best efforts. At about halfway to the ground, Promo heard and saw no more.

Chapter 13

MANY, MANY MEETINGS

Promo found himself in a bed. He assumed that he had died at the river crossing, and was now in wobbit-heaven. It wasn't of the "silver glass and a swift sunrise" variety, which was okay with Promo. It was as if he was in a nice hotel, or a really, really nice hospital.

"Where am I?" he asked aloud, in case someone from housekeeping was nearby.

"In the Riverdale Resort," said a terribly familiar voice. "It is the morning of October the twenty-fourth, although I don't think you have anything on your agenda for the day."

"Pantsoff? How did you get in my room?" said Promo.

"That's me! Sham let me in, and you're very lucky to be here!"

"Oh, yeah," said Promo. "I'm the luckiest guy in Wobbiton. I've been hunted, chased, stabbed and poisoned. And I fell off a horse, too. What happened after that? Am I still dying?"

"No, you're not dying. You're going to be just fine. Many of us had given you up for dead, but not me, never. It's a good thing the Executive Riders delayed capturing you. Those guys always gloat."

"We never could have escaped without Slider and Garfunkel," said Promo. "You know, Pantsoff, it would have been nice if you had turned up, too."

"Yes, I had to reschedule our rendezvous," said Pantsoff. "The craziest thing happened. I'll have to tell you all about it sometime. Suffice it to say I was trapped in a meeting that ran long. The important thing is that the project is still moving forward. Thanks, to an extent, to Slider."

"Slider's a great guy, as Big People go," said Promo. "I didn't know there were Big People like him. I thought they were big and stupid and mean like Bill Furface, or big and stupid and evil like the Executive Riders, or big and stupid and self-absorbed like you, or just big and stupid, like Barleycorn Butterface.

"You may think Barleycorn is stupid, and you could use his head to knock down a brick wall, but he mixes an excellent Mai Tai. As for Slider, please don't tell anyone, but Orogarn, son of Orogarni, is one of the kings from olden times."

"Really! I thought he was just a Ranger."

"Just a Ranger! Where do you think those guys come from, anyway? They are the last of the Men Of The Northwest. They're all dangerous, tall, and good-looking. Although Slider is the handsomest of them all."

"Tell me about it!" said Promo. "And he's great in a fight, even with just a half-a-sword. Will there be other Rangers helping out on this project? A dozen of those guys could do anything."

"You're right, that would be great, and I almost have a soft commitment from a number of them. They could be joining the project any day now."

"So I can take it easy!"

"Sure, for now," said Pantsoff.

"Did Sham and Mary and the other one make it?"

"Yes, and Sham has hardly left your side. I told him to go get me a bucket of ice while I stayed with you. Usually I can't even get him to go down to eat in one of the restaurants. He insists on ordering room service so he can eat here, and it's putting us way over budget."

"Speaking of which," said Promo. "I have a bunch of receipts from *The Dancing Doughnut* to give you. Did you know they charged me for the room damage from the Executive Riders?"

"Hold on to those receipts. Enron is going to reimburse everyone's expenses all at once. You can give them to him."

"That's not what you said before."

"No, but this will be better. And you can claim the trip as a deductible on your taxes. By the way, I had Enron remove the splinter of Vorpal Blade from your shoulder while you were unconscious. I have Power Of Attorney over your health care. There's a copy of the document in the envelope I gave you at Bug End."

"I didn't sign anything like that!"

"No, I forged your signature. I didn't want you to worry. Good thing, too. That splinter was headed straight for your heart. We either had to remove it surgically or embed a magnet in your chest, which was an idea of mine."

"Surgery sounds more reliable," said Promo.

"Perhaps. If the splinter had made it to your heart, you would have become a Mini-Wraith. For all eternity you would have accompanied the Executive Riders, fetching coffee for them and making their travel arrangements. You survived the splinter far longer than most. I knew you wobbits were tough, which is exactly why I recruited you for this project."

"How horrible! Running errands forever! But the Riders were destroyed in the flood, so I'm safe, right?"

"Oh, you're fine. Wasn't that flood something?"

"Yeah! Was that your work?"

"Partially. Enron did the rising water, the waves, and the fierce, foamy kayakers. I did the roaring, splashing, watery sound. I should probably point out that the Riders weren't destroyed, exactly. They were certainly inconvenienced though, and they won't be back for a while."

"Crap! Will they come after me here in Riverdale?"

"Of course not! No Rider would dare come here. At least, not for now. They're afraid of powerful Elf-lords like Enron and Garfunkel. Anyway, you're feeling better now?"

"Sure, I guess."

"Your color is good," said Pantsoff. But in a rare unspoken thought, he said to himself "Promo's color is a little faded in his left hand. I wonder if it will ever become transparent? I suppose he could paint it, or wear a glove. Maybe he'll become like a glass, filled with a clear light, or a jar filled with spare change. I could really go for a cup of coffee right now. I wonder---"

"Pantsoff?" said Promo.

"Splendid!" said Pantsoff. "You look splendid! Never better! Now get some rest. You've got a big conference coming up."

Without any further conversation, Promo was asleep. No one had ever acted so quickly on advice from Pantsoff.

Promo recovered at Riverdale. It was, as Bulbo had said time after time, "perfect, if a little expensive, whether you liked sleeping, or breakfast buffets, or salsa lessons, or spa treatments, or just sitting in the lobby staring at people."

Promo had been napping when he discovered Sham holding his slightly transparent left hand, stroking it.

"Sham! What are you doing?"

"Mr. Bunkins, sir!" He let go of the hand, blushed and turned hastily away. "Mr. Pantsoff asked me if I thought your hand was looking a little more opaque since the surgery. I was just seeing to it, sir."

"And how do you think it looks?"

"It looks splendid, sir. Much improved. Before the surgery, one could practically read a newspaper through it. I've set out your clothes for the meeting, sir."

"Very good, Sham." Promo dressed, and Sham brushed imaginary lint off the brand-new corduroy pants, little waistcoat and wool jacket that had been provided by the Hidden Valley Haberdashery For Boys And Wobbits in the lobby of the resort.

"Allow me to walk you to the meeting, sir." They went down a hall to a grand staircase. "It's a big house, this, and very peculiar. And there are elves everywhere! Elves doing the housekeeping and bringing the room service, elves at the front desk and the bell station, elves managing the restaurants." Sham opened the doors to the Elbowpad Room. There sat his friends.

"Hooray!" cried Puppy. "Make way for Promo, CEO Of The Ring!"

Everyone in the room at once glared at Puppy and said "Hush!"

Puppy sulked and said "I forgot that I'm not supposed to talk about anything evil, even though I was just kidding. I'll shut up now."

It was early evening, and light appetizers were served, along with a limited selection of beer and wine. "Will there be dinner?" said Promo to Mary.

"No," said Mary. "Pantsoff thought he could save some money by sticking with crudites, cheese and crackers. Maybe we can go out afterwards for some pizza or something."

The ballroom was filled with folk: Enron was there, and Garfunkel, and Pantsoff. Pantsoff never looked especially good, at best he could look professional, but next to the elves he looked absolutely shabby. They were tall, with beautiful skin and hair, stylishly dressed and very well spoken. Enron was as venerable as a successful CEO and as ripped as a warrior. He was the manager of all Riverdale, and mighty among elves and men. Nobody messed with him.

Promo was whisked past the wobbits and seated at the head table. Near him was a woman so beautiful that Promo forgot all about Maude, the Dude's Special Lady. She was so beautiful she had to be an elf. She was even more beautiful than the male elves, and that's saying a lot. Her appearance was queenly yet kind, young yet old, tall yet short. Promo was looking at one whom few mortals had seen, Ayiem, the Morningstar of her people, daughter of Enron.

It was awkward for someone like Promo to be seated among so many folk of such great beauty. He felt that if anyone noticed him at all they would ask him to leave. It didn't help that he had to sit on a stack of books to reach the table. But after a few quick beers he began to feel a little less self-conscious. As he looked around for someone to chat with, he saw the other wobbits were seated near the door at the kid's table. There was no sign of Slider.

Next to Promo on the right was a dwarf of important appearance. He had a long, white, french-braided beard. He wore massive, iron-bound wingtips. His sportcoat was made of chainmail and around his neck was a solid gold necktie. This dwarf business-wear was so striking that Promo actually stopped eating to look. The dwarf eventually noticed, and turned to Promo.

"Perhaps you should paint a portrait, wobbit," he said. "It will last longer."

"I'm sorry to stare," said Promo. "I've never seen anyone wear so much metal. My name's Promo Bunkins." He reached out to shake hands.

"Of course you are," said the dwarf. He put a business card into Promo's hand. "I am Groin, board-member of Smithibank. As you know, we are now called Smithi Financial Solutions."

"Groin! You know my Uncle Bulbo!"

"Yes. And I know you, Mr. Bunkins. That would explain our friendly, informal interaction. Normally we dwarves are all business. I understand you are Bulbo's adopted heir. May I ask who is handling your investments?"

"I'm doing it myself, actually. It's mostly in gold and collectables."

"I had heard you were more diversified, at least into jewels. I believe you wobbits refer to them as 'jools.'"

"Not all of us," Promo said. He glanced around for someone else to talk with, but could find no one. "So, how are things at Smithi?"

"Never better. Smithi Financial Solutions is the wonder of Little Earth. Dwayne is still King and CEO at One Smithi Plaza in the Only Mountain. Crawlin, Gori, Tori, Beefi, and Bufu are all on the board of directors with me and are utterly irreplaceable. Fatso is now so morbidly obese that he needs six personal assistants to help him get from his corner office to the board room."

"That doesn't sound good."

"No," said Groin. "We've been begging him to hire a dietician and trainer, or maybe even a life coach, but he won't hear of it. He's doing better than Borin, Wheeli and Deali, though. They're still dead."

"Indeed. But that's not all of Borin & Company, is it? Let's see, there's Crawlin and Fallin, Gori and Tori and Rori, Beefi and Bufu, Loin and you, Wheeli and Deali, Fatso, and Borin Oakmanfield. That's all thirteen. So what happened to Fallin, Loin, and Rori?"

"I was hoping you might know," said Groin. "They went on a business trip and have not been heard from for years. At Smithi we have a strict policy of responding to all messages within ten months, so I fear something is wrong. I had hoped they were here in the Hidden Valley, entertaining clients at the Last Waffle House, although that is not the case."

Groin's face suddenly glowed with fake enthusiasm. "But let me tell you some more about how great Smithi Financial

Solutions is doing. Our home office at the Only Mountain is more luxurious than ever. We're doing so well that there's even been a trickle-down effect into Lake City, which is enjoying an economic boomlet. Their beer and ale distributorships show clear sales upticks."

"Really! Bulbo always described that whole area as completely dreary."

Groin looked Promo and practically smiled. "You loved Bulbo very much, didn't you? I mean, not *in* love with him, but just the normal love between a wealthy, eccentric benefactor and his adopted heir."

"Well, sure, um, I guess so. Yes."

"What a character," said Groin. "But enough sentiment. I need to glad-hand some clients and prospects"

Eventually the waiters with appetizers stopped coming, and a band set up on a small stage. They began playing some standards. Enron buttonholed Promo and pulled him over into a corner.

"This is a wonderful resort,' said Promo as Enron was about to speak. "And the bruschetta I just had was fantastic. But look at this," he said, pointing at a lumpy pile of linen at their feet. "Your servers shouldn't leave dirty tablecloths and napkins here in the corner. Could we find a better place to talk?"

Enron crouched down by the pile and spoke to it. "Wake up, superstar. You're on in a few minutes. And Promo is here."

The pile moved, startling Promo. It revealed large furry feet and a face.

"Bulbo!" cried Promo, who jumped back.

"Hullo!" said Bulbo. That is how wobbits say Hello. "How have you been, Promo?"

"Bulbo, what are you doing here?"

"Freeloading, mostly. Enron has comped me my room and all my meals. I still have to pay for incidentals, but it's been great. Riverdale is a wonderful place to sit and think, or mostly just sit. Right now I'm getting ready for Open-Mike Night; I'm doing the opening number. Hey, Enron, have you seen Orogarn? He said he would help me with this last verse. I can't figure out a rhyme for al-u-minium. Can you get him for me?"

Enron stepped away to find Orogarn, and Bulbo leaned close to Promo.

"You still have It with you, I suppose?" he said confidentially.

"What?"

"Come on! Do you have the You-Know-What?"

"Oh, The Ring," said Promo. "Yes, on a chain around my neck. They made a new one for me while I was recovering from my surgery. Although there was nothing wrong with the chain I had. In fact, it seemed to repair itself every time I broke it. And I don't know how they handled The Ring when they put it on the new chain, since everyone's made such a big deal that only I should touch it. And I wonder who was guarding it while I was unconscious? It's all very strange."

"Would you show me the new chain, Promo?"

"The chain? Sure, whatever," said Promo as he fished into his shirt and pulled out The Ring. As he held it up, he couldn't help but notice that Bulbo had transformed into something that looked like the "after" version of the Picture Of Dorian Gray. Bulbo reached out a bony, bloody claw towards The Ring, and hissed. Promo prepared to administer a necessary sucker-punch, but Bulbo drew away. He appeared normal once more.

"Bad idea," he said to Promo. "Forget I asked. So, how are things in Wobbiton?"

Promo put The Ring away, and went with Bulbo to the bar. The elf-waiters were no longer taking drink orders, but a cash bar was still available. They had a few beers and charged them to Bulbo's complimentary room. Soon the unpleasantness with The Ring was forgotten. As they chatted idly about the doings back home, Slider stepped up. He was wearing fresh, clean clothes, possibly for the first time in years.

"What is this," he said, "a family reunion? You guys should be mingling!"

"I thought you were going to help me with my song," said Bulbo.

"I wish I could, Bulbo, really I do, but I think you're supposed to be on stage right now." Garfunkel, who was emceeing the event, had just introduced Bulbo. Bulbo scurried to the stage and cleared his throat as the band started his number. He began singing:

There was an Elf-lord from Nantucket
Whose---

"Thank you, Bulbo, thank you," said Enron, interrupting. "Bulbo Bunkins, everyone. Isn't he great?" He whispered to Bulbo fiercely, "I know this is a private party, but I'm running a family resort here! Like I've told you a million times, I will not have you doing any of your blue material in Riverdale."

Promo came up and took Bulbo's arm. "Let's get out of here, Bulbo. This isn't the right venue for you."

As they walked out, they noticed Slider sitting with Aiyem Morningstar. He had ordered a chocolate fondue that they were sharing as they stared into each other's mutually beautiful eyes.

"Ignore them," said Bulbo. "They'll be carrying on like that for the rest of the night."

Sham met them outside the ballroom. "I expect you'll be retiring, sir," he said to Promo. "I've taken the liberty of turning down your bedspread. I'll be sure to brush your little waistcoat for your big meeting tomorrow."

"Will Groin be there?" said Promo absently.

"The guy from Smithi Financial Solutions?" said Bulbo. "I expect so. He's been after me for decades. Wants to become my financial advisor. Now he'll be after you, too, Promo."

But Promo wasn't listening. Ever since he saw them together, Promo had been wondering about Slider and Aiyem. The experience left him feeling vaguely disappointed.

Chapter 14

THE EXPOSITION OF ENRON

The next day Promo awoke to a cheerful, professional wake-up call and healthy, low-fat breakfast. He would have preferred Riverdale's famous waffles, but he was heading into a big meeting with Enron that included breakfast, a full lunch, and both morning and afternoon snack breaks. He was encouraged by the volume of free food, but unnerved at the prospect of being stuck with Pantsoff and Groin for a full day. Perhaps the meeting would end early.

At the grand staircase Promo saw Bulbo talking with Pantsoff. Before he could vanish by using either his wobbit vanishing skills or The Ring, Pantsoff saw him.

"Promo, my lad!" Pantsoff said. "I believe Bulbo, you and I are all headed to the same place! How did you sleep? You look great. We're meeting in the Elbowpad Ballroom again. We don't want to be late and miss the team-building activity at the beginning!" Promo smiled weakly, like someone who had recently been hunted, chased, stabbed and poisoned.

Pantsoff led the wobbits as they hopped down the stairs that were just a little too big for them. They were joined by Sham, who followed discretely.

When they entered the ballroom, they saw Enron and several others seated at tables. In the front of the room was a podium and an easel with a pad of chart paper. The first chart read *Welcome To The Representatives Of All The Free Peoples Of Little Earth.* On a table nearby were piles of handouts awaiting distribution. There was a table in the back with coffee and little doughnuts brought direct from *The Dancing Doughnut Inn*.

"Outside catering!" said Promo to Bulbo.

"Yes," said Bulbo. "Enron was furious when Pantsoff told him that many of today's attendees had become tired of the menu at The Last Waffle House. Lunch will feature vegetarian chili catered by The Incredible Bjork. I've heard it's very good, but I've never had a chance to try it."

As he looked around, Promo saw Garfunkel and Groin. Slider was at a table by himself with his back to the wall, as was his custom. They all had folded paper cards in front of them with their names, to create the illusion that they all knew each other.

They went to Enron, and Promo asked "Do we need to take any handouts?"

"No," said Enron, "they'll be distributed during the meeting. Just make name cards for yourselves and come sit next to me. Feel free to get some of those overpriced doughnuts. Pantsoff paid to have coffee brought in, too, as if we couldn't brew it here. What is wrong with that guy?" Promo had planned to submit his receipts to Enron that morning, but he decided it might be better to wait.

Enron stepped to the podium. "Everyone, could I have your attention please. I'm sure you all want to get out of here on time tonight, so we should get started. Garfunkel, please hand out the agenda if you would."

He then flipped to the second page on the chart pad, which read *Great Peril, Urgent Errand.* "Allow me to introduce Promo son of Drono. He has come here on an urgent errand at great peril to himself. Stand up, Promo."

"I am standing up," said Promo. Everyone laughed politely at the traditional gag.

"But seriously," said Enron, "Little Earth is really in a tight spot, and I'm glad you're all here to provide your various reports and expertise. First, we should go around the room and introduce ourselves. As an icebreaker, please also tell the group which of Smoron's servants you like fighting the most. I'll go first. I'm Enron, and I like fighting Executive Riders." Everyone applauded warmly and nodded in agreement.

"Humph. I guess I'll go next," said a dwarf sitting next to Groin. "My name is Grimli, I'm with Smithibank, and I like slaying hobgoblins." Applause and agreement from the room.

"It looks like it's my turn, eh?" said an extremely good-looking elf with a complicated hairstyle, dressed in a jerkin of orange plaid. "Okay, well, I'm Landolakes, and I work at the Murkywood Forest Wood-Elf Lodge. My dad's the king there, don't you know. I like hunting giant spiders."

"Let's keep this moving," said a man, an actual human man, in an expensive raccoon skin coat. He was ruggedly good looking, and wore a silver-tipped stadium horn slung over his shoulder. "My name's Beeromor. I like killing anything that comes from Bordor." The applause was a little tentative, since it sounded he was bragging.

The introductions continued with Groin, Garfunkel, Slider, and a number of other elf and dwarf celebrities. Everyone tried to remain patient, until eventually they were done and Enron returned to the podium. He flipped to the next chart on the pad, which read *Dwarf Concerns: 1) Fallin in Moreo, 2) Executive Riders, 3) A warning.* He invited up the first speaker, Groin Of Smithi Financial Solutions. Groin stepped behind the podium, couldn't see over it, and then stepped to the side.

"Again, I'm Groin of Smithi Financial Solutions. Garfunkel is passing around my handout." The first page was identical to the chart.

"I'll start with a little background information. Some time ago, many Smithi shareholders wanted us to diversify after the dragon Smog caused a market adjustment. They wanted less exposure to the risks of mortgage and commercial lending. There had been interest in reopening our mining operations at Moreo. This location could have become a destination resort for dwarves all over Little Earth. It also could have provided us with much-needed office space for the region west of our headquarters at the Only Mountain.

"Under earlier leadership we had run into some delays on a similar project in Moreo: we dug too deep and awakened a nameless fear. Since the fear we awakened had no name, it was very difficult to discuss, and even harder to eliminate. But years later, some of our board members felt that we had the resources to return successfully to the Moreo project.

"My colleague Fallin was named project manager, and he assembled a team which went to Moreo. Initial reports were very encouraging, but then we stopped receiving them. That was about thirty years ago. Fallin likes to work independently, but it's unusual for him to not check in with his project sponsors at least once every seven years to share his progress. Please take a look at the second page of your handout."

Everyone turned the handout to page two, which was a portrait of an elderly, tough, and affluent looking dwarf. At the top were the words *Have You Seen This Dwarf?* and at the bottom was the name *Fallin, son of Funding,* and some contact information.

"The only discussion of Moreo since then has been from Smoron." said Groin. "He had one of his Executive Riders come to meet with Dwayne, the Smithi CEO. The Rider said that Smoron wanted to create a new synergy through cooperation between Smithi Financial Solutions and Bordor. He wanted to leverage our expertise at working with wobbits. He said Smoron was looking for one wobbit in particular, possibly with an offer of employment, as he put it. Dwayne used the old dwarf negotiating trick of not talking, so the Rider continued. It turns out that what he really wanted was a ring in the wobbit's possession that he said belonged to Smoron. He said if we could get him a meeting with the wobbit that had stolen this ring (his words, not mine), he would give us back three of our old Really Great Rings, as well as complete control of Moreo's mines, resort facilities, and offices, free of any nameless fear. He went on to say that if we refused, things would not go so well. Then, as if we might not understand that he was threatening us, he hissed right at Dwayne. Can you imagine the nerve of that guy?"

There were general murmurs of "Yeah, I hate it when they do that." Then Groin continued.

"Dwayne didn't get to be CEO by making hasty decisions, so he told the Rider, 'I'll need some time to present your offer back to my board of directors. They will want to review this matter. They are conservative, and your offer is risky.'"

"'It isn't risky at all,' said the Rider."

"'Yes it is,' said Dwayne."

"'No it isn't,' said the Rider. The negotiations continued like this for some time. The Rider eventually lost interest and left, but he returned to make the same offer twice during the next three quarters.

"Dwayne himself asked me to take time out of my busy schedule to give Bulbo this warning: Smoron wants you badly enough to offer us Moreo and three Really Great Rings to get you, so watch out. In consideration of your service to Borin Oakmanfield and Smithibank, we will, of course, not bring you to Bordor. I'm also here to get some details about the ring Smoron is after. He's been pressuring the Mayor of Lake City just as he pressured us, and we're afraid they might accept Smoron's offer before we do. He's even started to assemble troops at the border near the Only Mountain. He says it's only a training exercise, but we've all heard that before. That's it, everyone. I look forward to your comments." Groin then bowed and returned to his seat.

"Thank you, Groin," said Enron. "As it happens, I'm next on the agenda, and my presentation may provide some of the information you seek regarding The Ring." He turned to the next chart on the easel: *The Juan Ring- An Overview.*

Garfunkel passed around Enron's handout and many of them took notes on it as Enron began speaking in his rich tenor voice. He told them of Smoron, and the Really Great Rings, and their manufacture in the world long ago. He spoke of the elven designers of old and of their friendship with Moreo. He detailed, with many bullet points and graphs, how their quest for new processes and markets was used by Smoron to ensnare them. At that time he still claimed to be working in partnership with the elves, but all along he was busy stealing their intellectual capital. He then betrayed them, designing a master ring of his own that would dominate all other rings. He sent the work south to cut costs, bringing back the components to Mount Dum-Da-Dum-Dum and assembling the ring in the fiery Crotch Of Doom. This outsourcing cut costs so deeply that The Ring came to be named after the southerner that fabricated the parts: The Juan Ring.

Enron then told of the elves wisely hiding their rings, while the dwarves lost theirs and the kings of men were destroyed by these deadly accessories. He provided a first-hand account of Smoron's defeat by the Next To The Last Alliance, which startled Promo.

"You were there, Enron?" he said, unable to wait for the Q&A session at the end of the presentation.

"Oh yes," said Enron. "I've been in the business as long as anyone, for thousands of fiscal years. I've seen it all, done it all, and I know everyone."

"And he's only a half-elf," Bulbo whispered to Promo. "Imagine what he'd be like if he was pure elf!"

"Wow!" said Promo quietly.

Garfunkel interrupted. "If there are no further questions, could we please limit our side conversations?"

Enron continued. "I was there. I saw Ellen-doll and Gil-Gameshalad fall. I saw Nasal, the sword of Isadora, break in two. And I saw Smoron defeated by a clever low blow from a man with only a half-a-sword, who then took The Ring for his own." He pointed at Beeromor, who had raised his hand discreetly. "You have a question?"

"Back home in Dongor everyone knows The Ring was destroyed," said Beeromor. "But you're saying Isadora took it?"

"Yes," said Enron. "Isadora kept it, but the original plan was that it was to be taken back to the Crotch Of Doom and there destroyed. Sure enough, changing the plan cost Isadora his life in a surprise attack, and The Ring was lost. The pieces of his sword were brought here by a lone survivor who told me the story of the ambush. Smoron was defeated but not destroyed. And the whole affair put a strain on the various joint enterprises of elves and men. We haven't worked together successfully since then." He then pointed at Groin. "A question?"

"No, just a comment. Elves and men have worked together since then, along with the mighty dwarves of Smithi Financial Solutions, when we defeated the Moisty Mountain Goblins at The Battle Of Six Or Seven Armies. And we all made a fortune on that battle, too, from the dragon-hoard we split up!"

"Yes," said Enron, "but that was a long time ago."

"Not that long ago, eh?" said Landolakes. "I was there, and so was Groin and Mr. Bunkins."

"Please," said Garfunkel. "If we want to be able to go home to our kingdoms on time, we can't have all this cross-talk."

"Thank you, Garfunkel," said Enron. "As I was saying, The Ring was not destroyed, but since it was lost Smoron no longer had power over the three Really Great Rings of the Elves. Now that The Ring has been found, though, there will be problems."

"Are there any other questions, or comments? No? Does anyone want to take a break, or check your messages?" Promo looked around hopefully, but everyone wanted to keep going. "Then let's proceed with our agenda." He turned to the next chart on the easel, which read *Ad Hoc Report From The City Of Minas Plussign.* "Please give our speaker your full attention. Beeromor, do you have a handout to distribute?"

"No, my horse was delayed out of Minas Plussign and I didn't have time to prepare one. I'll just use this chart, and you can take notes if you want." He turned to the chart and wrote *Dongor Defends All Little Earth* underneath the *Ad Hoc* line. "My father's kingdom of Dongor defends all of Little Earth."

Beeromor turned back to the chart and on the next line wrote *East Giliath Fallen To Executive Rider.* He then said "The suburb of East Giliath has fallen to an Executive Rider leading an army of evildoers."

"I hope he doesn't just read each of his charts to us," said Bulbo quietly to Promo.

Beeromor wrote on another line *My Brother Dreamed A Poem.*

"This sounds interesting," said Bulbo.

"Shh!" said Garfunkel.

"My brother dreamed a poem after we led a forlorn hope unit to cover the main retreat out of East Giliath. We held back wave after wave of goblins, hobgoblins, and hemogoblins, and then cut the bridge we were defending. That night my brother had a crazy dream about a poem. We thought you should hear it, Enron, since you're really smart and everything. Here goes." He pulled out a scrap of paper and read aloud:

Seek for the Sword that was broken
In Riverdale it dwells
There shall some meetings be taken
With lots of elf and dwarf swells
Jargon and poems will be spoken
A wobbit will sing with the band
The Juan Ring will maybe awaken
And recession will be at hand

My father is Denosaur the Lord of Minas Plussign and the Vice-Ruler of all Dongor. He's the smartest guy in town, and he couldn't figure this dream out, so I've come here to Riverdale to ask around."

"Maybe this will help," said Slider, who stood, walked to the handouts table in front, unsheathed his half-a-sword and dropped it on the table. Then he took off his scabbard and upended it, dumping the pointy half of the sword on the table, too. "It was like this when I got it."

"What?" said Beeromor. "I thought you were a busboy!"

"You should have paid attention during the introductions."

"This is Orogarn," said Enron, "son of Orogarni, descended from Isadora, Ellen-doll's son, of Minas Plussign."

Promo looked carefully at the notes he had been taking. He drew a few lines and then furiously circled something. "Hey! That means that The Ring belongs to you! Smoron isn't out to get me after all, he wants you, Slider! Here, take The Ring!"

"No way!" said Beeromor. "The Ring belongs to me!"

"Settle down, you two" said Slider. "Promo, you have to hold onto the hot potato a while longer."

"Yes, Promo, show us The Ring," said Pantsoff. "But keep hold of the chain."

Promo worked the chain off over his head, struggling to get it past his nose. "It's a little tight," he said to Enron.

"Behold," said Enron. "The Juan Ring."

"I don't get it," said Beeromor. "How did a wobbit end up with my ring? And how could a busboy with a broken sword save Minas Plussign?"

Bulbo was feeling ignored, so he stood up, climbed onto the table and began reciting:

All that is gold does not glitter
Not all those who wander are lost
You can't tell a book by its cover
A rolling stone gathers no moss
Renewed shall be blade that was broken
The crownless again shall be king
Overnight his best dress shirt is soakin'

'Round the collar shall be no more ring

"There you are!" said Bulbo. "We can't explain it any more plainly than that." Then he whispered to Promo. "What do you think? I wrote that a while ago. I really feel it captures Slider's spirit. Pantsoff seemed to like it"

"The rhythm seems a little forced," said Promo. "And I'm not sure if I would have thrown in the word 'soakin' just to have a rhyme with 'broken.'"

"Thanks for the introduction, Bulbo," said Slider. "Yes, it's a tough, lonely life in the Rangers. We don't get all the glory like you lads do in Minas Plussign. We spend most of our time out in the rain, crouching in foxholes, waiting to ambush trolls and goblins. We try not to mind when people assume we're hoboes, about to panhandle them for a cup of coffee. Beeromor, your men keep Smoron bottled up in Bordor, it's true, but the Rangers look after everything else. We keep the wilderness safe and clean of monsters. Being the Chief Ranger is like being King Janitor, and there's always a mess that needs mopping up. Now it sounds like the real mess is oozing towards Dongor, and though some of my men might call it 'Mission Creep,' it looks like my new assignment is to clean up that mess before it gets there."

"Wait a minute!" said Beeromor. "How do we know this ring isn't forgery? I'm sure there's money to be made selling counterfeit magic rings. And where is Saccharine The White? I thought he was the wizard that knew all about the Really Great Rings!"

"I can explain everything," said Bulbo. But Enron cut him off.

"Let's get back to the agenda," he said. "Garfunkel, hand out the Memo Of Galadtameecha." As stated in the agenda, soon everyone was reading the memo, with its account of Bulbo stealing the Ring from Gol-Gol. There many startled reactions from the readers.

Soon everyone (except Beeromor) was finished reading. Enron turned to the next chart which read *Ring Update* and asked Promo for his report of The Ring's trip from Wobbiton to Riverdale. There were no handouts, and Promo kept it short.

"Thank you for your concise presentation," said Enron. "Your brevity is an inspiration to us all. Next on our agenda..." He turned to a new chart that had only the name *Pantsoff* on it, with no information. "I assume you've prepared no handouts, Pantsoff?"

"Correct, Enron!" said Pantsoff as he stepped to the front of the room. "To truly understand our situation, you need to understand what was happening in Murkywood while most of you were getting rich from the dragon-slaying project I managed."

Bulbo sighed loudly, sat back, and folded his arms. Many others in the room did the same.

Pantsoff ignored the non-verbals and continued. "Bulbo and the dwarves were working as a self-directed team while I was dealing with the urgent and important matter of The Neccomancer. The White Council was trying to take action against him, but Saccharine, a known pacifist, insisted that we leave him alone. He kept presenting 'legal' and 'moral' issues that made assassinating The Neccomancer seem unacceptable. We all knew that it was only a matter of time before The Neccomancer regained enough of his former market share to rebrand back to his old name, Smoron. When we finally made our assault on his headquarters at zero dark thirty that fateful morning, he was able to escape and relocate to his newly redecorated offices in Bordor."

"Doesn't the memo we just read it say that his escape was your fault, Pantsoff?" said Promo as he nudged Bulbo.

"That memo reflects an certain elvish bias. I remember the escape quite a bit differently, and I am working on a minority report that will be attached to the main memo. But to get back to my main point, Smoron soon took up residence in the Dark Office of Bordor. We were concerned that he was trying to locate and acquire The Juan Ring once more. The White Council met in this very ballroom to discuss our next steps, but Saccharine assured us that The Ring was lost forever."

Pantsoff almost seemed regretful for a moment. "I never should have listened to that guy. He's very persuasive, you know. Perhaps things would have been different if---"

"Our dilemma is in fact almost entirely your fault," interrupted Enron. "But it is also true that Saccharine is a great salesman. It is said that he once sold a universal life insurance policy to an elf."

"A dread salesman indeed," said Pantsoff. "And despite his confidence and isolationism, I worried. During my studies of wobbits I noticed a spike in the chatter of known spies and evildoers all around Wobbiton. Even the birds and the beasts began acting suspicious. I saw one hummingbird leaving a secret message at a dead drop. I finally called in Orogarn and his Rangers for backup.

"Hummingbird!" said Slider. "I should have killed that bird when I had the chance."

"At Orogarn's recommendation," said Pantsoff, "we began a long executive search for Gol-Gol. For someone that's been alive for so long, he was hard to locate. He keeps a very low profile. The hunt took months."

"You quit searching after only a week," said Slider. "I continued, and found him."

"Yes, we found him," said Pantsoff. "But I broke away from the search temporarily to follow another lead. I went to the Minas Plussign Public Library to do some important research on how I might conclusively identify The Ring. Believe it or not, Lord Denosaur was not entirely happy to have me reviewing his special archive of Juan Ring books and periodicals. He said an irresponsible researcher had damaged the collection by eating, drinking and smoking while handling some rare files years earlier. I promised him I would do none of these things. After I paid some late return fines for a few scrolls I borrowed previously, Denosaur granted me access to his archive. There, among the memos and three-ring binders, I found a journal written by Isadora himself." Pantsoff produced an ancient book.

"Did you take that from my father's archive?" said Beeromor. "You can't check a book out of a special collection!"

"And I fully intend to return it," said Pantsoff. "Here's what it says." He undid a tiny lock on the cover, and then flipped around in the pages. Seemingly at random he began reading in a bored, sing-songy voice.

Dear Diary: Today I won the Really Great Ring from Smoron, blah blah blah. I, Isadora, blah blah blah---

"Ah! Here we are! I had to skip ahead a little."

The Ring was hot when I first took it, as hot as a glede---

"When I first read that, I left the archive, went to the reference department, found a dictionary, looked up the word 'glede,' and found out it meant 'an ember.'"

"We figured that out from the context," said Groin.

Pantsoff continued reading.

---but as the ring did cool verily, I saw the engraving begin to fade. I shall copy down the writing forthwith, even though I know not the language in which it is written, lest I am unable to find a translator before the words fadeth altogether. Mayhaps if The Ring was re-heated, like unto a slice of leftover pizza, the engraving would be refreshed.

"There is a Post-It stuck to the next page. It is Isadora's copy of the engraving," said Pantsoff. "The rest of the pages are blank. I left Minas Plussign with this information, caught up with Orogarn, and then we found Gol-Gol."

"I found Gol-Gol," said Orogarn, in an attempt at accuracy. "Once I caught him, and Pantsoff heard that Gol-Gol was in my custody, he left Minas Plussign. I didn't wait for him to begin conducting the interview. Of course, Gol-Gol refused to cooperate. He bit me whenever he could, and kept hitting me on the head with a huge mallet. I tried to threaten him with extraordinary rendition to Murkywood, and that's ultimately what I did, turning him over to the Wood-Elf authorities. Even that failed to produce any useful intelligence regarding The Ring. Eventually Pantsoff arrived, checked into the Murkywood Wood-Elf Lodge and took over the interrogation."

"I tried the 'Good Shirriff, Bad Shirriff,' technique on Gol-Gol," said Pantsoff. "I brought him some coffee, we went out to lunch, caught a couple of shows, and I learned a few things. Most interesting was the fact that Gol-Gol has lived for a very, very long time, which is a known side effect of The Juan Ring."

"What did Isadora write on the Post-It?" said Promo. "Did it match the engraving on The Ring?"

"I'm getting to that! I later gave The Ring Isadora's suggested re-heating test, and yes, Promo, the engraving matched Isadora's Post-It. It read as follows---

Ash bag dekafstarbuk, ash bag koolatta,
Ash bag wakawaka argh barnumstiki krimpedges

"That's enough!" said Enron, who was visibly upset. "Like I told Bulbo, this is a family resort. We can't have any more talk like that! Keep it up and the only business I'll be able to get will be at spring break, or from tattoo conventions."

"My apologies," said Pantsoff. "Would it be okay if I repeated it translated?"

"Go ahead."

"Thanks. Translated it reads:

Juan Ring to lay them off, Juan Ring to find them,
Juan Ring to hire them as temps
and with a contract bind them

"There it is then," said Pantsoff. "By the way, I also learned that Gol-Gol visited Bordor, and he told them everything. Smoron has been out to get The Ring and Promo ever since. He may even know they're both here in Riverdale. Does anyone have any questions?"

"I'm glad Gol-Gol is still being detained," said Beeromor. "That could be helpful, at least."

"Agreed," said Slider. "He's still with the Wood-Elves and he's not going anywhere."

"I guess this would be a good time for my presentation, by golly," said Landolakes. He found a blank chart on the easel and wrote: *Alas! Gol-Gol has escaped!*

"Alas!" he said. "Gol-Gol has escaped!" Everybody gasped.

"What?" said Slider. "I kept him secure for weeks as we hiked through the woods, but you couldn't keep him from escaping from the dungeons of your resort?"

"It's been done before!" said Groin as he flashed a "thumbs-up" to Bulbo, who smiled and returned it. (For more about Groin and Bulbo's thrilling escape, order your copy of The Wobbit A Parody from Amazon.com now!)

"Finally," said Pantsoff, "there's a mishap that isn't being blamed on me! If we are unable to defeat Smoron, it can only be the result of Gol-Gol's escape. Please, Landolakes, how did this critical failure take place?"

"Okay, so, we Wood-Elves are big believers in rehabilitation through sport, don't you know. Pantsoff, after you checked out of the lodge we enrolled Gol-Gol in all of our most popular activities: hunting, fishing, camping, grilling. Come winter we were going to start him on hockey, curling and ice-fishing. But that's not going to happen, eh? During one of our hunting classes he climbed up into in a deer blind and wouldn't come down. We brought him some tuna hot dish, a few beers and something to read, but in the night some porcs attacked and he escaped with them. They were huge, for Pete's sake, bigger than any goblin, almost as tall as Groin."

"About four feet tall?" said Slider, jotting down some notes. "Long arms? Hairy ears?" Landolakes nodded. "Sounds like some of Smoron's porcs, all the way from Bordor. There's a conspiracy at work here. Smoron wants Gol-Gol to remain at large."

"Maybe this will work out in our favor," said Pantsoff.

"How?" said Enron.

"I don't know. I'm just brainstorming. That reminds me, you were wondering about Saccharine The White. I'm afraid he might not be as reliable a team member as we hoped."

"There I was," said Pantsoff. "It was June, and I was attending my triennial meeting with one of my brother wizards, Raggypants The Brown. It was a casual event at Evenstarbucks Coffee. While we were waiting for our cappuccinos, he gave me alarming news."

"'The nine Executive Riders have been deployed!' he said. 'But I have no idea why. Wherever they go, they ask for a place called Wobbiton. I've never heard of it myself. Have you?'"

"'Yes, I was just there. It's not that hard to find. Thank goodness Smoron won't reimburse the Riders for purchasing maps. How did you find out about this?'"

"'From Saccharine The White. He said he'd be happy to have a meeting with you, if you're willing to bring some doughnuts.'"

"This was good news," said Pantsoff. "Saccharine is the Head Wizard of The White Council. Raggypants is solid, too, don't get me wrong. He is a master of herbs and spices, and of changing colors of things, which is great if you're making some stew or redoing your apartment. And he can talk to the animals, just imagine it! Chatting with a chimp in chimpanzee! But Saccharine has spent his whole career becoming an expert on Smoron and The Juan Ring. He planned the mission to assassinate Smoron in Murkywood, which, since it failed, should have made me suspicious. Anyway, Raggypants said he had to get home and do his hair, it really needed a washing. After that he had an appointment with the King Of The Hedgehogs. I asked him to tell the King and all his other animal friends to bring any news of Smoron or The Ring directly to Saccharine at his Eisentower office. He said he would, and then he wished me well and left, taking his cappuccino with him."

"I jotted down a quick note for Promo to update him on our next steps, and visited Whee to leave it for him there. Then, after a few cocktails, a very pleasant dinner, and quiet night at *The Dancing Doughnut*, I left immediately to meet with Saccharine The White."

"It's a long ride to Eisentower, all the way at the end of the Moisty Mountains. When I got there it struck me as odd that the gatekeepers were hideous porcs, and it made me a little uneasy when they clanged the gate shut behind me, but I proceeded. I didn't want to let my nerves to get the best of me."

"Saccharine met me in the lobby, signed me in, got me a visitor's badge from the porc at the reception desk, and took me to his office."

"'So you have come, Pantsoff. Bwa-ha-ha!' he said. He laughs coldly like that all the time."

"'Yes, I've come for your aid, Saccharine The White.'"

"He said 'Have you indeed, Pantsoff The *Grey*! But aren't you Little Earth's greatest project manager, the master of fireworks and popcorns of all kinds? Why come to me now, after months of enjoying your per diem so lavishly in Wobbiton and Whee?' He's not exactly a people person, so when he talks like that I try to not take it personally. But he has a lovely speaking voice."

"'Nevertheless,' I said, 'we need to work as a team on this situation. Raggypants tells me that Smoron has deployed the Executive Riders!'"

"'Raggypants The Brown!' he said. 'Raggypants The Tree-Hugger! Raggypants The Housepainter! Raggypants The Sous Chef! He was barely smart enough to entice you here, Pantsoff The Grey, and here you'll stay. For I am Saccharine The Wise, Saccharine The Ring Maker, Saccharine Of Many Colors!'"

"At least someone around here is embracing diversity," said Promo quietly.

"'It seems Saccharine The Humble is out of the question,' I said."

"'Enough about me!' he said. His voice started to sound less crazy and angry. "Let's talk about you. Aren't you interested in taking your career to the next level, Pantsoff? You don't want to be a project manager forever, do you? Things are happening right now, Pantsoff! Change is everywhere! Befriend change and make it your slave! Wouldn't you like to be the next Head Wizard of the White Council? That would make you Pantsoff The White! And I would run all the holdings of Bordor! We would share The Juan Ring! You could wear it every other day, on even numbered days of the month! Tell me yes, Pantsoff! Be my partner. Tell me where I will find The Ring!"

"'You're a terrific salesman, Saccharine,' I said. "But I don't think it would work out."

"'Don't let the presumptive close of my sales pitch offend you, Pantsoff. Did I talk features instead of benefits? What do I have to do to make this sale? Where is The Ring?"

"'Never kid a kidder, Saccharine. We can't use the Juan Ring together. That timeshare condo we co-owned didn't work out, so how could this possibly succeed?'"

"'Suit yourself. I know you don't want to join with Smoron, and you've refused my generous offer, so that leaves the third choice: you stay here in Eisentower until you tell me the location of The Ring. That will give me a chance to think of a fitting punishment for the insolence of Pantsoff The Grey. Bwa-ha-ha!"

"'Oh yeah?' I said, but I knew my words were empty. I thought of a number of snappier comebacks during my imprisonment, but by then it was too late."

"He took me to a garden area on the roof of the building. The view was incredible, although it was then that I noticed that the local woods had been cut down, and in their place were factories for weapon manufacture, barracks for legions of porc warriors, and kennels for litter after litter of rargs. He imprisoned me, there on the roof. I paced back and forth hoping it wouldn't rain. Later he came up and made the whole sales pitch all over again, but with charts and handouts."

"A sales pitch?" said Bulbo. "Wasn't there some sort of Wizard's Duel, with the two of you magically flinging each other back and forth?"

"There was no duel," said Promo. "Just Pantsoff resisting the greatest sales pitch in Little Earth! I saw the whole thing in a dream! It all seemed so real. Pantsoff is telling the truth."

"Thank you," said Pantsoff. "I was in a tight spot. But as luck would have it, Raggypants remembered to have all the birds and beasts bring updates to Eisentower. By the end of the summer, The King Of The Eagles stopped by with a progress report. I asked him if he could give me a lift."

"'I thought I was done doing favors for you!' he said. 'We said we were even after I rescued you twice during your dragon-slaying project.'"

"'We might have said that, so maybe I'll have to owe you one after this. Come on, Beaky!'"

"He agreed, of course, and took me to meet with the horse-lords of Hohum. They were so pleased with some consulting I did for them that they gave me their best horse, named Thermofax, to speed me on my way. I took the horse and rode for Wobbiton, and then Whee, and then Carrottop, where the Executive Riders finally caught up with me. We had a huge, explosion-filled battle and I moved on the next morning, reasonably assuming the Riders to be defeated. I rode around for a while until Thermofax had to get to a critical appointment of his own. He thanked me for riding him, galloped off, and then I walked the rest of the way here."

"That's what happened? Really?" said Slider.

"Of course!" said Pantsoff. "More or less."

Enron turned the page on the easel to a chart that read *Recommendations.* There was a lot of blank space on the page.

"We now have all the known facts," he said. "I'd like each table to brainstorm some ideas, and then present their best recommendation to the entire room." He used their birth-dates to arrange everyone randomly into new table groups. They hated getting up and moving to new tables, but it had to be done. In fifteen minutes, each group presented their ideas.

Garfunkel's table suggested that they contact Jeff Bombadowski at his bowling alley home and give the Juan Ring into his care. "The Dude abides, after all" said Garfunkel.

Enron wrote *1) Give Ring To The Dude* on the chart, but not everyone was excited about the idea.

"The Dude?" Pantsoff said. "He's a great guy, but not super-responsible. He would probably leave it somewhere by mistake. Who knows what would happen then?"

Promo's table gave their idea. "The Ring would be safe here in Riverdale. Why don't I just leave it here?" said Promo.

Enron wrote *2) Leave Ring In Rivendell.* Then he said to Promo "There's no way I'm going to let that happen. I'm trying to run a business here. Next?"

Groin spoke for his table. "We think the Ring should be dropped into the sea. Preferably into a very deep spot. There it would lay undisturbed until the end of time."

Enron wrote *3) Drop Ring Into Sea.*

"Really?" Slider said. "It took your table fifteen minutes to come up with that? We already know Smoron's got willow trees and hummingbirds working for him. Don't you think he could hire a kraken or a mackerel, too? Come on!"

"Another conspiracy theory? Then what's your idea?" said Groin.

"Drop it into the Crotch of Doom," said Slider, "where it was assembled. The one place where it can be melted into something less dangerous, like a magic cufflink. You can't do anything with one cufflink."

"Couldn't we just smash it with a hammer?" asked Grimli, the younger dwarf.

"Not with my hammer, you won't," said Groin. "The Ring can't be smashed. That's why I'm for dropping it into the sea."

Enron wrote *4) Drop Ring Into Smoron's Fiery Backyard.* "I have my doubts," he said. "But it looks like we're agreed that The Ring must be hidden forever or destroyed. Only an idiot or a lunatic would think otherwise."

"I have an idea," said Beeromor. "Who says it has to be hidden or destroyed? Why don't we use The Ring against Smoron? One of us can wield it. We're all good guys, right? What could possibly go wrong if we're well-intentioned enough?"

"I'm not going to wear it," said Enron. "I saw what happened when Isadora tried that. No thank-you."

"I'm out," said Pantsoff. "I've already got one of the Really Great Rings of the Elves, although I'm not supposed to talk about it. I wouldn't take another ring. I don't want to look greedy."

"Maybe my dad could wear it," said Beeromor. "He's perfect for that! Or I could wear it! I'd be unstoppable!"

Enron wrote *5) Give Ring To Beeromor*,

"That secret Elf-ring of yours, Pantsoff," said Groin. "Couldn't we use it against Smoron along with the other two Elf-rings?"

"Like Pantsoff said, we're not supposed to even discuss the Elf-rings," said Enron. "And anyway, those rings don't work like that. They aren't useful for battle or commerce or even management. They are more about soft skills, like healing and communication and saving the whales. They'd be of no use against Smoron. And if he regains The Ring, our rings would only be turned against us, for hurting and arguing and destroying the whales. He will use them to eliminate every competitor in every imaginable market, and monopolize the sale of all goods and services. His tyranny of Little Earth will be vertically integrated. That is his purpose."

"And if we destroyed the Juan Ring," said Groin. "Or threw it into the sea?"

"We're not going to throw anything into the sea," said Enron. "And as for destroying The Ring, we don't really know what will happen if that plan succeeds. We hope it would not be anything bad."

"So destroying The Ring may be a bad idea, too?" said Groin.

"Destroying The Ring is perfect!" said Pantsoff. "It's a bad idea among many bad ideas, so Smoron will never see it coming. It will give us the all-important Element Of Surprise!"

Enron turned to the chart, read the choices aloud, put it to a vote. In the end, everyone voted for Choice Number Four except Groin and Grimli, who stuck with Number Three because it would be less expensive.

"It is resolved," said Enron. "We will destroy the Juan Ring by throwing it into the Crotch Of Doom. But who will do it?"

"Very well, you can stop hinting!" said Bulbo. "I'll undertake this heroic quest. The media attention will help me sell my autobiography, but now I'll have to write a new ending. It's too bad, too, because I really wanted to use *That'll do, Pig. That'll do.* Oh well. When would be a good time for Promo to turn over The Ring to me? I assume I'll have to sign for it, or something."

"No, Bulbo," said Pantsoff. "Thanks for your interest, but we'll be going in another direction on this."

"Really?" said Bulbo. He paused. "I know! You're going to have Beaky, The King Of The Eagles, fly to Bordor. He could drop The Ring into the Crotch Of Doom from a great height! You're a genius! It will be fast and foolproof."

"No, we were thinking of having someone like you walk into Bordor with it. Like you, but younger. No offense."

"That's age discrimination!" said Promo. "They can't do that to you, Uncle Bulbo!"

The doors to the ballroom opened, and lunch was brought in. Bacon-lettuce-and-tomato sandwiches from Farmer Lamprey, and vegetarian chili from Bjork's Farm. Promo completely forget about planning a lawsuit against the White Council for ageism. He really enjoyed the chili. As they finished their coffee and a light dessert, Enron returned to the podium.

"This afternoon," he said as a few smokers straggled back from outside, "we must choose who will take the Juan Ring to Mount Dum-Da-Dum-Dum in Bordor, and there, cast it into the Crotch Of Doom. I hope we can make our decision soon and get done early. Who will take The Ring? We're looking for a young version of Bulbo. The candidate should be good at sneaking, and have experience with the Juan Ring if at all possible. A volunteer, preferably." Everyone looked at Promo.

"I will take The Ring," he said. "But I do not know the way."

"Excellent!" said Pantsoff. "Promo will carry The Ring. We do everything we can to provide him with a map."

"I'm relieved," said Enron. "This way we won't have to resize the chain The Ring hangs on."

"Lord Enron," said Sham, who had been absolutely quiet all morning. "May I inquire as to whether Mr. Bunkins will be traveling alone?"

"Sham Sammich!" said Enron. "What a wonderful, selfless act on your part. You will certainly accompany him! Someone has to keep him on task."

"Oh," said Sham, quietly. "That's not what I meant, but yes, of course..."

Chapter 15

THE RING FLIES SOUTH FOR THE WINTER

Right before Happy Hour, the wobbits called an informal meeting of their own. Mary and Puppy were furious.

"Since you two weren't mentioned this morning," said Bulbo, "I assume Promo and Sham will be going on without you. You'll be sent home, probably with some lovely parting gifts."

"This is so bogus!" said Puppy. "What do you mean we're not going with Promo?"

"Yeah!" said Mary. "You need me! What if you have to hire more horses? Or organize another house-warming?"

"What are you talking about?" said Promo. "You hated the first part of the journey! Puppy, how many times did you tell me you were bored?"

"So you expect us to go back home?" said Puppy. "Home is even more boring! And there's no one like Maude at home. Or Aiyem Morningstar. Or Orogarn, for that matter."

"True," said Promo. "But what about the danger? Being eaten by trees or buried alive by wights? Not to mention the Executive Riders! Who wants to get stabbed with a magic, poisoned dagger?"

"The danger is exciting!" said Mary. "It's extreme! Thanks to you, we've discovered our inner thrill-seekers! We can't return to a normal life! We won't!"

"And if I go home, I'll have to do my income tax," said Puppy. "I want to put that off as long as possible. Give me Executive Riders every time."

"I'll have to re-grout all the bathroom tiles at Buckiebrand Hall," said Mary. "If I go with you, someone else might do it."

"We've got to go with," said Puppy. "You'll need someone with intelligence in the party."

"No you won't," said Pantsoff as he walked up uninvited. "Intelligence won't matter. All you need to do is walk east until you get to a volcano, and then throw The Ring into it. But on the way, it will still be helpful to have a couple extra wobbits in the party to draw fire away from Promo. You two were excellent decoys during the trip from Wobbiton to Riverdale, so I'm recommending you for the job all the way to Bordor!"

"We win again!" said Mary.

"Yay!" said Puppy.

"That's not official," said Pantsoff. "We need to do some focus groups and send out surveys. There's a lot of opinions we need before anyone goes anywhere with The Ring."

"Has there been any more thought about asking the Eagles to do it?" said Bulbo.

"The consensus is that the Eagles have been overused already," said Pantsoff. "The Free Peoples Of Little Earth are getting tired of the Eagles. And of course, Eagles are exactly what Smoron will be looking for. They rescued Borin & Company when the goblins had us trapped in the fir trees, they showed up in the nick of time to win the Battle Of Six Or Seven Armies, and their King extracted me from Saccharine's rooftop prison. Enough is enough. Trust me, Bulbo, the Eagles are out of this project."

As they waited on Enron and the many decisions that had to be made in the days that followed, the wobbits wasted time at the resort as best they could. They tried every cocktail available, they saw every show and cabaret act, and they gambled in the casino until Enron forbade their use of IOUs.

Beeromor spent most of his time in the health club, and Grimli tried to grow his financial advisor business by having prospect meetings and investment seminars. They had hoped to return to their kingdoms after Enron's big meeting, but were content to stay put in their complimentary suites.

Slider and Landolakes went out on patrol, looking for news about Smoron. They discovered that all the horses of the Executive Riders had been killed in the magic tsunami. There were no dead Riders to recover, though, only a few shoes and a necktie that they had lost in their defeat. By December some of the surveys were being returned, and the numbers from the focus groups were being crunched.

Enron called the wobbits in for a meeting to give them his decision. There were no handouts.

"Promo and Sham," he said, "you will be traveling as part of a very small project team. I've spent a fortune keeping everyone here at the resort, so I simply can't afford to a host of elves in armor to send with you. And with all those warriors you would lose---"

"We would lose the Element Of Surprise, yes," said Bulbo. "So who is going?"

"The Superfriends Of The Ring shall be nine." said Enron. "That seems only fair, since there are nine Executive Riders. There will be Promo and Sham, as agreed. Pantsoff will accompany you, since that will ensure that he leaves my resort. For the rest, I will be sending you with some of Little Earth's brightest and best: Landolakes of the Wood-Elves, Grimli of the dwarves, and Orogarn of the men. This mess is all his ancestor Isadora's fault anyway."

"Slider is coming! Hooray!" said Promo. "But didn't he say he was going to help Beeromor in Minas Plussign?"

"I say a lot of things," said Slider. He had been observing unseen from a stand of potted plants in the corner. "We'll see how it goes. My priority remains looking after you, Promo. All other concerns are secondary. Beeromor can come with us and we can drop him off in Dongor on the way."

"That leaves just two positions open," said Enron. "We really don't have enough time to search for candidates, to say nothing of reviewing resumes, conducting interviews, and completing background checks. If only we could fill these positions internally."

Mary and Puppy waited, holding their breaths. Did Pantsoff forget to recommend them to Enron?

"Mary, Puppy, I don't suppose you would be---"

"We'll do it! Yay!" they cried. Puppy ran back and forth waving his arms in joy.

"Very good," said Enron. "Tomorrow you'll each get a contract that I'll need signed and returned in forty-eight hours. You might also want have a lawyer put your affairs in order before you set out. Payment of your bills while you're gone, creating a power of attorney, signing a last will and testament, that sort of thing."

"Yay!" said Puppy.

Nasal, Slider's highly collectable antique broken sword, was brought by Enron to the Riverdale Swordatorium for repairs. It was one of many shops at the resort, and the salesmen there sold overpriced swords to vacationing rubes. But they also were highly skilled in reforging high-end weapons like Nasal, and they soon had it completely rebuilt.

"I rename you Da-doo-ron-ron, The Flame Of The Northwest," said Slider. He expertly waved the sword about. "A full-length sword! This is going to take some getting used to."

"The reforging is flawless," said Enron, "and the new runes add some stylish updates to a classic weapon."

"Absolutely beautiful. I should have had these repairs done years ago. What was I thinking?"

"Better late than never," said Enron.

Bulbo met with his nephew in private that same day, and Promo got some hardware upgrades of his own. Bulbo opened up two dusty, battered, leather cases. Each had a highly specialized piece of equipment form-fitted inside.

From one, Bulbo removed a large knife. Like the knives from the real baroow, it amounted to a short sword for a wobbit. It had a ruby red handle. "This is Stink. It is an Elf Army Knife, you see, you can tell by the small runes at the base of the blade. This main blade folds in," he said, as he demonstrated. "There are many others that fold out, a small blade, a pliers/wire-cutter, a scissors, a can opener, all kinds of tools." He gave it to Promo.

"And here," he said, "is my First Class Mail Shirt. It will turn away any blade or arrow, and you can wear it under your shirt. It breathes well, you can layer it, and it wicks moisture away. But don't tell anyone you've got it on. I don't want them teasing you about it. Most of them aren't wearing armor. I fancy it could even turn the blades of the Executive Riders."

"Really!" said Promo. "It's too bad you didn't give it to me back in Wobbiton, before one of those guys stabbed me."

"I'm sorry about that," said Bulbo. "I have trouble letting go."

"Yes," said Promo. "I've noticed."

Promo put on the Mail Shirt and then put his shirt, little waistcoat, and wool jacket on over it. Then he tried out the corkscrew and the screwdriver on his Elf Army Knife. Bulbo sang quietly to himself:

Sitting in the morning sun
I'll be sitting here when evening comes
Watching as the guests check in
And I'll watch them
when they check out again, yeah

I'm sitting in the lobby all day
Watching the guests walk away
I'm just sitting by the fire all day
Wasting time

I left my home in Bug End
I'm in Riverdale, I'm here to stay
No projects or adventures
Since I gave my magic ring away

I'm sitting in the lobby all day
Watching the guests walk away
I'm just sitting by the fire all day
Wasting time

"You're overworking that refrain," said Promo.

"It's a work in progress," said Bulbo.

It was a cold day in January when they were to depart. Enron had given them a few days off for the holidays, but they had to stay at the resort so there hadn't been much point. It was just before dusk when they all met in the lobby before setting out.

Enron had them all stand together for a group portrait, wobbits in front. While it was being sketched, he said "You shall be...The Superfriends Of The Ring." He wished he hadn't, because he didn't care for catchphrases.

Everyone did a final equipment check. The Company took no warhorses, lances or catapults, relying on the aforementioned Element Of Surprise. Stealth and secrecy were critical. Since all of the non-wobbits were professionals, they all brought their own gear. Slider had Da-doo-ron-ron, but carried no backup weapon, and wore his usual tattered greatcoat. Rangers felt that the shields and armor used by traditional troops were inappropriate for their role as irregulars, working behind enemy lines. "Our only chance is in striking swiftly and silently, without warning."

Beeromor carried a well-worn, custom-built sword with a matching shield, and wore his raccoon-skin coat. His silver-tipped stadium horn was in his hand. He yelled at the top of his voice "Here comes Dongor! Boo-yah!" and then honked the horn mightily. Guests all the way from the front desk to the lounge were startled, wondering if this was the fire alarm.

"You idiot!" said Enron as he went to calm his paying customers.

"Fine," said Beeromor. "I won't honk the horn again, even if it kills me."

Grimli alone wore non-secret armor. He had a chainmail shirt, a plate armor jacket, trousers of fine steel mesh, and socks of lacquered leather. Any time he moved suddenly he made a clanking sound. Dwarves rarely had the Element Of Surprise. When they did, it was due to their shortness, or because they had tunneled beneath their enemies. He carried a broad-bladed axe.

Landolakes wore a plaid elven hunting outfit. He had a bow and quiver, and a long white hunting knife. Sharpshooting and cut-throat ambushes were his preference, but for traditional battles he carried a sharpened hockey stick and wore the fiercely painted goalie mask, as did the rest of his kind.

The wobbits carried the swords that the Dude gave them from the wight-treasure. Puppy had to be reminded to put on a coat. Promo wore his secret First Class Mail Shirt, and carried Stink in his pocket, with all the blades and tools closed into the handle. Sham carried an omelet pan as a backup weapon. In his pack were the rest of his pots and pans, a few extra hankies for Mr. Promo, some salt, some salt substitute for Mr. Promo's blood pressure, some tobacco, some chewing gum if Mr. Promo wanted to quit smoking, and a lint-brush for Mr. Promo's dandruff. He had forgotten to pack any rope but decided "Perhaps we can pick some up on the way."

Pantsoff bore his staff, which was an upgrade of the wand he had carried during his project with Bulbo and the Dwarves. At his waist he had the elven-sword Hamstring, stolen from some trolls. He wore the usual big wizard hat. He felt it was part of his image.

Waiting outside was the pony they bought from Bill Furface. Even though he was overloaded with elven gear and supplies, he looked better than when they first saw him. Sham named him Furface, which was a bit of an insult to the pony. He was going to miss Riverdale as much as anyone else in the Company.

As they stood together in the turnaround outside the front door, Enron said a last few words. "You should march at night to avoid detection. By the way, I feel it only fair to point out that your contracts allow you to leave the project whenever you want. Just bear in mind that your final paycheck will be forfeit if you fail to provide us with at least two weeks notice."

Grimli scowled. "Winners never quit, and quitters never win" he said.

"Maybe," said Enron. "But it is wise to take things one day at a time."

"Monkey see, monkey do," said Grimli. "I'm here for the duration, Mr. Bunkins. You shall have me, and my axe."

"And my bow, don't you know," said Landolakes.

"And my sword," said Slider.

"And my sword, too," said Beeromor.

"And my sword and staff," said Pantsoff.

"And my short sword," said Mary.

"And my omelette pan, sir," said Sham.

"What are you guys talking about?" said Puppy.

"I'm sure you need to get going," said Enron. "Please don't be late on my account."

Bulbo yelled from his fireside chair in the lobby "Good luck! Promo, be sure to keep a diary! I'll ghostwrite your autobiography when you return."

"Shall I ever see Uncle Bulbo again?" said Promo.

Mary and Puppy both pantomimed hanging themselves.

They headed south, staying west of the mountains to avoid Smoron's spies. They marched in a line, with Pantsoff in front in case they ran into anyone from the media. Slider was next, to keep Pantsoff pointed in the right direction. After everyone else came Landolakes, with his bow ready for either porcs or venison.

The beginning of the journey was cold and dreary. Mary and Puppy were having trouble adjusting to sleeping during the day. Promo couldn't sleep at all when he realized he forgot to give Enron his receipts.

After about two weeks they could see mountains ahead of them, at bedtime, during the day. "There they are!" said Grimli. "The mountains of Zither, Shabaz, and Zigzag. Among my kind, we---"

Puppy interrupted him, as he commonly did. "Hey Slider, what are you looking at? Why aren't you looking at the mountains? What do you see, Slider? Slider?"

"I don't like the look of that cloud." said Slider. Everyone looked, but most couldn't see it. After a few minutes of staring he said "That's no cloud! Everyone hit the deck!" Moments later, a huge flock of hummingbirds hummed overhead, glancing around ominously.

"Smoron's spies," said Slider. "We'll have to be very careful around birds from now on, and not just hummingbirds. Others birds known to be on his payroll include the Booby, the Titmouse, the Woodcock, and the Titpecker."

"So now what?" said Puppy.

"We will continue on to the Mountains," said Slider. "To Caradtable, right over there."

"Is that what Grimli was talking about?" said Mary.

"I don't know," said Puppy. "I wasn't listening."

"If we're going through the Caradtable Mountains, it's going to be very cold." said Beeromor. "We'll want to be able to light a fire if it's a matter of life or death. We should gather some firewood and each carry a bundle of it."

"A faggot?" said Grimli.

"No," said Beeromore. "I have a girlfriend back home."

"You misunderstand me," said Grimli. "I meant we should each carry a bundle of sticks to burn."

"Yes, that's what I said," said Beeromor.

With a fully-loaded pony and a bundle of firewood each, in the middle of the night, they began their climb into the mountains. It started snowing, which was cheerful for a moment, until they realized there would be no opportunity to make snow-angels during their climb. The path got steeper as the snow got heavier. Soon it was neck-high on the wobbits, which is not that deep, unless you're climbing a mountain with a full pack in the dark.

"I hate to be the one to say it" said Beeromor, "but we can't go on. We ought to quit for the night."

"I knew it," muttered Grimli.

"All right," said Slider. "We'll sleep right here. Wobbits, you should sleep standing up so we can find you in the morning."

They tried to sleep, but the snow actually did threaten to bury the wobbits alive.

"I guess this is the life-or-death situation we were waiting for," said Beeromor. "Caradtable hates us. Permission to light the fire, Pantsoff? Or should we wait until the weakest among us dies? I figure that's Puppy, but it might be Promo. Well?"

"Permission granted," said Pantsoff. Slider sighed. He had a hard time remembering that Pantsoff was actually the manager of this project. Pantsoff took one of the bundles, held it in the air, and shouted *Presto Change-o!*

The sticks burst into flame and Pantsoff quickly put them down. Flames soared into the air, and then spelled out *Pantsoff Is Here!* "Pretty impressive, yes?" he said. "This is the first time I've been able to advertise in this region!"

The fire helped to keep the wobbits and Grimli from being buried in snow, but it was still bitterly cold. As Sham started to turn blue, Pantsoff reached into his coat and pulled out an elegant, understated hip-flask. He took a sip and handed it to Sham.

"One sip only. It is called *mirrortile*, the hundred-proof cordial of the elves. Caradtable won't kill us tonight." Sham gratefully took a sip.

"I got it from Garfunkel, he said you wobbits liked it."

"Like it? We love it!" said Puppy as he grabbed it from Sham. Mary grabbed it next, and then Promo.

"Pass that over here, little feller," said Landolakes. "This stuff will keep you warm and no mistake." He took it and sipped. "We drink it when we go ice-fishing, ya hey!"

"What the heck are you talking about?" said Grimli. "Give me that!" He grabbed the hip-flask and drank, as did the others. It was dawn before they knew it.

Everyone survived the night, thanks to the faggots and the cordial, although some of them were a little headachy that morning. The snow had stopped, but it was piled high all around them.

"Hey there, Pantsoff!" said Landolakes. "Why don't you do some more magic and get us out of here! Turn your staff into a snow blower or something!"

"Typical amateur!" said Pantsoff. "I thought Wood-Elves understood magic. You ought to know it doesn't work like that!"

"If you ladies are done yapping, let me show you how we do snow removal in Dongor! Boo-yah!" Beeromor charged into the snowbank headfirst, creating a path of sorts.

"I'd better go keep an eye on our Grunt," said Slider, who joined in digging a path.

Landolakes watched for a minute. "You two are as slow as molasses! This must be your first snow flurry, eh? Instead of digging through it, we Wood-Elves just walk over it!" He stepped up and walked smoothly across the snow, and soon was past the digging of the other two. Then he was gone.

"An Elf who's light on his feet," said Pantsoff. "Why am I not surprised?"

"I bet he's a terrific dancer, too," said Grimli.

The men were still digging and yelling things like "Boo-Yah!" and "Ding-Hao!" and "Hoo-Wah!" when Landolakes returned.

"Hey there, I'm back! For Pete's sake, look how hard you're working. Don't worry, though, you're almost through. The snow bank is pretty narrow."

"I knew it!" said Grimli. "Caradtable is trying to trick us into turning back."

"Yes, and it's worked. We're leaving as fast as we can," said Slider.

"Hurry up you guys," said Puppy. "I hate this mountain!"

"Yeah!" said Mary. "We hate it! We want to get out of this snow!"

"Yeah!" said Puppy. "Get us out of here! Now!"

"Here," said Slider. "I can help. Puppy, take my hands. Great. Now, Beeromor, you take his ankles."

"Hey!" said Puppy. "Cut it out, you guys!"

"Follow my lead, Beeromor," said Slider. They started swinging Puppy back and forth.

"One!"

"Two!"

"Three!" Together, they threw Puppy over to the other side of the snowbank.

"Come here, Mary!" said Beeromor.

They gave Mary the same help, and then dug the rest of the way. When they broke through, they found the two young wobbits having a snowball fight. The rest of the party followed behind, including Furface the pony. As they looked back at their campsite down the path through the snowbank, they saw the little circle quickly smashed by a suspiciously sudden avalanche.

"We're going, we're going," said Grimli. "Caradtable has trouble taking 'yes' for an answer."

The Company slowly made their way back down the mountain. Caradtable had defeated them. The score was Evildoers: One, Superfriends: Nothing.

Chapter 16

JOURNEY TO THE CENTER OF LITTLE EARTH

It was evening after a long day of marching when Pantsoff called for a meeting. Everyone attended. Puppy interrupted with a question.

"How about a little more of that *mirrortile*, Pantsoff?" he said.

"You weren't going to drink the rest by yourself, were you?" said Grimli.

"Fine," said Pantsoff. He passed it around after taking his sip. "Here. As for our situation, I have safely led us out of the mountains. Now, since I value your opinions, I want your input before we continue. The only way by which we can continue is unpleasant, very dangerous, and Slider is against it: we must journey through the Mines Of Moreo. It's full of narrow bridges, crumbling staircases, and sudden drops in the darkness. And lots of goblins, probably."

"Sounds good to me," said Grimli. "It's a dwarf's paradise! I'll go, Pantsoff, to look upon the Halls Of Derwin, if you can find the Doors That Are Shut."

"What?" said Beeromor.

"The doors to Moreo are hidden," said Pantsoff. "Hidden, and magically locked. But it's nothing I can't handle. I got my team past the magic doors of the Only Mountain quite easily on Bulbo's adventure."

"No," said Promo. "Bulbo got your team past those doors. You weren't even there."

"What are you, my biographer?" said Pantsoff. "Trust me, I can get us into Moreo."

"This sounds like a really bad idea," said Beeromor.

"Okay," said Pantsoff. "We'll put it to a vote. Who says we avoid Moreo, even though there is no other path available?" Puppy and Mary raised their hands.

"And who says we enter Moreo?" Pantsoff and Grimli raised theirs.

"And who abstains?" Beeromor, Landolakes, and Slider raised their hands. They were actually for avoiding Moreo, but they didn't want to vote along with Mary and Puppy.

"Promo, Sham, what about you?" said Pantsoff.

"Oh, let's get it over with," said Promo. "I say we journey through Moreo."

"And I'm with Mr. Promo," said Sham. "Of course."

"The two of them should only count as one vote," said Mary.

"Words hurt, Mr. Mary," said Sham.

"It's resolved, then," said Pantsoff. "We head towards Moreo first thing tomorrow. The door used to be in the next mountain over, about fifteen miles to the southwest. I know you're all tired from our escape from Caradtable. This is a perfectly safe place to camp for the night." Rargs howled in the distance.

"Listen to that wind!" said Pantsoff. "Bundle up, everyone, and sleep tight."

"You're kidding, right?" said Slider. "You've been chased by rargs, so you should know what they sound like. We can't stay here. Let's at least find a defensible position. High ground. Trees to climb. Anything!"

"Let's dig some trenches," said Beeromor. "A rarg's bark is worse than his bite."

"True," said Slider. "But in the Rangers we always say 'Don't look a gift rarg in the mouth.' I think we should get out of here."

"We should have stayed in Riverdale," said Puppy.

"Mr. Pantsoff knows how to escape rargs," said Sham. "Stay close to him, Mr. Puppy," said Sham. "But watch out for his backswing if he draws that sword."

Slider found some high ground within a handy ring of stones, and led the party there. They built a fire, and soon saw glowing rarg eyes all around them. Everyone drew a weapon, stood in a circle and faced out. A rarg stepped into the light. Then it fell dead, with an arrow in its throat. Landolakes had loosed his bow.

"I'm gonna go get that rarg," he said. "Their meat's pretty good in a stew, you know." But before he could make any more dinner plans, the other rargs attacked. Beeromor hacked and hewed at them, and Gimli chopped them into firewood-sized pieces with his axe. Slider had to choke up his grip on Da-doo-ron-ron now that the sword was returned to its original length, but he soon got the hang of it, slaying many rargs as they leapt over the stone ring. Landolakes shot twenty-two, despite having only twenty arrows.

Pantsoff decided to use magic instead of his sword, for fear of hitting Mary and Puppy who were clinging to his legs. With a shout of *Expecto Patronum* the rarg chieftain burst into an explosion of popcorn. A combination of cheese and caramel popcorn fell to the ground, as the remaining rargs panicked and ran off.

The Superfriends took a minute to catch their breath. Landolakes went looking for the juiciest of the slaughtered rargs, but was disappointed.

"What sort of monkey business is this, eh?" he said. "The carcasses are all gone! Even the popcorn has vanished!"

"These were the worst kind of rargs: magic rargs!" said Pantsoff. "They disappear when you kill them. Our hopes of stew were in vain, Landolakes. Let's get some sleep, and then move on right after breakfast."

They ate some poached eggs, and walked, and shortly after a late lunch arrived at a large cliff face with a stagnant, nasty pond in front of it.

"I'm pretty sure the doors are here," said Pantsoff. "They're really quite amazing. Built as a bi-partisan venture using Elf know-how and Dwarf financing. Those were the days."

"Until those stupid Elves ruined everything," muttered Grimli.

"Oh, sure," said Landolakes. "The Dwarves are always the victims."

"Break it up, you two," said Pantsoff. "Take the gear off Furface and divide it up. We're going to turn him loose."

"You betcha, Pantsoff," said Landolakes. "That pony's too smart to go into some dwarf sewer."

"Shut up!" said Grimli. "Wait until you see how beautiful Moreo is!"

Pantsoff stood staring at the cliff face as the others repacked their knapsacks. "I just don't get it. The doors should be right here."

"What's your plan?" said Slider.

"I think we'll just wait and see," said Pantsoff.

The sun went down. "Still nothing?" said Slider to Pantsoff, who hadn't moved.

"Maybe you're right," said Pantsoff. "This is hopeless. We should just go back to Riverdale and await the end." He turned and sat on the ground, and put his head in his hands.

The moon came up, and shone upon the cliff face. The outline of a beautifully engraved double door appeared in silver. "Pantsoff, look at this!" said Slider.

Pantsoff turned, and then leapt up. "I knew it! Moon letters! And just where I expected them, too!" A tree motif with Elvish writing appeared.

"The symbol of the Regular Elves!" said Landolakes.

"Not the Wood-Elves?" said Promo.

"No, my people had nothing to do with this. It's a little too flashy for our tastes, don't you know." said Landolakes. A moment later, a dollar sign appeared among the trees.

"The emblem of Derwin, the father of all Dwarves!" said Grimli.

"What does the writing say?"

"Nothing important," said Pantsoff. "Just *The Doors Of Derwin, Lord Of Moria. Say The Magic Words And Enter.* And the smaller letters underneath say *All Deliveries In Rear.*"

"And what are the magic words?" said Beeromor.

"Beats me," said Pantsoff. "Grimli, what are the magic words?"

"Why would I know?" said Grimli. "I'm a busy and important dwarf! I've spent my life building my investment business. When would I have time to vacation in Moreo?"

"Landolakes," said Pantsoff. "How about you?"

"Nope," he said. "Like I said, I'm a Wood-Elf. We're completely different from Regular Elves."

"Anyone else?' said Pantsoff. "No? Okay, I once knew every spell of Elves and Men and Porcs for this purpose. Let me try one."

Hocus pocus!
Open sesame!

Nothing happened. "Anyone else want a try?' said Pantsoff. Mary and Puppy kept busy throwing rocks into the foul pond nearby. They were fascinated by the strange ripples and bubbles in the water that seemed to be unrelated to their rock-throwing.

"Wouldn't it be funny if you literally said 'The Magic Words,' and then the doors opened?" said Promo.

The Magic Words! said Pantsoff in a voice loud enough for the doors to hear. They immediately opened, swinging inward.

"That was the next thing I was going to try," he said.

"I guess the Elves and Dwarves of old had a sense of humor," said Beeromor. "Although I'm not a fan of practical jokes."

"Furface, listen carefully," said Sham to the pony. "We're going into the mine over here. You should go back to Riverdale, and then head to the Dude's bowling alley. There you can hang out with Fatty Pumpkin. That's what I would do if I were you, anyway."

"Let's go, everyone," said Pantsoff. "Nothing can stop us now!"

A slimy, gross tentacle flew out of the water and wrapped itself around Promo's ankle. It began dragging him to the pond.

"Yuck!" cried Promo. He took out Stink, his Elf Army Knife, opened the first tool available, which was the corkscrew, and began poking desperately at the suckered monstrosity around his naked ankle. Slider, Landolakes, Beeromor, and Grimli were pushing and shoving each other to have a chance at fighting the tentacle. Fortunately, dozens more flew out of the pond a moment later, so everyone was able to participate, except Furface, who decided to get started on his trip to back to Riverdale.

"Use your bow, Landolakes!" shouted Grimli as he chopped a tentacle. "Shoot at it!"

"And lose my arrows?" said Landolakes as the hacked with his hunting knife at another. "No way! Maybe you should throw your axe at it!"

Promo used the pliers tool on his knife to pull the last of the nasty suckers off his ankle. The rest of the foul tentacle had been pureed by the Company, who were now busy keeping all the other ones away from the ringbearer.

"Why don't you turn it into popcorn, Pantsoff?" cried Slider.

"You should have spoken up sooner!" said Pantsoff from the doorway. "No time! Follow me into the mine! Flee, you fools!" He grabbed Promo's hand and yanked him into the doorway. The other wobbits quickly followed. The rest of the Company backed in as they fought. Tentacles crowded the magic doorway trying to reach Promo. Then they suddenly gave up, and grabbed the double doors instead. They pulled them shut with a slamming noise that only can be made by stone doors.

"I feel like I've been thrown out of a bar that caters only to giant squid," said Mary.

"Listen!" said Pantsoff. There was a crashing noise outside. "The creature is piling boulders against the door!"

"That's stupid!" said Grimli. "The doors open in. They can't be blocked from the outside."

"Of course it's stupid," said Pantsoff. "It's a giant squid. But we weren't going to be leaving Moreo through those doors anyway. Follow me."

The wizard held his staff aloft. At the top a slowly spinning blue light appeared, allowing them to see, more or less. They walked up some steps.

"The giant squid almost dragged me to a horrible death," said Promo. "Why would that make me hungry?"

"Maybe you have a taste for calamari?" said Pantsoff.

"No, but some of that *mirrortile* to help steady my nerves would be nice." Everyone else admitted to feeling a little shaken up, so they all had a sip. There wasn't much left.

After a light snack, they moved on. Pantsoff was in front, in one hand holding his staff, and in the other, the sword Hamstring. It was made by the Elves for the ancient wars of Gondola, and they knew it as MC Foehammer. Behind him was Grimli, and behind him was Promo, holding his Swiss Army Knife with the main blade open. Promo's knife, Stink, was also of ancient Elf manufacture, so it and Hamstring both would glow if there were porcs or goblins near. Of course, to benefit from this feature, one would have to carry the weapon around with the blade out. And it didn't work very well if you were outdoors in direct sunlight. Nor did it alert anyone to the presence of rargs or giant squid. Behind Promo went Sham, then Landolakes, then Mary and the other one, then Beeromor, and finally Slider, sneaking around at the back of the group.

After several hours of walking, they came to an opening into three passages. Despite his claims of having been to Moreo in the past, Pantsoff had no idea which path to take. He hoped the answer would come to him in a dream, so he told everyone to make camp.

To the left was a great stone door, partially open. Promo peeked in but Pantsoff stopped him. "Be careful, Promo, about going into any of these rooms. They could be dangerous. Send Puppy first. Oh, Puppy! Come here! We've found something interesting you should see!"

Puppy hurried over, and then burst into the potentially dangerous room. There were no porcs or goblins, but there was a huge opening in the middle of the floor. It may have been a well or perhaps a great, dwarven toilet. Either way it had been unused for centuries, but Puppy almost fell into it. After the initial near-death terror wore off, he quickly become bored. He picked up a rock and carefully dropped it in. He unpacked and then came back to hear a distant *ker-plunk* echoing up from the depths.

Pantsoff heard the noise, and glared at Puppy. "Did you drop something into that well? What is it with you and throwing rocks?" he said. "Do you want another giant squid to come after us? Knock it off!"

Then there came out of the depths faint taps: *Tap tap tap, tommm tommm tommm, tap tap tap.* Then they stopped.

"Sounds like a distress call!" said Beeromor.

They started again more slowly: *Tap tap tommm, tap tap tommm, tap tap tommm, tap-tommm.* Then it stopped.

"That one sounded like a song," said Mary. "'Jingle Bells,' I think."

It started a third time: *Tap tap tommm tommm tommm tommm, tap tap tommm tommm tommm tommm.* Then silence.

"My turn, my turn!" said Puppy. "That one was 'Happy Birthday To You!'" Then the tapping died away and was not heard again.

"Get some sleep, everyone," said Slider, who took first watch.

Pantsoff took last watch. The Company woke to find him completing a magic spell of divination at the three passages.

...Eenie, meenie, miney, mo!

"I've found the correct passage!" he announced. They had some pancakes and then began marching for a second day. Even though Pantsoff assured them this was the right passage, marching through it in the darkness was boring and terrifying at the same time. When they finally stopped walking after a long, dreadful day, Promo was curious about Moreo and the dwarf life-style.

"Grimli, did dwarves really live in this dark, scary place? And why?"

Grimli looked at him sadly. "Back in the old days, Moreo was full of light and music and business. We've always wanted to rebuild it. The dwarves used to be great. It reminds me of a song." He rose and began singing in a deep voice.

Once we built a tower to the sun
Brick and iron and stone

Once we built a tower, now it's gone
Buddy, can you spare some gold?

Once we dug a fortress underground
In the great days of old
Now the garrison is not around
Buddy, can you spare some gold?

Dwarves in armor suits
Gee, we looked swell
Bearing some ancient dwarven grudge
Hosts in iron boots
Went stomping to war
I sold them doughnuts and fudge

I can't quite remember
They called me "Al"
It was Al, I've been told
Say, don't you remember
I'm your pal
Buddy, can you spare some gold?

"Moreo is a fortress?" said Promo. "Isn't it a mine?"

"It was a fortress, and a corporate headquarters, and a resort, and a mine," said Grimli.

"Very dwarvish, eh?" said Landolakes. "Why is it deserted now?"

"We delved too deep," said Grimli. "We were digging for Invincibilium, a metal valuable beyond measure. It's lightweight, easy to forge, takes a sharp edge, it can be flexible yet very strong, it never tarnishes and it doesn't show fingerprints. As the dwarves of old dug for it, they disturbed Derwin's Bane, whatever that is. They fled the thing, and no new Invincibilium was mined after that. And almost all of the existing supply was acquired by Smoron through sharp dealing. The elves once used it, too. With it they made Moon-Letters, like the ones outside, the ones that the giant squid smashed. It is said that Borin Oakmanfield gave Bulbo a First Class Mail Shirt made of Invincibilium."

"Yes," said Pantsoff. "I never told Bulbo, but it was worth more than all of Wobbiton put together!"

Promo felt anxious about wearing something so valuable, as if it should be kept in a safe place. Then he wished he was in a safe place. Then, for only a moment, he thought he saw two pale glowing eyes peering at him, and he wished the Company hadn't stopped for the night. He lay there, worrying, until he convinced himself the eyes were just a dream.

That morning Pantsoff greeted them all cheerfully. "We'll be out of Moreo by nightfall. I personally guarantee it! Today's going to be a great day!"

They were about to get started when Puppy cried out from a nearby room "Hey everyone, come check out this funny looking thing!" The others came in and saw an oblong block of black stone, about the length of an average dwarf.

"It looks like a tomb!" said Promo. He couldn't help notice the dwarven letters carved on it.

Without being asked, Pantsoff read:

HERE LIES FALLIN
SON OF FUNDING
LORD OF MOREO

Grimli looked up at the stone ceiling and howled "Nooooooooo!" Then he slowly banged his helmeted noggin upon the tomb, making a mournful clonking sound.

Chapter 17

A BRIDGE TOO FAR FOR PANTSOFF

The Company Of The Ring stood around the tomb of Fallin. It was pretty awkward.

"We're all very sorry for your loss, Grimli," said Promo.

"On behalf of the entire Company," said Pantsoff, "I'd like to extend our deepest condolences to you and to the entire Smithi Financial Solutions family. I'm sure that if Fallin were alive today, he'd want our project to succeed. We should probably be moving---What happened in here?"

Pantsoff was just noticing the scattered, dusty armor and weapons. This was fairly common decor for any room in a dwarf corporate setting. There were also tables and chairs and decaying books, so the room may have been Fallin's Tomb as well as a break room or coffee area. Less common for a dwarf office were the piles of dwarf and goblin skeletons that Slider had noticed. He was examining them closely, and could see that some still had their hands around each other's throats.

"I'm not a shirriff," he said, "but upon examining the evidence, I see signs of a struggle. The cause of death generally seems to be blood loss due to wounds from arrows, battle-axes and scimitars. And possibly biting."

"Maybe there are some clues in here," said Pantsoff as he pulled at a massive, iron-bound book titled "Ledger, by Gori for Smithi Financial Solutions." It was being held by the headless remains of Gori. The skeleton wouldn't let go, so Pantsoff had to put his boot on its shoulder for leverage. He gave it another good tug, one of the arms broke off, and the book came free.

"You knew Gori from the dragon adventure, didn't you, Pantsoff?" said Promo. "He's dead, Fallin's dead, but you don't seem very upset."

"What's done is done," said Pantsoff. "Let's see what Gori's ledger can tell us."

November tenth he read. *Fallin, Lord of Moreo was killed while working at his desk. A goblin shot him through his window from outside. If only he hadn't insisted on a corner office. We killed the goblin, but---*

"You aren't going to read that whole boring book out loud, are you?" said Puppy. He and Mary were playing hacky-sack with a dwarf skull. Pantsoff kept reading.

We cannot get out. We cannot get out. We cannot get out. Pantsoff turned the page. *We cannot get out.*

"He goes on like this for a while. I'll skip ahead. Ah! Here we are. *They have taken the conference room and the supply closet. The pool is up to the wall at our secret entrance. The giant squid got Loin yesterday. Drums, drums in the deep. Goblins have broken in. Oh no! They've cut off my head!* That's pretty impressive writing," said Pantsoff.

"We dwarves keep very thorough documentation," said Grimli. He nodded proudly. "But I wonder what he meant by *We cannot get out."*

Grimli had barely spoken these words when a noise came echoing out of the darkness, like a huge kettle drum played in a novelty song, a deep *boinnng. Boinnng, boinnng* it rolled again. Then there was a great noise of echoing feet and harsh cries.

"So that's what Gori meant," said Grimli.

"Quick, barricade the west door," said Pantsoff. "Leave the east door unblocked!"

"Which way is east?" said Mary. "I'm a little turned around."

"Over here! Barricade this one!" said Pantsoff. The Company started piling furniture, armor, and skeletons in front of the door. Soon everything that could be picked up had been put into the barricade. "Draw your weapons, everyone!"

Hamstring was glowing, and so was Stink's main knife blade. The enemy outside became very quiet, and suddenly the door was flung open. It opened away from the barricade. Goblins and a troll peered in.

"The door opens out?" said Slider.

"Who's dumber, eh?" said Landolakes. "Pantsoff or the giant squid?"

"Shoot at them, Landolakes!" said Pantsoff.

"Too bad no one else on our team has a bow, eh?" said Landolakes as he shot a couple of goblins.

"Slider, how did you hunt deer at Carrottop without a bow?" said Promo as he dodged a goblin arrow.

"I used a sling," said Slider.

"Shouldn't you be using it now?"

"No, I'm much better with my sword," said Slider as he charged the goblins. A few of them had pushed through the office furniture, but they were killed as Slider thrust Da-Doo-Ron-Ron through all three of them at once.

Soon more goblins had broken through. With a great sweep of his weapon, Slider cut the head off one, after cutting the head off another with his backstroke. Beeromor picked out and killed all the biggest goblins, some of them more than half his height. Landolakes quietly dispatched the unwary ones with his hunting knife. Grimli hewed the legs from under a goblin who was about to leap down on Mary from atop Fallin's tomb. Sham whacked one with his omelette pan.

The troll that accompanied the goblin patrol was slowly forcing his way through the furniture as well. Beeromor swung at him. He struck too close to the hilt of his sword, and it fell from his pained, shaken hands. The troll, unharmed, was sticking his fat, naked foot past the barricade when Promo saw him. Ignoring the fact that he was the most important member of the party, Promo charged, and stabbed the troll's foot with Stink. The creature bellowed, pulled back his foot, and ran away.

"Good hit, kid!" said Slider. "You have a fine blade! Don't get cocky."

As Slider was paying a nice compliment to Promo, the enemy captain approached quickly. He wasn't a goblin, but a huge porc-chieftain, a giant among porcs, almost as tall as a short man. He rushed through the remains of the barricade, his slicked-back hair and his greasy complexion glinting in the dim light. He glanced around with his shifty eyes, and then lowered his sawed-off halberd and charged straight at Promo. The point caught Promo on the right side and pinned him against the wall. For the final blow, the porc was drawing a cruel-looking box cutter from its scabbard when Slider brought Da-Doo-Ron-Ron down on his head, parting the porc's hair perfectly and permanently.

Boinnng, boinnng went the drums in the deep.

"Now!" cried Pantsoff. "Fly, you fools!"

"I wish he'd stop saying that," said Puppy as they ran.

Slider went to carry Promo when he noticed an absence of blood or wounds. "I thought you'd be dead!" said Slider.

"No, although I've been hearing that a lot lately," said Promo.

"Indeed, sir," said Sham. "One hates to pry, sir, but might I inquire as to why you're not---"

"Come on," said Pantsoff back over his shoulder.

They ran for about an hour, and then noticed that they weren't being chased. They stopped in a huge atrium for a moment to catch their breath.

"Like I was saying, Promo," said Slider. "How is it you're not wounded? That spear-thrust would have skewered a wild boar!"

"Skewered boar!" said Landolakes to Grimli. "Makes you hungry for some home cooking, eh?"

"What's your secret, Promo?" said Beeromor.

"Time for a quick meeting, everyone," said Pantsoff, interrupting. "I've saved our project from the goblins, and we're about to leave Moreo. At the end of the atrium are some crumbling stairs that lead to a very narrow bridge over a terrifying abyss. On the other side of the bridge is the east exit of Moreo. We're practically outside. Once everyone is ready we can calmly---"

Boinnng, boinnng! rolled the drums. The party ran for the stairs, but not before seeing countless goblins, and behind them, a great, dark, man-shaped being. It had a head of a slightly dopey lion, wings that seemed somehow butterfly-like, and big, fluffy, furry feet. The wings were huge, but it was as flightless as an emu. It roared gratuitously, and carried both a whip and a sword, both flaming. The whole thing was wreathed in a dark fire, which must have been mostly smoke.

"On, no!" said Landolakes. "A Bakshi! A Bakshi is come!"

"Dewin's Bane!" cried Grimli.

They ran for it, without being told. It's not easy to run down stairs under the best of circumstances, but when you have short wobbit legs, and you're terrified by a monster chasing you and by the abyss below you, and the stairs are collapsing, and there's no bannister, the whole process can be pretty unnerving. With all of Grimli's talk of the Wonders Of Moreo, the workmanship wasn't very impressive. Incredibly, Promo and the others made it past the falling stairs to the narrow bridge and across. But Pantsoff stopped in the middle of the bridge and waited. Slider went back to him.

"What are you doing?" Slider said. "The exit's right over there!"

"Fly, you fools," Pantsoff said yet again. Slider shrugged and followed orders.

The Bakshi reached the bridge. Pantsoff stood in the middle of it.

"You cannot pass!" he said. "You cannot pass for three reasons, and excuse me for not having any handouts. Reason One: I am the Servant of the Secret Popcorn, wielder of the Flame of Orville. Reason Two: The dark, smoky fire will not avail you, flame of Kartun."

The Bakshi slowly stepped forward, unimpressed. He roared a couple of times, and then raised his sword tentatively.

"Reason Three: You cannot pass!" Pantsoff then struck the bridge with his staff, which wiggled for a moment. Then, before the Bakshi could bring down his sword, the bridge turned into kettlecorn.

The Bakshi flapped its wings uselessly and started to fall. Then it changed strategy and struck at Pantsoff with his whip, which was unnecessary because he was falling, too. From the cloud of falling popcorn, the party could hear Pantsoff cry for a final time "Fly, you fools!" And then he was gone.

"That was the best presentation Pantsoff ever made," said Slider. "He's never been so persuasive. But now we must obey his last order, the often repeated 'Fly, you fools!' There's the Exit sign, over there. Run!"

The *boinnng, boinnng* rolled on, but with a little less enthusiasm.

"With Pantsoff gone, I'm in charge here," said Beeromor. "Follow me to the exit!"

"Are you kidding?" said Slider. "I'm trusted by the ring-bearer, I'm the King, and I could beat the crap out of you. Follow me."

"Have it your way," said Beeromor. He and the rest of the party followed Slider through the exit and out of Moreo. The dazzling effect of stepping from underground into sunlight reminded the wobbits of when they would step out of the Dude's bowling alley to get some fresh air before lunch. They ran until they were out of the range of any crossbow-armed goblin hit-men.

The *boinnng, boinnng* rolled more quietly in the distance, and then faded.

Chapter 18

LOTHLORILAND

"Farewell, Pantsoff," said Slider. "We should never have entered Moreo. Alas that I must now speak the words 'I told you so.'"

"Farewell, Pantsoff." said Promo. "Shall I never see your bushy mustache again?"

"You won't," said Mary. "Assuming he's dead, that is."

"Move 'em out, boys," said Slider. "We've got places to go and rings to unmake."

The Company went east, down the road from the Moreo Gates. It was rough and broken, but was clearly once a great Dwarf Turnpike. They passed magnificent, ancient toll booths, which were found on every road built by dwarves.

"I shall take you by the road that Pantsoff chose," said Slider. "I hope to come to the woods where the Silverloaf Creek flows into the Great Big River."

"There lie the woods of Lothloriland, don't you know," said Landolakes. "Fairest of the dwelling places and theme parks of my people. There are no trees like those of that land. In autumn the leaves of the *melvyn* tree turn gold, but do not fall until spring, which allows them to be gathered with the first Mowing Of The Lawn. This eliminates much needless raking and yard waste removal. The trunks of the trees are grey and smooth, so smooth that they look fake, but they're real, eh?"

For some time Sham and Promo had been struggling to keep up with the others. It may have been their short legs, combined with the wounds that were starting to accumulate on

Promo. Sham was wounded too, a scratch on the forehead. A goblin thrust with an ice pick had slipped past Sham's parry with the omelette pan.

"Sorry, guys," said Slider, who went back to them. "In the excitement I forgot about your skewering, Promo. Sham, you're still bleeding, too. Why don't Beeromor and I carry you for a while."

"Great," said Beeromor. "I get the one with the heaviest knapsack."

"Yay!" said Puppy when he saw the wobbits riding on the men's shoulders. "We're having chicken-fights! My turn next!"

They walked in this way until late afternoon, when Slider and Beeromor were both ready for an early dinner. They stopped and Grimli fetched water and kindled a fire, while Mary and Puppy were sent on a snipe hunt "for dinner," just to get them out of everyone's hair. Slider tended to the wounded, examining Sham's forehead first.

"You're lucky, Sham!" he said. "This wound isn't deep, and there's no sign of poison."

"Poison, Mr. Slider?"

"Yes. The goblins of the Moisty Mountain Gang use many dirty tricks. They often rub garlic on their blades to spread infection. They have even been known to use hollow point arrows, which create horrible wounds. But this one should heal well. Let's look at you now, Promo."

"Actually, I'm feeling a lot better. I just need some rest and a square meal. No need to examine my wounds. I'm good."

"Nope," said Slider. "Take off the coat, jacket, little waistcoat, and shirt. You need a thorough examination." Promo stripped to his waist, and Slider laughed out loud.

"Get a look at this, guys!" said Slider.

"That's a First Class Mail Shirt!" said Grimli. "Pure Invincibilium! You can't get those anymore! I've never seen anything like it!"

"An arrow-proof vest!" said Beeromor. "The oldest trick in the book. No wonder you looked so brave fighting that troll! You're wearing 'dwarf courage!'"

"Slider, you're going to look at this wound, right?" said Promo as he removed the armor. "It's kind of weird standing here topless while you guys chat."

"Oh, sure," Slider said. When he took a good look at Promo, he was startled.

"Promo, you're a mess! This bruise from the spear-stab on your right side looks bad. The other bruise on your left side from where you hit the wall looks even worse. Then there's the Vorpal blade wound in your left shoulder, which is mostly healed but you'll have that scar forever. And there's nothing I can do about the partially transparent left hand. What are you going to look like by the end of this journey? For now, I can treat the wounds with some leftover doublemint leaves from Carrottop. They'll make you smell better, too. Seriously, though, we were just giving you the business about the vest. I wouldn't wear it, but for civilians, amateurs and high-profile targets like you, it's a good idea. Wearing that armor is absolutely nothing to be embarrassed about."

"I agree," said Beeromor. "It wouldn't have saved you from the giant squid, but there'll probably be more arrows coming your way. Heck, I'd shoot at you if I were a goblin."

They made stew with some more of the doublemint leaves. After they ate they were on their way once more. Grimli walked with Promo, just get a break from walking with Puppy and Mary.

"It sure is dark," said Grimli. "It must be pretty late. It's quiet, too. That invincibilium shirt you have is great! So, what arrangements have you made for your retirement?" Despite being the principal member of his own investment business, The Grimli Group, he was very bad at small talk. The other principals of other investment groups at Smithi Financial Solutions were just as bad, being dwarves, so it usually didn't make any difference. It was just a little difficult for him when there was no actual business to discuss.

"I'm not making any long-term plans right now," said Promo. And it was dark, and quiet, too, but not as quiet as Grimli thought.

"I keep hearing footsteps behind us," said Promo. He checked Stink compulsively to see if there was a tell-tale glow, but there wasn't. Did that mean there were no enemies around, or just no enemy goblins?

"Good to be cautious!" said Grimli. "Goblins will sometimes pursue an enemy for years if they have a fallen *capo* to avenge. *Vendetta*, they call it."

"Great!' said Promo.

They approached some very tall trees with smooth, grey trunks that looked fake in the darkness.

"Beauty! We're here!" said Landolakes. "Lothloriland at last!"

"I don't know," said Beeomor. "I have a bad feeling about this."

"What are you talking about?" said Slider.

"Back home there's all sorts scary stories about this forest," said Beeromor. "And here I am about to walk into it. I don't know."

"Yah hey, those trees are pretty scary," said Landolakes. "Tell you what. If you still feel afraid once we're in, maybe you can ask Promo to lend you his arrow-proof vest!"

"Shut it, nature-boy," said Beeromor. "Let's go." Then he discreetly worked his way over to Slider to have a few words.

"Just between you and me," he said, "man to man, I'm not a big fan of elves. Or dwarves or wobbits for that matter. Smoron is an elf, I've heard, and the elves should be the ones to put him down. These elves don't have the best interests of men at heart."

"My job," said Slider, "is to help Promo get The Ring safely to Bordor, where it can be destroyed. If you can't do your job or you need a diversity seminar, that's your affair. Now let me get back to protecting the ring-bearer."

They soon heard the music of a waterfall running sweetly nearby. "Do you hear that, eh?" said Landolakes. "That's the voice of El Nimrod, the enchanted elf-stream. There's a song about the elf that this stream is named after."

"Oh no!" said Puppy.

"The song is sad, and very long, and I can't remember the end, and a lot of it is in elvish. Here, let me sing it for you, then. It will help us pass the time as we walk for the next two hours or so."

There was an elf named Nimrod
Who---

"Stick 'em up!" said a voice in the trees. "One move and you're all dead!"

"What a relief!" said Puppy.

"Quiet you!" said the voice. "Drop your weapons!" But before any weapons could be dropped, the voice started laughing. Other laughter came from trees all around the Company. Landolakes looked up and spotted the voice's source.

"Oh, real mature, you guys," he said. "I can see you up there, Haldol, and you're not funny."

"Boo-hoo, Landolakes!" said Haldol. "Stop being such a big baby and come up. We need to talk with you and Promo. By the way, that wobbit next to Promo wheezes so loudly we could shoot him in the dark!"

"It wasn't me," said Sham. "My breathing is utterly quiet, like all wobbit butler-gardeners. With all due respect, the breathing noise comes from Mr. Grimli. I believe he may have hay-fever."

Haldol let down a rope ladder. Promo climbed up after Landolakes, as terrified by the ladder as he was by the collapsing staircases of Moreo. Even more than most wobbits, he disliked heights. The ladder ended in a platform in the middle of a huge tree. Promo struggled to lift himself off the ladder and up onto the platform, so Landolakes helped him. Standing behind a counter amid the branches was the elf that led the prank "ambush."

"Welcome to Lothloriland!" he said. "I'm Haldol, and you must be Mr. Bunkins. How many of you will be staying with us?"

"Nine," said Promo. "No, eight. Me and my butler, a couple more wobbits, Orogarn and another man, and Landolakes here."

"I forgot to offer my condolences," said Haldol. "I'm very sorry to hear about Pantsoff. He did some work for us a while back. I'm sure he'll be missed."

"Thanks, that's very kind of you."

"And Orogarn, son of Orogarni, is a member of our Platinum Circle," said Haldol. "He'll be staying on the Concierge level. But you only listed seven guests. Who is the eight?"

"Grimli, of Smithi Financial Solutions."

"What, a dwarf? Are you sure he'll like it here, Mr. Bunkins? Wouldn't he be more comfortable in a dwarf establishment? I understand there are plenty of vacancies at Moreo, and---"

"He's staying here, with us," said Promo.

"Very well," said Haldol. "I'll have a bellhop show you to your trees and help you with your luggage."

The wobbits had a tree all to themselves, but they were a little uncomfortable with it. There was no railing of any sort on the edge of the platform where they slept. Puppy felt a morbid desire to throw himself over the edge. He kept this desire to himself.

It was the middle of the night when Promo awoke. He heard steps and harsh voices below him, and assumed it was some Lothloriland guests returning to their trees after a night of partying. But he caught a few words and they all involved killing, which seemed odd, especially since it was a weeknight. He quietly opened the knife blade on Stink and saw a bright glow: goblins! The glow faded as the goblins walked past. But Promo still had an uneasy feeling. The feeling intensified when he heard soft footsteps, then climbing, and then saw two pale eyes looking over the platform. Then they vanished.

A moment later there was a knock on the platform. Haldol was on the rope ladder, and stuck his head up. "Has anyone been bothering you, Mr. Bunkins?"

"There were some goblins," said Promo, "but they seem to have gone."

"My apologies. We get all kinds here. You won't be seeing them again. Anything else?"

"Just a pair of glowing eyes. Not a goblin's, though."

"And not a friend of yours?"

"No!"

"I'll alert security. I got a glimpse of him and almost assumed he was a wobbit. Then I noticed his upper body strength as he climbed your tree, and I knew I was wrong. Please let us know at the front desk if there are any more disturbances."

"Thank you," said Promo, and he went back to sleep.

Early the next morning the Company had a meeting scheduled with the owners of Lothloriland. There was to be a discussion about modifying the project plan to account for the loss of Pantsoff. Everyone met in the lobby with Haldol, who took them to the Managers's Office. On the way they came to a river.

"The Manager's Office is just past the Celephant River," said Haldol. "Let me help you across." He threw a rope to an elf on the other side. They pulled it tight and tied it at both ends.

"Now what?" said Grimli.

"Just walk across, then!" said Landolakes. He stepped out onto the rope and effortlessly walked to the other side.

"You're kidding!" said Grimli.

"No, it's easy!" Landolakes walked easily back.

"You guys really like to rub it in," said Beeromor.

"We are happy to accommodate our guests that need a little extra assistance," said Haldol. "We have umbrellas to help you balance, if you wish. Or you may use a unicycle if you'd like to ride across."

"Haldol, why don't you throw across a couple more ropes for these folks to hold onto?" said Landolakes.

They threw two more ropes as hand-holds. Slider crossed with ease.

"Couldn't you throw some more ropes," said Grimli, "and build an actual bridge?"

"I knew I'd need rope," said Sham.

Eventually, even Grimli was able to walk across. But there were issues to address before the meeting. They were about to enter a graceful building through a door marked Authorized Personnel Only.

"The Manager's Office is in this limited access area, but we're happy to make an exception and allow you all in," said Haldol. "Your dwarf, however, will have to go blindfolded. We can't take the chance that he'll see any documents that are for *Internal Use Only.* There's a lot of Proprietary Information he might read."

"Oh, come on!" said Promo.

"I will not go blindfolded!" said Grimli. "The only time I wear a blindfold is when I'm swinging my battle axe at a pinata.

Will there be a pinata at our meeting? No? Then I'm not wearing a blindfold."

"I'm really sorry about this," said Haldol. "Personally, I have no problem with you being here. But I could get fired for even letting you in. It's an elf policy, that's all. It's not personal."

"You're just following orders?" said Promo. "What's next? Are you going to point at a sign that says *No Dwarves Allowed* and tell us we have to obey? Okay, then we'll all wear blindfolds."

"Sure," said Haldol. "That's fine with me."

"Even Landolakes," said Grimli.

"What?" said Landolakes. "Grimli, you hoser! I'm an Elf! What a load of hooey this is!"

"It's not personal," said Grimli.

Haldol summoned some elves from housekeeping to provide blindfolds and then to lead each member of the party. They passed through the door and were well on their way when they were stopped. Haldol was reading a memo that had been hand-delivered to him.

"I've just been informed via memo from Lady Galadtameecha that you are all to walk free. Even the dwarf Grimli. The Lady has heard from Riverdale about some new shit that has come to light. No hard feelings, Grimli?"

"Hmph," he said. The blindfolds were removed, and they saw they were in a huge office area with many cubicles.

"The Lady's office is this way," said Haldol. They continued walking until they reached a great corner office, separated by a glittering glass wall from the cubicles.

"Her office isn't in a tree?" said Promo.

"Oh, no," said Haldol. "Trees are just for the guests. We're running a business here!" Through the windows on the far walls, Promo could see all of Lothloriland. The great, phony-looking trees, the mighty thrill rides, the edutainment venues, the restaurants and snack bars, the information kiosks, and the countless gift shops. It was all without decay and very, very clean. Inside the office stood Galadtameecha and her husband.

Chapter 19

THE BIRDBATH OF GALADTAMEECHA

"Lady Galadtameecha," said Haldol. "Everyone's here for your 10:00."

"Please come in," said Kelophane, the Lady's husband. "Have a seat over here, Promo." The Company entered one by one. Kelophane spoke very slowly. Promo figured maybe this was because he was immortal, and consequently never in a hurry. He also was very good at winning friends and influencing people, because he greeted each of the party by name as they entered his wife's office.

"Orogarn, son of Orogarni! So glad that you could visit us again."

"Landolakes, great to see you! How are things up north?"

"Grimli of Smithi Financial Solutions! A pleasure to meet you."

Once everyone was seated, Galadtameecha stood to speak to the party. She was incredibly beautiful, but this was offset, or possibly augmented, by the impression she gave of incredible power, age, and wisdom. And she apparently could read one's innermost thoughts, even the most fleeting ones. Which could be embarrassing for many of the guys she spoke with.

"On behalf of all Lothloriland, The Happiest Place On Little Earth, allow me to extend my deepest condolences regarding Pantsoff." She spoke to the company slowly, as slowly as her husband. Promo was beginning to wonder if the elves were making fun of them.

"Would you tell me how it happened?" she asked. "We've heard about your journey, but received no details about Pantsoff."

"Alas, he fell in Moreo," said Slider. "So that the rest of us might escape from a Bakshi."

"Indeed, I saw in Moreo that which haunts our darkest dreams," said Grimli. "I saw Derwin's Bane."

"Saw it? Stirred it up, you mean," said Kelophane. "You should never have entered Moreo. Whenever disaster strikes, there's a Dwarf involved."

"Actually, it was a wobbit," said Grimli. "Puppy here stirred up the Bakshi, as well as a giant squid, a troll and some goblins," said Grimli. "Ha-haaa!"

"Hey," said Puppy. "It was an accident."

"Never mind that," said Kelophane. "The Dwarf is going to be nothing but trouble. This is what we get for marketing to a diverse group of guests."

"Quiet, husband," said Galadtameecha. "Do not repent of embracing change, or of welcoming the Dwarf. Grimli just wanted to see his ancient home. Why wouldn't he, after seeing with his own eyes the peaks of Zither, Shabaz, and Zigzag. Tall do these mountains stand in his dreams."

The Dwarf, hearing the names of his three favorite mountains, looked up and met the Lady's eyes. It was as if he expected to see a hated competitor, but instead was greeted by a profitable client. Wonder came into his face, and he smiled.

He rose clumsily and bowed in dwarf-fashion, saying "Lady Galadtameecha, do you do your own investing?"

"My apologies, Grimli," said Kelophane. "I've been under a lot of pressure lately."

"Thank you, dear," said Galadtameecha. "Since Pantsoff isn't here, I should tell you that there were a lot of us on the White Council that voted for him to be Head Wizard, even though Saccharine The White was the winner. I'm wondering now if it was a good idea to have Saccharine adding up the ballots. Anyway, there is still hope left, even without him. I'm happy to support this project, but I will not advise you, nor will I help you understand what was, or is, or might be. I will, on the other hand, provide you with some confusing images which may or may not help you in your decision making. Also, I will warn you that this project stands on the edge of a knife. Stray but a little and it will fail. Yet hope remains while all the Company is true."

Beeromor fidgeted furiously, looking at his boots. Mary blushed deeply.

"Why don't you relax for the rest of the day." said Galadtameecha. "My husband will give you passes to the theme park, as well as some meal vouchers. I have some other business to attend to, so you can break for lunch, and then later I can have some one-off meetings with a few of you as needed. I think we've accomplished everything we needed to for today. Thanks, everyone!"

At lunch, the party shared their thoughts and feelings. "Mary, why did you blush during the meeting?" said Puppy. "We were all really embarrassed for you."

"I felt as if I was having that dream that bothers Promo so much. The one where he's giving a speech to a meeting of shirriffs, but he has no pants on."

"Mary!" said Promo. "Shut up!"

"It's okay," said Puppy. "We all know about it. Well, all the wobbits do, and now so does everyone else."

"As I was saying," said Mary, "I felt rather embarrassed. It was as if, within my pantsless dream, she was offering me a kilt. How about you, Beeromor?"

"Keep your accusations to yourself, half-pint!" said Beeromor. "No temptation could ever cause a man of Minas Plusssign to be untrue to his word." But of what passed through his mind, and what Galadtameecha offered him, he would not say.

"No one accused you of anything, Beeromor," said Promo.

"What about you, Mr. Mail Shirt?" said Beeromor. "What did she offer you?"

"None of your business!" said Promo.

"Watch out for her, shorty. Invincibilium will be no protection if Galadtameecha wants something from you. Among my people there are legends that she lives in a gingerbread house where she fattens up little children and eats them. "

"Whoa, whoa, whoa!" said Slider. "That's enough badmouthing of the Lady!"

"I didn't say I believed the legends," said Beeromor.

They remained some days in Lothloriland, but no one could be sure how many. As in Las Vegas, the ownership made it difficult for guests to keep track of time. The Company did little but eat, drink, rest, walk among the amazing trees, ride the roller coasters, rent the paddleboats, snack, and browse the gift shops, and it was enough.

Since it was the self-proclaimed Happiest Place On Little Earth, Lothloriland never encouraged mourning, but everywhere there were elves singing of Pantsoff, or *The Grey Project Manager* as they called him.

Promo thought it would be nice to whip up a quick song honoring Pantsoff, but he didn't want to bother writing any music. Instead, he just wrote some lyrics, or "words" as the wobbits call them, to create a quick "Sung To The Tune Of." Like everyone else, he used the melody that Puppy used in his drinking song.

A check ignored, an unpaid bill,
If someone else was paying he
Would always eat and drink his fill
As if the food and drink were free

He always had an anecdote
To share on subjects far and wide
You soon would learn them all by rote
Unless you found a place to hide

"Very good, sir, although I shouldn't share your song with Mr. Puppy. You know how he feels about that melody." said Sham. "I've taken the liberty of writing a verse of my own."

To popcorn he would change his foes
To caramel corn, or Cracker Jack
Or cheddar cheese, to charm the nose
Or Extra Butter, by the sack

"Not bad, Sham," said Promo. "I always enjoy writing 'Laundry List' songs if I can't come up with anything else."

"How very kind of you to say, sir."

As the butler and the heir critiqued each other's songwriting, Lady Galadtameecha approached. She spoke no word, but beckoned them. They went to an enclosed garden behind a stand that sold little hamburgers. *I'll have to tell Slider about this, he loves greasy little burgers* thought Promo. In the garden the Lady stood in front of a low pedestal with a large, shallow bowl atop it. She filled it with water from a pitcher.

"She wants to show us a bird-bath?" said Promo quietly to Sham.

"I suspect there may be more here than meets the eye, sir," said Sham.

"Here is the Magic Mirror Of Galadtameecha," she said. "I have brought you here so that you may look in it, if you will."

How odd, thought Promo, *that she named it after herself. That would be like if Bulbo had named Stink his "Elf Army Knife Of Bulbo." Whatever. I guess you can do that sort of thing when you're the Queen Of The Elves. Whoops!* He suddenly realized that Galadtameecha was talking to him.

"--- even the wisest cannot always tell," she said. "Do you wish to look?"

Promo didn't answer. He was using a trick that Bulbo would use when he was caught not listening. Something usually would happen to get Bulbo off the hook before he had to admit he was daydreaming.

"Lady Galadtameecha," said Sham, "Begging your pardon, madam, but may I have a look?"

It worked! thought Promo.

"Certainly, Sham Hammich," she said with a smile. "Please be sure to keep your hands, feet and face out of the water at all times." She cleared her throat and then spoke the magic words:

Mirror, mirror, on the ground
Who's the greatest elf around?
Show this wobbit scenes of home
His father's stuck there all alone.

Sham looked into the water. At first he saw a commercial for a nearby Lothloriland gift shop that sold nothing but suspenders, or "braces" as the wobbits called them. The commercial suddenly vanished and he saw Bug End. But it was a different Bug End. Virginia's Beauty Shop and Promo's condo beneath it were both gone, and so was the Hammich home that should have been next door. Gone too were the laundromat across the street and the Smithibank branch on the corner. In their place stood a Dragon Donuts, a Trollbucks Coffee, a Burger Wight, and a First Bank Of Bordor.

"Oh, no!" he said. "Mr. Promo, we must return home at once! What has happened to my father?"

"Steady, Sham," said the Lady. "The Mirror sometimes shows things that will happen, or sometimes things that will never happen, and sometimes it just makes up crazy stuff at random."

"Very well, madam," said Sham. "What is the use, then, of looking in the Mirror at all?"

"You were the one that wanted to look, Sham," she said. "You should have seen the expression on your face. Hilarious!"

"Ah!" said Sham. "A practical joke. Very humorous, madam."

"Promo," she said. "How about you?"

"Sure," he said. "I'll be a good sport. Too bad Puppy and Mary aren't here."

Promo stepped up to the Mirror as the Lady reminded him "Please keep your hands, feet and face out of the water at all times. I'm sorry, but our insurance requires me to say that each time someone looks." She then spoke the magic words:

Mirror, mirror, on the ground
Who's the greatest elf around?
Show this wobbit anything
To help him melt down Smoron's Ring.

Promo looked. There was an ad for the evening's all-elf musical revue. Then he saw an old, bent figure that he assumed was Pantsoff. But the figure was dressed in white, and his staff was white with a sleek, professional appearance. Pantsoff's staff looked like something he might have picked up under a tree after a storm. Was Promo seeing Pantsoff after a makeover, or was it Saccharine The White?

The Mirror did a dissolve to a montage sequence: the sea at night, then a storm, then a tall ship, then a white fortress, then a banner on the ship with an emblem of a tree, then the smoke of fire and battle, and then a small ship sailing away.

"That seems pretty encouraging overall," said Promo. "Thanks, Galadtameecha, I guess we'll be going back to---" Promo looked back at the Mirror, and saw a single, lidless Eye, with a black slit for a pupil. The Eye was rimmed with fire, as if by infection. It glanced this way and that, searching for something. Then Promo heard a deep, hollow, raspy voice-over.

"We interrupt this divination to bring you a live update from Bordor. Smoron is restlessly searching, with his single, horrible eye, for the Juan Ring. The Ring is thought to be in the possession of a wobbit, Promo Bunkins of Bug End. Turn yourself in, Promo! We just want to talk!"

The Ring, on its the new chain made in Riverdale, grew heavier, and drew Promo's face closer and closer to the Mirror. The Juan Ring was about to touch the water when Promo felt the Lady and Sham grab him and pull him away. The Eye and the voice-over vanished.

"Hey!" the Lady said. "Twice I told you to not touch the water! Do I need to put up a sign?"

"You didn't say that the Juan Ring shouldn't touch it," said Promo. The Lady shook her head.

"Was that the voice-over of Smoron?" said Promo.

"No, he's too busy to do his own media work. That was probably contractor voice talent, reading copy that the Executive Riders created."

"Where did they get that guy?" said Promo. "He was so raspy!"

"Yes. Some doublemint tea would have helped." said the Lady. "Too bad Smoron refuses to use it in Bordor. He says it may have side effects, and it requires further testing."

"I never noticed that ring you're wearing," said Promo. "It looks great with your dress. Is it new?"

"No," she said. "But now that you've seen the Eye you can see my ring. It's one of the Elven Really Great Rings. It is called Enya, the Ring Of Adamantium, and I am its keeper."

"Oh, like Pantsoff! He had one, too. I wonder who has the third one?" said Promo.

"Sir, I believe Mr. Pantsoff told us about his Ring in confidence," said Sham.

"Don't worry, Sham," said the Lady. "Pantsoff wasn't very discreet. His Ring was Little Earth's worst-kept secret."

"Shall I never hear him say embarrassing things about me again?" said Promo. "Hey! I've got an idea! Galadtameecha, since you've already got one of these Rings, couldn't I just give the Juan Ring to you?

"Me, with the Juan Ring? That's an interesting thought. Let's see, I could destroy Smoron, and rule all of Little Earth with wisdom and patience. And if anyone got in my way, I could destroy them, too."

She suddenly was nine feet tall with lightning shooting out of her eyes. *She really carries off that look quite well* thought Promo.

"All shall worship me and despair!" she said. It was as if everything but the Lady had disappeared. A moment later, though, things returned to normal.

The Lady suddenly stopped being scary and totally hot. She reverted back to being incredibly powerful, ancient, wise, and totally hot.

"Phew!" she said. "I will stay on as CEO of Lothloriland, and remain Galadtameecha. I have passed the test. I'm glad there were no essay questions."

Chapter 20

FAREWELL TO LOTHLORILAND

After her meeting with Promo and Sham, the Lady called a late meeting with the entire Company. When they had all arrived at her office, she got to the point immediately, although still speaking very slowly.

"Thank you for all coming here on such short notice. Now is the time for those who wish to continue their Quest to harden their hearts and leave this place. Those who no longer wish to go forward may remain here, for a while."

"What?" said Puppy.

"She said if we don't want to go on the dangerous quest we can stay here," said Mary.

"Stay here, in Lothloriland?"

"Yes, Puppy," said the Lady. "Of course, we'll arrange for anyone that stays to actually become part of the Lothloriland family."

"We'll be given elf wives?"

"No, you'll be given jobs. Something rewarding, where you can reach your full potential. In your case, probably in housekeeping or food services."

"I guess I'll go forward with the um, Quest. Mission. Thing."

The others agreed with him. Mary in particular wanted to avoid a lifetime of honest work in the hospitality industry.

"What's your next step in the journey?" said the Lady.

"Pantsoff never told us," said Slider. "Whenever I asked him, he said the project plan was only available on a 'need to know' basis."

"That sounds familiar," she said as she looked at Kelophane. He nodded his head. "In that case, I suggest you travel by boat down the Really Great River. It will be less toilsome than marching, and you will be able to catch up on any paperwork you might have. We will provide the boats at not cost to you, but we will be submitting an invoice to Enron."

"That sounds fine," said Slider. "Just send it to Riverdale. Thank you."

"Very good," said Galadtameecha."Come to the Paddle Boat Rental Pavilion tomorrow, and we will meet you on the river for a farewell luncheon. I've authorized late checkouts for all of you, so you don't have to be out of your rooms until noon.

Slider insisted that the Company meet in the lounge over drinks to try to formulate an actionable plan. He had to promise to pick up the tab, to get full attendance.

"Does everyone have a drink?" said Slider. "Great. As I said before, I'm only paying for the first round, and if you want appetizers you're on your own. So, before Pantsoff fell into the abyss, I had planned at this point in our Quest to join Beeromor in his journey to Minas Plussign. I figured that would be as good a place as any for my inevitable duel with Smoron. But Promo, if you don't plan on coming with Beeromor, then I don't know if I can leave you to journey to Bordor on your own. No offense, but you'd never survive. You probably couldn't even find the place. Not even if Sham came with you."

"If neither the Ring nor Orogarn will come with me to Minas Plussign," said Beeromor, "then I will go there alone. If you only wish to destroy the Juan Ring, then you have no real use for my leadership or my awesome fighting prowess. But if you seek to destroy Smoron's evil empire, then it would be stupid to throw The Ring away."

"Did you just say it would be stupid to destroy The Ring?" said Promo.

"What? No!" said Beeromor. "I said, um, that it would *super* to throw The Ring away. Why? Did you really think I meant that you should give me The Ring, and we could all go to Minas Plussign, and then we could destroy Smoron once and for all, and exploit his existing capital to make New Dongor the economic center of Little Earth? No! I would never say that!"

Beeromor's rant struck Promo as odd, and perhaps dangerous. But Slider said nothing, and was focussed on double-checking the bar tab. The bartender announced "last call," but no one of the Company wanted to stick around. They were going to have a big day tomorrow, and had to pack in the morning.

Packing was made more complicated by the many gifts of food and clothing the elves provided. Haldol brought a gift bag to each room. The food was mostly in the form of little cookies, individually wrapped. Grimli ate one immediately.

"Not bad!" he said. "These would be great with some peanut butter on them. What are they? In Lake City near the Only Mountain, they make a snack bar like this called *crap.* Fallin and the dwarves ate it while hunting the dragon." He ate another one in one bite.

"Easy there!" said the elf. "We call these cookies *limpa* or wayrations. They are made in the magical kitchens of the Ceebler elves for use by college students. One of them will keep a freshman attentive and productive all day. We're trying to expand our market to include travelers and warriors, so we'd be interested in your feedback. Wayrations contain no animal fat, sodium, fructose, gluten, chemicals, artificial colors or preservatives, which is why they are so small and lightweight. Thanks to a proprietary process, they will keep indefinitely while sealed in their wrappers. Whatever you do, though, don't get ammonia on them."

The clothes the Elves provided just didn't look right on Grimli, or on the wobbits. The only member of the Company that looked good in his Elf-issued skinny-jeans and graphic tee was Landolakes. But each of them looked good in the special cloak they were provided. The cloaks were warm in the outdoors, but breathed well indoors. It was hard to tell their color, which shifted to match the surroundings. In an office they looked dark grey, but if you were in a factory or a warehouse the collar turned blue. In a shop or restaurant a name tag would appear on the breast.

"Are these magic cloaks?" asked Puppy.

"No, they're just well-made," said Haldol. "You probably buy all your clothes off the rack."

Elf bell-boys brought all the luggage to the Paddleboat Pavilion, where three sleek paddle-boats awaited them. There were also coils of rope that immediately caught Sham's eye. He inspected one and then spoke with Haldol.

"May I say, Mr. Haldol, that this is the finest rope I have ever seen. I've been a rope hobbyist for years and I've never seen anything like it. Not at the rope shop I visit, nor in the pages of Rope Digest, Ropes Of The World, Weekly Rope or Rope Enthusiast. How is it made?"

"If only I had time to tell you!" said Haldol. "Too bad you won't be here next Tuesday. We're offering a rope-making workshop. Perhaps some other time."

He then spoke to the entire Company. "These are our famous paddle-boats, uniting traditional craftsmanship with state-of-the-art design. They've been painted with a charming lily pad pattern that is excellent camouflage. They're guaranteed to be absolutely unsinkable, but they tend to capsize easily, so avoid any horseplay."

"Oh!" said Mary. "These look like the Pedalo boats they rent at the Buckieland Park District Lagoon! They're really fun for about fifteen minutes, and then they become totally exhausting."

"You sound like an expert," said Haldol. "You and Puppy can share a boat with Beeromor. Grimli and Landolakes can share another, and Slider will go with Promo and Sham."

The boats were packed and the Company got underway. Landolakes and Grimli kept going in circles at first, but they soon got the hang of it. They approached a swan-shaped paddle-boat crewed by Kelophane and Galadtameecha. As soon as the Company was within earshot, she began singing:

I sang of leaves in trees gone by
When there was wind that blew the branches
I sang of Kelophane, my guy
I sang of woods and farms and ranches

He slept forever at my side
He made me smoothies in the blender
We took eternal life in stride

He's neither borrower nor lender

But the Riders come at night
In their suits of dark grey flannel
Worse than troll or porc or wight
But all nine look just the same.

And now The Ring will be denied
And all our summers turned to winter
We'll take a west-bound cruise some night
Our time was up once Promo came.

"She's implying that the Elves are finished once we destroy The Ring, and it's all my fault!" said Promo.

"Oh, no sir," said Sham. "I think the Lady just used that last line to make the rhyme scheme work. It all sounded ad-libbed. I wouldn't take it personally, sir."

"Yes. Her imagery was all over the place."

They came to a bay with a lovely little dockside restaurant. A private room had been reserved, and there were more parting gifts waiting there.

"You really shouldn't have," said Slider. "We didn't get you anything."

"Oh, please," said the Lady. "It's the least we could do, what with you going off to destroy the most evil object in existence and break up Smoron's attempt to monopolize all of Little Earth. Lunch is on us. Order whatever you like." She handed him a menu.

After a very nice luncheon, Mary and Puppy started chanting "Gifts! Gifts! Gifts! Gifts!" Galadtameecha had Kelophane bring each gift to its recipient. They let Mary and Puppy open theirs first.

"Belts," said Mary. "You gave us silver belts. Thank you." Puppy thanked the elves as well, but their hearts weren't in it.

"They each have a golden flower for a clasp," said Kelophane. "Just like mine!"

"Yeah, great," said Puppy. Slider opened his gift next.

"A new sheath for Da-Doo-Ron-Ron!" he said. "It's perfect! Thank you!" he tried it out, and it was truly perfect.

"The sword that is drawn from that sheath will not be broken, even in defeat!" the Lady said.

"I appreciate the vote of confidence," said Slider. "Wait, there's something else here in the bottom of the gift bag!" He opened a small box, and within was a silver brooch with a green stone.

"I gave this brooch to my daughter Kelebrain, and she gave it to her daughter Aiyem Morningstar. And now it comes to you, my future grandson-in-law!"

"No way!" said Puppy in an unfortunately loud stage whisper to Mary. "The Lady is Aiyem's grandmother?" Once he realized that everyone had heard him, he said more quitely, "Mary, this is so weird!" Beeromor opened his gift next, without being invited.

"A golden belt. Thanks," he said. Then he muttered "I've probably got a dozen of these at home."

"His belt is gold, but our belts are silver!" said Puppy to Mary. "Probably because we're just wobbits." Landolakes was next. His gift was a professional-grade elf longbow and a quiver of matching arrows.

"Oh, beauty!" he said. "I can't wait to go hunting with this! Thanks, you two!" Mary and Puppy made disappointed noises because they didn't get awesome gifts.

"Sham, go ahead and open your gift." she said. "Don't be shy."

"Very good, my Lady," said Sham. Inside his gift bag was a small package. He unwrapped it and found a high quality gift box, the kind that you have to pay extra for in the finer Lothloriland shops. He opened the box and inside there was... a box. A beautiful little grey wooden one with the Lothloriland logo on the lid. It appeared to be made of wood from a *melvyn* tree.

"My Lady, it's lovely! How thoughtful! A box for Mr. Promo's tie clasps! Thank you so very much!"

"Actually, Sham, the gift is inside the box."

"Ah, of course." He opened the box. "It's filled with fine grey soil! My Lady, it's wonderful. Again, thank you!"

"Sham, that earth is from my orchard. It won't help you on your journey---"

"Oh, thank you, My Lady!"

"Let me finish, Sham. Your gift won't keep you on your road or defend you from any peril---"

"Just like my gift," said Puppy very, very quietly. Mary and Beeromor both rolled their eyes in discreet agreement.

"But if you carry it through the rest of your project and see your home again at last, sprinkle this earth in your garden. It may, perhaps, reward you."

"I'll look forward to that as I march into Bordor and back, My Lady. Thank you."

"Grimli you're next" Galadtameecha said. He held only an envelope, which he opened.

"A gift card?" he said.

"Yes," she said. "We didn't know what to get you. But that's a special card. You can use it to get anything you want from Lothloriland. What would you like?" He blushed.

"I'd like a lock of your hair, or even just one hair. Or a baby tooth. Some fingernail clippings. Anything! Can't you see that I love you?"

"Amazing are the Dwarves!" said the Lady. She didn't want the situation to become any more awkward than it already was, so she spoke a little more quickly than normal. "They can be charming and disgusting, rude and courteous, humble and demanding all at once. Here, Grimli, let us meet halfway." She undid her hair, and then with a tug and a grimace pulled out three golden hairs. "But tell me, what will you do with such a gift?"

"I will treasure these hairs, in memory of your words to me at our first meeting." He gave her the card. "And if ever I return home, I will have them bronzed."

"Of course you will! Who hasn't opened their gift yet?" the Lady asked. "Promo, you're last. Open yours." He opened a little package that held a small stoppered bottle. He hoped it wasn't after-shave.

"In this phial is caught the light of the star Earandeye." said the Lady. "May it be a light to you in dark places, when all other lights go out. It will look brighter without the sun shining directly on it."

It was a very sunny day, so Promo held the phial under the table for a moment. "It does look brighter! Thank you." He bowed, but could find no other words to say. He was too busy wondering about Bordor, and exactly how soon the lights would go out.

Thank-yous and goodbyes were said, and everybody got into their respective paddle-boats. As the Company went forward and the Lady and her husband want back to the office, she sang another number. This time she sang in elvish. Promo couldn't understand a word of it, and the tune was really sad. He could have used something a little more encouraging.

They went around a bend in the river, and could no longer see Lothloriland. Promo had hoped to return there someday, but never did because of his other responsibilities. And he didn't want to leave Lothloriland at that moment. Neither did anyone else. Grimli was inconsolable.

"Face the facts, Grimli," said Landolakes kindly. "She's married, eh? And you're a workaholic, lots of late nights with your investment group. Besides, do you really think you're her 'type?'"

"You mean, am I an Elf?" Grimli said. "I get it. I just can't help but wonder, you know, if things had been different..."

"Of course," said Landolakes. "But you have those three hairs, eh? Pretty nice!"

"Yes, I suppose so," said Grimli. "Hey, careful! You're rocking the boat! These things are tippy, aren't they?"

The Company pedaled until their legs became sore, but kept going. The little paddle-wheels in the back of each boat turned and turned. The trees they passed appeared less beautiful as they went forward. Promo was worried, but it was getting dark, his stomach was still full from lunch, and it wasn't his turn to pedal, so he soon fell into an uneasy sleep.

Chapter 21

THE REALLY GREAT RIVER

"Good morning, sir!" said Sham. "I trust you slept well. We have a big day of pedaling ahead of us, so I've brushed out your magic cloak. It's a remarkable thing sir, these cloaks attract absolutely no lint, and very little dandruff. Magic indeed! Come have a warm at the fire. I'll see about your breakfast."

They saw no sign of the enemy that day, or the next. The dull hours passed without event. East of the River the land was desolate and grey, or sometimes brown, but to the west there was green grass. The long-term effects of Smoron's poor environmental practices in the east were obvious.

Sham looked from bank to bank uneasily. He felt the Company was very vulnerable, in their three sleek but small paddle-boats in the midst of shelterless lands, on a river that was a frontier of war. Slider and Beeromor felt the same insecurity. Landolakes was busy listening to Grimli drone on about the imagined break-up of his imagined relationship with Galadtameecha. Mary and Puppy spent most of their time splashing each other.

After four days of this, Sham thought he was having boredom-induced hallucinations when saw something strange in the water. He said nothing, not sure if it was his place to point out his amateur observations to trained professionals like Mr. Slider or Mr. Beeromor.

That night, when everyone was done eating their wieners and toasted marshmallows, Sham thought he might talk to Mr. Promo about what he saw.

"I saw the funniest thing in the water about an hour or two before we stopped, sir," he said. He was trying to ease into the subject.

"Really?" said Promo. "Like a jester, or a fish wearing a little hat?"

"Not exactly, sir. Not 'ha-ha' funny. Funny as in 'Beeromor has a funny look in his eye.'"

"Sure, funny as in 'strange' rather than 'humorous.'" said Promo. "Tell me about it."

"Well, sir, I saw what looked like a log---"

"That's not humorous, nor is it strange."

"---A log that was drifting faster than the boats. It was coming from behind and catching up with us."

"Sham, that could have been some tricky currents."

"Yes, sir. Or it could have been the log's webbed feet, which it used like a duck."

"I see your point, Sham. Ducks are funny. I remember a joke Uncle Bulbo used to tell about a duck that walked into a tavern---"

"Indeed, sir, but the point I'm making is that it was neither a log nor a duck. And it had pale, lamp-like eyes."

"Of course!" said Promo. "Gol-Gol! It wasn't my imagination! I thought I saw him following us in Moreo and in Lothloriland. I didn't say anything because I didn't want everyone to worry."

"As you wish, sir."

In the middle of the night, Sham quietly woke Promo. "Excuse me, sir, but I've been restless tonight and I couldn't help but notice the appearance of two pale, lamp-like eyes in the water near the moored boats."

Promo found Stink, opened what turned out to be the Phillips screwdriver, closed that tool, and then opened the main blade. It wasn't glowing, so he shook the knife vigorously. It still didn't glow, so he knew the thing in the water couldn't be a goblin. He looked for the eyes again, but they were gone. Slider stepped over.

"Promo, why have you drawn your Elf Army Knife?" he said.

"I saw Gol-Gol," said Promo. "I was going to try to catch him, or something,"

"Yeah, good luck with that," said Slider.

"You knew about Gol-Gol, Mr. Slider?" said Sham.

"I'm the greatest tracker in Little Earth, Sham. Yes, I knew. So did Grimli. You knew Gol-Gol was following us, didn't you, Grimli?" Grimli sat up in his blankets.

"I have the eyes of a hawk, the ears of a fox, and the beard of a goat," said Grimli. "Of course I knew he was following us! Landolakes, you saw him too, right?"

"How could I not notice him, eh?" said Landolakes. "I know all about him. He was a prisoner of the Wood-Elves. And I've spent most of my life listening for approaching giant spiders. They're way quieter than Gol-Gol. I keep hearing him sniffling. Beeromor and I were talking about that hoser, weren't we, eh?"

"When you're a Captain of Minas Plussign," said Beeromor, "you learn a few things about watching out for ambushes and enemy scouts. I knew about Gol-Gol, but I didn't want to say anything until I brought you his head. You know, after I killed him. Then, Promo, you'd see things clearly, and you would give me The Ring!"

"What?" said Promo.

"Never mind that last part. Hey!" Beeromor said to Mary and Puppy. "You two saw Gol-Gol, didn't you?"

"Yeah. We've been seeing him since Puppy woke up all of Moreo. Why?"

"No reason," said Beeormor. "And you're the last to notice we're being followed, right, Sham? You finally figured that out? Hilarious!"

"Yes sir," said Sham. "Quite funny."

"Okay, back to bed everyone," said Slider. "I'll keep watch, and tomorrow we'll see if we can break away from him. We'll be pedaling extra hard!"

The next day the pedaling was fast and furious, and went on into the night, and they saw no more of Gol-Gol. They once more traveled at night, messing up everyone's sleep schedule and making the pedaling even more boring. This went on tediously until the seventh day.

In the early morning the Company saw that the riverbanks were becoming steeper and the country was becoming hillier. As they made camp, Slider saw a tough-looking hummingbird hovering above them, and then flying south. Landolakes saw it, too.

"There's no way that bird's searching for nectar to sip around here, don't you know. There's no flowers for miles."

"He looked like trouble to me," said Slider. "Let's stay under cover until dark."

On the eighth night of their journey, they had to pedal close to the eastern shore to avoid some rapids. As they did, under suspiciously bright starlight, they were spotted and fired upon by a squad of porcs. One of their arrows struck a paddle-boat, another just missed Slider, but a third hit Promo in the back. It bounced off his First Class Mail Shirt, but it hurt a lot.

"I'm no expert," said Promo, wincing, "but this seems a perfect spot for an ambush. Do you think Gol-Gol was part of it?"

"Maybe he was," said Slider. "This is exactly where I would have attacked. But whoever planned the ambush isn't as good as me. If he was, we'd all be dead. Our magic cloaks and the lily pad camouflage of the paddle-boats may be defeating the archers' aim. Anyway, we better get out of here. Pedal, all of you! Pedal to safety!"

The paddle-wheels of the three boats churned wildly, and no more arrows fell among them. Landolakes sought to return fire. He stood in the paddle-boat, something only Elves can do. Turning back, he drew an arrow, but could acquire no target. A sudden feeling of dread swept over him. At that same moment, Promo felt the old war wound in his shoulder act up.

Elbowpad Gilletrazor! Landolakes said as he looked up. Above them was a great winged creature. No one could see it clearly. It could have been an evil pegasus, or a evil pterodactyl, or a huge, evil hummingbird. It was definitely evil.

Landolakes' brand-new longbow of Lothloriland twanged mightily. The airborne enemy swerved, and then crash-landed on the east side of the river.

"That was a great shot, my friend!" said Grimli.

"But what did I hit? It wasn't an eagle, that's for darn sure."

"It reminded me of the Bakshi, but everyone knows they don't fly."

They journeyed on without incident for another night. The next day Mary and Puppy insisted on sleeping in, so the Company took the night off and pedaled the following day. Slider had planned to make this part of the trip by daylight anyway. That afternoon they saw why.

The riverbanks grew to cliffs on either side. In the distance Promo could see what looked like two pillars. As they pedaled slightly nearer, he saw that the pillars were two vast figures. The likenesses of two kings had been carved in the rock. They both had expressions and body language that seemed to say *You're not supposed to be here!*

Slider had the Company stop pedaling for a moment so they could admire the unfriendly monuments. "Behold the Argonauts, the Public Works Projects Of The Kings," he cried.

"They must have cost a fortune," said Grimli.

"My tax dollars at work!" said Beeromor.

"They kind of look like Slider," said Grimli. Slider was trying to pose like the stone figures, but remained seated in his paddle-boat.

"I get it, he's king," said Beeromor. "He needs to give it a rest."

Slider soon realized it was time to get back to work. They pedaled past the great monuments, and then rested in the shadow of the hills beyond. The tenth day of their journey was over. They had to now choose between going east or west. The last stage of their Quest was before them, which would amount to 66% of their total adventure.

Chapter 22

THE END OF THE SUPERFRIENDS?

They camped on the shore, and Promo was on first watch for the night. Slider was restless, so he came over to chat.

"Can't sleep?" said Promo.

"No. I have a bad feeling about this," said Slider. "Check Sting and see if it detects any goblins." Promo got his Elf Army Knife and opened the main blade. There was a very faint glow.

"That's not good," said Slider. "How exactly does the Goblin Detector feature work? Does a faint glow mean there are just a few goblins nearby, or could it mean there's a great mob of them, but they're across the River? Or could it be one really huge hemogoblin in the general vicinity?"

"I don't know," Promo said. "Uncle Bulbo had this thing for years, but he never created a User's Manual, or even a Quick Start Guide."

"In case there's something nearby let me take watch," said Slider. "We'll have to be extra-careful tomorrow."

The next day they had a breakfast meeting to determine who would be going where. Promo was first on the agenda.

"I know we're pressed for time," he said. "But I could really use an hour or so to do some brainstorming. Just on my own."

He was reluctantly given an hour, after which he was to present his ideas back to the group. He walked off into some trees trying to get out of sight. But Beeromor watched him carefully, and he had that funny look in his eye. Not "ha-ha" funny, either.

As he walked, Promo had the feeling he was being watched, or stalked. He turned, expecting to see Gol-Gol, or an Executive Rider, or a wight, or even a killer tree. But there was Beeromor, smiling and kind.

"Hi," he said. "I was worried about you being alone and unguarded. While I'm here, though, do you mind if we kick some ideas around? I've been working on a plan that I think you'll like."

"I appreciate your help," said Promo as he sat down. "But I really wanted some time alone. Soul-searching, that sort of thing. You understand. So thanks for dropping by..."

Beeromor didn't take the hint. In fact, he came up to Promo and sat next to him. "Please, Promo, just hear me out. I've got something in mind that you'll love!"

Promo said nothing, but Beeromor still didn't get it. "How about this, Promo. Let me at least see The Ring. You know, for old time's sake."

Remembering how this scenario went with Bulbo and with Galadtameecha, Promo responded quickly. "No, that's not a good idea."

"Sure," said Beeromor nonchalantly. "Whatever. But did you ever wonder what we could accomplish if, instead of destroying The Ring, we actually used it against Smoron? Nothing could go wrong!"

"You were at the meeting at Riverdale," said Promo. "You know as well as I do that all the experts agree on destroying The Ring. It's our only choice."

"Unbelievable!" said Beeromor. "You really would listen a roomful of Little Earth riff-raff? You know about elves, right? They started this whole thing in the first place! And dwarves? You're going to trust a couple of bankers? Or a wizard, who's so smart that he got himself killed? Or maybe a homeless guy who claims to secretly be a king? You're going to take their word over mine? You can't destroy The Ring! There's only one thing to do!"

"Thanks, Beeromor, this has been really helpful."

"You'll come with me to Minas Plussign?" Beeromor said, with the funny look back on his face.

"Kind of, yes."

"Great!" said Beeromor. "Lend me The Ring. Just until Smoron is destroyed and I rule all of Little Earth. Then I'll give it right back to you. We could destroy The Ring together!" He reached toward Promo like he was reaching for a burrito.

"Sure, let me get it out for you," said Promo. He quickly pulled it out by its chain and put it on his finger. The uncanny chain did not need to be broken or unclasped, it just let go of The Ring, so that Promo wouldn't have to walk around with his hand up by his head.

"Hey!" said Beeromor. "Where did you go, you little runt! Come back! Come back here, shorty, so I can take The Ring and kill you! Kill you, kill you all, and rule Little Earth! Come back! Please! I just want to talk!"

He lunged at Promo, or where Promo had been moments ago. Promo was no longer there. Beeromor lunged again, hoping to get lucky, but missed. He lunged a third time, but tripped on a tree root and fell, face first, into a cream pie that was to have been Promo's breakfast.

Beeormor stood up and wiped the whipped cream from his eyes with two fingers of each hand. He flicked the pie filling onto the ground, and then realized what he had done. Like the whipped cream, the funny look was no longer in his eyes.

"What have I done? Promo! Come back! It was temporary insanity, but it's gone now! I've been under a lot of pressure lately. It was stress! I'm fine now! Come back!"

There was no answer. Promo was running faster than any wobbit had ever run, which isn't really that fast at all. He couldn't hear Beeromor, not because he was far away, but because he was deafened by the sound of his own heavy breathing. To make matters worse, he was running uphill.

He came to the summit of Armon Henner, the Hill Of Hearing And Sight, the ancient watchtower. Slider had spoken about it, but Promo hadn't expected a great stone chair to sit in.

"How can you keep watch when you're sitting down and comfy?" he thought. "I'd fall asleep." He sat, just to see if it still worked. Sure enough, he soon saw plenty, and he didn't like any of it.

Everywhere there were signs of war. Promo had visions of all Little Earth in chaos. The Moisty Mountains were crawling with goblins wielding their wickedly curved straight-razors. In Murkywood, the Wood-Elves hurled special curling-stones at giant spiders. Smoke rose on the borders of Lothloriland. Horsemen were galloping on the grassy plains of Hohum. Rargs were being taken on walks all around Eisentower. From the havens of Harrods, ships of war were putting out to sea. Out of the East, Men were moving endlessly, speaking with their terrible east coast accents.

Suddenly, Promo felt The Eye. It had become aware of him. It was searching for him like a finger, poking and prodding.

Two powers strove in Promo, one urging him to take off The Ring, the other urging him to check in with Smoron. They were in the form of two tiny figures, one on each of his shoulders. The one on his right shoulder gained the advantage by using his harp as a weapon, hitting the other on the head. *Take it off, you idiot! Take it off now!* the harpist screamed. Promo was convinced, and he removed the ring.

His visions of war stopped, but he still had a great view from the hill top. It was a good place for introspection. "Beeromor never wanted to come to Bordor anyway, which is for the best. The temptation of The Ring is too much for him. The Ring will probably take hold of Grimli next, or maybe Landolakes, so I'm not sure I want them with me, either. I know what to expect from Mary and Puppy, but who cares? Since the goblins keep shooting specifically at me, it appears those two aren't even useful as decoys. Slider will be needed in Minas Plussign, especially if Beeromor goes berserk again. And Sham, well, I still don't think it's fair that he should be mixed up in this. He should be back in Wobbiton, drinking beer with Rosie O'Cotton.

"This is a job I have to do on my own, and it's not going to get any easier if I wait," said Promo. "Shall I ever see any of the Superfriends again? Pantsoff, I think I shall miss you most of all." Promo put The Ring back on his finger.

He vanished thinking "I hope Smoron doesn't start looking for me again. I gotta remember to take this Ring off as soon as possible."

At the camp, the Company was wondering what to do. They didn't want to pester Promo, but they were starting to wonder if he was okay. And when he came back, then what?

"I want to go to Minas Plussign," said Landolakes. "That's where the fighting will be, don't you know."

"I agree," said Grimli. "But if Promo wants to go to Bordor I'll go with him. A deal's a deal."

"Fair enough," said Landolakes. "If everyone else wants to

go to Bordor, I guess I'll tag along."

"Begging your pardon, sirs, but I don't think you understand what Mr. Promo is doing," said Sham. "If I know Mr. Promo, I'm sure he's trying to build up the courage to take The Ring to Bordor. And he'll want to do it by himself. He has no interest in putting any of us in danger, just as he has no plans to go to Minas Plussign. Speaking of which, where's Mr. Beeromor?"

At that moment, Beeromor reappeared. He looked grim and sad. "What's wrong, Beeromor?" said Slider. "And why is there pie in your beard? Have you seen Promo?"

"Have I seen Promo?" he said. "Yes and no. I saw him at the start, but then he disappeared. He must have put The Ring on. I thought he would come back here."

"What did you do to him?" said Slider.

"Nothing! We just talked. It got a little heated. You know how passionate I am. I may have spoken out of turn, and then he vanished."

"Quick!" said Slider. "Use the Buddy system and search for Promo in pairs!" They all ran off shouting. All except Sham, and since his Buddy was Promo, no one noticed.

"If I was Mr. Promo, what would I do?" he said. "I'd go to the boats, take the gear I needed and start pedaling. I'm off!" Sham ran to the boats and saw that one was slipping into water with no one pushing it. "Mr. Promo!" he cried.

The paddle-boat was quickly in deep water. Sham chased after it, even though he was a dedicated non-swimmer, and he was carrying his huge knapsack. Soon the water was over his head, at least four feet deep. He looked up, perhaps for his last view of the sun, when he saw a now-visible hand reach very deeply into the water and pull him out.

"I had no idea your arms were so long, sir," he said.

"I suppose you'll insist on coming with me to Bordor?" said Promo.

"If it's quite all right, sir."

"Then sit next to me and start pedaling," said Promo. "I'm tired of going in circles."

They only pedaled as far as the eastern shore of the River, and landed the boat in an out of sight spot. Then, shouldering their burdens they set off, seeking a path that would bring them over the gray pinstripe hills, and down into the land of Shadow.

Acknowledgements

Thanks to my wife Mary Beth for her encouragement. Because of her I finished writing this book on time, more or less.

Thanks to my daughter Zoe for her belief in me as a writer, and for listening to me politely.

Thanks to my daughter Becca for cheering me up on a daily basis.

Thanks to Carsten Polzin at Piper Verlag for finding my first book on the internet, publishing it, and then asking me for this, my second book.

Thanks to Benjamin Chandler for his extensive comments from his second home in Slovakia, and for his excellent concept art.

Thanks to Jean Kloth for her razor-sharp editing and writing suggestions, even though she still has no interest whatsoever in Tolkien's writings.

Thanks to John O'Neill, my biggest fan in Scotland, for his notes and his constant support on Amazon.

Thanks to Stephen Lynch, my biggest fan in England, for his notes and for championing my book on the internet.

Thanks to Rick Kirk for his Tolkien insights and comedy-writing suggestions.

Thanks to Bill and Nick at Sign Express, Oak Park, Illinois, for their encouragement and promotional suggestions.

Thanks to the Hunger-Dunger Writer's Group, especially Lou Carlozzo for his free publicity, and James Finn Garner for his many tips on the business of writing.

Thanks to my friends at the Oak Park Public Library, especially Debbie, Martin, and Carolyn.

Thanks to Oak Park Writer's Group, especially Dan Montville.

About the Author

Paul Erickson's mission in life is to be the world's foremost Tolkien parodist. Erickson was born in 1959, and has lived his entire life in the Chicago suburb of Oak Park. He read The Hobbit in 7th grade, and then read Bored Of The Rings that summer. He spent most of his high school years playing Dungeons & Dragons and attempting to read The Lord Of The Rings. In college he worked at the Bristol Renaissance Faire, wearing tights and selling love songs. After earning a BA in Philosophy he went into banking.

In the late eighties he performed song parodies in comedy clubs with ace guitarist Steve Ginensky. In the nineties he parodied slam poetry as part of Team Chicago, winning the 1991 Poetry Slam Nationals. In 2009 his banking career was cut short when his employer went out of business. Fortunately, by that time he had finished reading The Lord Of The Rings. While in line at the unemployment office, he realized no one in the US had ever published a parody of The Hobbit.

He went to Starbucks with his MacBook and got to work, combining all his nerd knowledge of Middle-earth with his one real skill: writing parodies. In 2011, with the help of bestselling humorist James Finn Garner (Politically Correct Bedtime Stories) he published The Wobbit A Parody on Kindle.

The Wobbit A Parody was discovered on the internet and published as a German paperback in 2012 by Piper Verlag. They published Erickson's second parody, The Superfriends Of The Ring in October, 2013. Erickson's parodies are also available in Turkish and Russian.

Visit Paul: www.TheWobbitAParody.com

Like his Facebook page: www.facebook.com/TheWobbitAParody

31246246R00142

Made in the USA
Charleston, SC
11 July 2014